A POSSESSORY ESTATES
AND
FUTURE INTERESTS PRIMER
Third Edition

By

Peter T. Wendel
Professor of Law
Pepperdine University School of Law

THOMSON
★
™
WEST

Mat #40622461

COPYRIGHT © 1996 WEST PUBLISHING CO.

© West, a Thomson business, 2005

© 2007 Thomson/West

      610 Opperman Drive

      St. Paul, MN 55123

      1–800–328–9352

Printed in the United States of America

ISBN: 978–0–314–18369–9

 TEXT IS PRINTED ON 10% POST CONSUMER RECYCLED PAPER

To my lovely wife, Gerri —

for agreeing to share our life estates,

and for bearing our four beautiful remainders:

Carolyn, Paul, John, and Kristin

PREFACE

A complete study of the abstract beauty of possessory estates and future interests is best left to its own upper level course. The basic Property course and/or Wills & Trusts course is incomplete, however, without a two to three week introduction to the basic principles and combinations of possessory estates and future interests. This material provides just such an introduction.

Such an expedited coverage of such a complex and extensive area of law, however, inherently requires simplifications and generalizations. As you become more familiar with the material, you will begin to see the myriad of possible combinations of possessory estates and future interests. Although the material covers some of these combinations in footnotes, such complex combinations are generally beyond the scope of the introductory coverage. The goal here is to understand the basic principles and combinations of possessory estate and future interests necessary to understand the material covered in most Property courses and/or Wills & Trusts courses.

I wish to express my thanks and appreciation to the many people who contributed to this edition: to my colleagues, Dean Charles I. Nelson, for his contributions to the first edition of this book, and Professor Shelley Saxer, for her thorough reading of, and excellent comments and criticism on, earlier editions; to my research assistants over the years, Ms. Theona Zhordania-Taat, Ms. Jennifer Black, Mr. Jean-Paul Le Clercq, Ms. Krista S. Jacobsen, and Ms. Nathalie Schuler Ferro, for their invaluable research assistance and proofreading; to Cecilia and her staff at *Caffe Aroma*, for letting me use her neighborhood coffee shop as my 'office away from the office;' and to all of the students over the years who have endured my Property class and my experiments with how best to present the material. Their honest and thoughtful reactions to my different ideas helped to formulate this latest edition. In many respects this book is the product of years of shared learning process that naturally occurs in the classroom, and everyone's contributions make this book much better. I hope you find it useful in your studies.

Peter Wendel

Malibu, California
May, 2007

Table of Contents

Preface iii

Chapter 1
INTRODUCTION

I.   **OVERVIEW**...1

    A. INTRODUCTION 1
    B. HISTORICAL ROOTS...2
    C. INSTRUMENTS USED TO CREATE 2

II. **THE ANALYTICAL SCHEME**..3

    A. POSSESSORY ESTATES 3
    B. FUTURE INTERESTS..4
    C. THE ANALYTICAL KEYS 4

Chapter 2
THE FEE SIMPLE ABSOLUTE

I.   **OVERVIEW** 6

II. **THE BENCHMARK ESTATE**...6

    A. THE NATURE OF THE ESTATE 6
    B. THE WORDS OF PURCHASE 7
    C. THE WORDS OF LIMITATION...................................8
    D. ANALYZING THE POSSESSORY ESTATE 9

III. **THE MODERN TREND**..11

IV. **TRANSFERABILITY, DEVISABILITY, INHERITABILITY**....13

    Review Chart...14
    Chapter 2 Problem Set 15

Chapter 3
THE FEE SIMPLE DEFEASIBLES

I. OVERVIEW 17

II. ANALYZING THE FEE SIMPLE DEFEASIBLES......................17

    A. THE NATURE OF THE ESTATE..................................17
    B. IDENTIFYING EACH FEE SIMPLE DEFEASIBLE................18

**III. THE FUTURE INTERESTS WHICH FOLLOW A FEE
SIMPLE DEFEASIBLE** 25

    A. ANALYZING FUTURE INTERESTS 25
    B. SHIFTING vs. SPRINGING EXECUTORY INTERESTS..........30

IV. MODERN TREND..32

V. TRANSFERABILITY, DEVISABILITY, INHERITABILITY....34

    Recap Flowchart 35
    Review Chart..36
    Chapter 3 Problem Set 37

Chapter 4
THE FINITE ESTATES

I. OVERVIEW.. 42

II. THE NATURE OF THE FINITE ESTATES 42

III. DISTINGUISHING THE DIFFERENT FINITE ESTATES........43

    A. THE LIFE ESTATE 43
    B. THE FEE TAIL 44
    C. THE TERM OF YEARS 46

**IV. THE FUTURE INTERESTS WHICH FOLLOWING
A FINITE ESTATE**..47

V. THE MODERN TREND..49

VI. TRANSFERABILITY, DEVISABILITY, INHERITABILITY....49

    Recap Flowchart 51
    Test Grid 52
    Review Chart..53
    Chapter 4 Problem Set 54

Chapter 5
REMAINDERS: VESTED vs. CONTINGENT

I. OVERVIEW...58

II. THE TEST FOR VESTED REMAINDERS 58

    A. BORN AND ASCERTAINABLE.......................................59
    B. NO EXPRESS CONDITION PRECEDENT 60

III. DESTRUCTIBILITY OF CONTINGENT REMAINDERS.........65

IV. THE ALTERNATIVE CONTINGENT REMAINDER 70

    A. INTRODUCTION 70
    B. ALTERNATIVE PHRASING...73

V. PREMATURE TERMINATION OF FINITE ESTATE...............73

    A. METHODS BY WHICH FINITE ESTATE MAY END
       PREMATURELY 73
    B. APPLICATION TO ALTERNATIVE CONTINGENT
       REMAINDERS 79

VI. ALTERNATIVE CONTINGENT REMAINDER
     LOOK-ALIKE 80

VII. MODERN TREND 82

VIII.   TRANSFERABILITY, DEVISABILITY, INHERITABILITY 82

Chapter 6
ALTERNATIVE APPROACH FOR ANALYZING CONVEYANCES – LEAD WITH THE PARTIES

I.   OVERVIEW 84

II.   ALTERNATIVE APPROACH – LEAD WITH THE PARTIES .84

    Chapter 6 Problem Set 89
    Review Problem Set 1 93

Chapter 7
VARIATIONS ON THE EXECUTORY INTERESTS

I.   OVERVIEW 98

    A. REVIEW 98
    B. HISTORICAL BACKGROUND 98
    C. SHIFTING vs. SPRINGING EXECUTORY INTERESTS 99

II.   SPRINGING EXECUTORY INTEREST 99

    A. THE "FUTURE INTEREST ONLY" CONVEYANCE 99
    B. THE "GAP" SCENARIO 101

III. THE VESTED REMAINDER SUBJECT TO DIVESTMENT ..103

    A. THE REQUIREMENT OF A VESTED REMAINDER.............105
    B. THE EXPRESS CONDITION PRECEDENT
        REQUIREMENT 106
    C. THE CONDITION PRECEDENT MUST BE IN THE
        SUBSEQUENT CLAUSE 108
    D. EXPRESS CONDITION WHICH CAN BE
        EITHER A CONDITION PRECEDENT OR
        CONDTION SUBSEQUENT......................................110
    E. EFFECT UPON THE PRECEDING FINITE ESTATE.............112

IV. RECAP 114

    Chapter 7 Problem Set 115
    Review Problem Set 2 119

Chapter 8
DISTINGUISHNG CONDITION PRECEDENT FROM CONDITION SUBSEQUENT FROM DIVESTING CONDITION

  I. OVERVIEW 124

  II. REVISITING THE CONDITION SUBSEUQENT 124

 III. REVISITING THE CONDITION PRECEDENT.......................126

    A. REVISITING CONTINGENT REMAINDERS 126
    B. REVISITING THE DIVESTING CONDITION........................126
    C. ANALYTICAL KEYS 129

 IV. RECAP...132

    Chapter 8 Problem Set 134

Chapter 9
ONE LAST SET OF ESTATES: LIFE ESTATES DEFEASIBLE

  I. OVERVIEW...137

  II. THE LIFE ESTATE CUT SHORT BY DETERMINABLE WORDS OF LIMITATION 138

 III. THE LIFE ESTATE CUT SHORT BY CONDITION SUBSEQUENT WORDS OF LIMITATION 140

 IV. RECAP...141

Chapter 9 Problem Set 143

Chapter 10
MISCELLANEOUS COMMON LAW RULES REGULATING CONVEYANCES

  I. OVERVIEW...146

 II. RULES FURTHERING THE COMMON LAW
      INHERITANCE TAX 146

      A. THE RULE IN SHELLEY'S CASE 146
      B. THE DOCTRINE OF WORTHIER TITLE 150

III. THE RULE IN PUREFOY'S CASE.............................152

IV. MODERN TREND 153

      Recap Chart...155
      Chapter 10 Problem Set 156

Chapter 11
CLASS GIFTS

  I. OVERVIEW...158

 II. ANALYSIS 158

III. CLOSING THE CLASS 160

      A. NATURALLY/PHYSIOLOGICALLY......................160
      B. RULE OF CONVENIENCE 160
      C. RECAP..162

      Recap Chart...163
      Chapter 11 Problem Set 164
      Review Problem Set 3 167

Chapter 12
THE RULE AGAINST PERPETUITIES

I.   OVERVIEW 172

II. THE CREATE, KILL & COUNT APPROACH 173

    A. CONTINGENT REMAINDERS 176
    RAP & Contingent Remainder Problem Set 185

    B. EXECUTORY INTERESTS 188
    Executory Interests Problem Set 197

    C. CLASS GIFTS 199
    Class Gifts Problem Set 204

    D. MODERN TREND 205

APPENDIX A
ANSWERS TO PROBLEM SETS

Chapter 2 Problem Set 206
Chapter 3 Problem Set 208
Chapter 4 Problem Set 211
Chapter 6 Problem Set 215
Review Problem Set 1 218
Chapter 7 Problem Set 224
Review Problem Set 2 228
Chapter 8 Problem Set 233
Chapter 9 Problem Set 236
Chapter 10 Problem Set 240
Chapter 11 Problem Set 243
Review Problem Set 3 246
Chapter 12 Problem Set – Contingent Remainders 253
Chapter 12 Problem Set – Executory Interests 263
Chapter 12 Problem Set – Vested Subject to Open 269

Index 271

Chapter 1

INTRODUCTION

I. OVERVIEW

A. INTRODUCTION

O[1] owns Greenacres, a 200 acre farm:

GREENACRES

O decides she wants to give Greenacres to A and B. She comes to you for advice on how she can divide the property between them. One way is to split Greenacres in half, giving 100 acres to each. But just as property can be divided physically, property rights can also be divided temporally - over time.

The study of the temporal division of property rights is the study of possessory estates and future interests. The party who holds the right to take actual possession of the property *right now* holds the *possessory estate*. The party who holds the right to take actual possession of the property *in the future* (when a prior possessory estate ends), holds the

---

[1] "O" is the abbreviation for the original owner's/grantor's name. The material could use any name for the owner/grantor and other parties, but to simplify the analytical process the material typically will use a letter as a substitute for each party's name (after you get more comfortable with the material, the problem sets will introduce names). Anytime you see a capital letter in a conveyance, assume the capital letter is an abbreviation for a full name. O is the common abbreviation for the party who owns the property; A, B, C, etc., for the grantees typically. Obviously in the real world, any formal document would use the person's full name. In this example, O could be Olivia Olinich, A could be Andy Anderson, and B could be Betty Booqu. Assume each capital letter constitutes a person who is alive and who can be identified at the time of the conveyance.

future interest.[2] For example, O could give Greenacres "to A for life, then to B and her heirs."[3] A would hold the possessory estate (the right to possess Greenacres right now), and B would hold the future interest (the right to possess Greenacres in the future - upon A's death). This is but one example of how O could split the property rights temporally between A and B. There are many different ways property interests can be split over time. The different possible combinations of temporal estates, and how such estates are created, are the essence of the law of possessory estates and future interests.

B. HISTORICAL ROOTS

Possessory estate and future interests were first created during early common law in response to historical conditions and rules which existed at that time. Although most of these conditions and rules no longer exist, the terminology and basic combinations of estates which were developed then generally remain intact today. Analytically, however, it is possible to learn possessory estates and future interests without a detailed examination of their historical roots. This material will refer to the historical origins of the possessory estate and future interest scheme only to the limited extent that it aids in understanding the present terms and schemes.

C. INSTRUMENTS USED TO CREATE

Possessory estates and future interests can be created in a number of different written instruments. The simplest way to create the interests is in a deed, in which case they are known as *legal* possessory estates and future interests. Possessory estates and future interests are best understood, however, in the context of a trust. In a trust, the trustee holds legal title and

---

[2] Both possessory estates and future interests are *present* property rights in that the holder *presently* has the right to possess the land. The right to possess the land may be immediate, in which case the interest is a possessory interest, or it may be the right to possess the property in the future, in which case the interest is a future interest; in either case, the holder *presently* owns that right. Possession is not a mere hope or expectancy, it is a right and property interest. In the case of the future interest, full enjoyment of the right is delayed, but the right to possess the land in the future is a present right.

[3] Although possessory estates and future interests can be created in either personal property or real property, historically possessory estates and future interests were used primarily with real property. For many students, it is conceptually easier to think about the system of possessory estates and future interests in the context of real property. For that reason, for the most part the hypotheticals and problems will assume the property being conveyed is real property. It is recommended that you use this mindset as well in thinking about possessory estates and future interests – at least at the outset.

the trust beneficiaries hold the equitable interest in the trust property. Invariably the trust beneficiaries' interests are split over time into some combination of possessory estates and future interests.[4] Because trust beneficiaries hold the equitable interest in a trust, they hold *equitable* possessory estates and future interests (created in a trust) as opposed to legal possessory estates and future interests (created in a deed typically).

Overlapping the law of trusts onto the law of possessory estates and future interests, however, only further complicates the already challenging task of learning the latter.[5] To minimize the degree of difficulty associated with learning the basic possessory estates and future interests, the material will assume, for the most part, that the conveyance is in the form of a deed and creates a legal possessory estate and future interest. In the real world, however, it is extremely rare to encounter possessory estates and future interests outside of a trust.

II. THE ANALYTICAL SCHEME

Although it is important to know how to create (i.e., how to draft) possessory estates and future interests, the introductory coverage to possessory estates and future interests focuses primarily on how to *construe* possessory estates and future interests drafted by someone else.[6] In construing a conveyance,[7] there will be only one possessory estate, but there can be more than one future interest. Construing possessory estates and future interests involves properly analyzing (1) which possessory estate has been created, and (2) which future interest or interests have been created.

---

[4] For example, upon learning that he had terminal cancer, the patient established a trust for his benefit for the remainder of his life, then for the benefit of his wife for her life, and upon her death, the property is to be distributed outright to his children equally.

[5] Accordingly, most introductory coverages focus on *legal* possessory estates and future interests. In the real world, however, *legal* possessory estates and future interests should be discouraged. The disadvantages associated with *legal* future interests in land are so numerous that in England, the homeland of possessory estates and future interests, they are now prohibited as a general rule. Only *equitable* possessory estates future interests are permitted in England. EDWARD H. RABIN ET AL., FUNDAMENTALS OF MODERN REAL PROPERTY LAW 191 (4th ed., Foundation Press 2000).

[6] You should keep in mind, however, how you would *create* such possessory estates and future interests. Knowing the proper way to create the estates facilitates construing them.

[7] A conveyance is a generic term used to describe the different ways property can be transferred from one party to another: (1) either for consideration (a sale) or as a gift (a donative transfer), and (2) either inter vivos (while the grantor/transferor is alive) or testamentary (at the time of the grantor's/transferor's death).

A. POSSESSORY ESTATES

Proper analysis of the possessory estate involves two steps: (1) identify *who* holds the possessory estate, and (2) identify *which possessory estate has been created* based upon its duration. Different possessory estates last for different periods of time. For example, in theory a fee simple absolute lasts forever, while a life estate lasts only for the life of the grantee. Under the traditional common law approach, each possessory estate has its own *"words of limitation"* which indicate its *duration* and which *must* be used to create that possessory estate. In analyzing the possessory estate, the key is to focus on the express language of the conveyance to identify which words of limitation have been used. The words of limitation used will determine the duration of the estate, and the duration of the estate will help determine which possessory estate has been created and which future interest follows it.

B. FUTURE INTERESTS

Proper analysis of each future interest involves three steps: (1) identify *which* future interest it is; (2) identify *who* holds it; and (3) indicate the *duration* of the future interest (how long the party has the right to possess the property once it becomes possessory). For the most part, these last two steps are the same as for possessory estates. The challenge is identifying *which* future interest the party holds. The keys to analyzing *which* future interest it is are: (a) which possessory estate it follows, and (b) whether the grantor or a third party holds the future interest.

C. THE ANALYTICAL KEYS

Possessory estates and future interests are rather abstract.[8] The key is to focus on the *terminology* (at times it will seem like a foreign language), the *words of limitation* necessary to create the different estates, and the different permissible combinations of possessory estates and future interests. Analytically the best way to master possessory estates and future interests is to (1) group them into the different possible *categories* of possessory estates, (2) know which future interests go with which category of possessory estates, and (3) know how to distinguish the different permissible combinations of

---

[8] So abstract that parts of the prior paragraphs no doubt seemed incomprehensible. Do not worry if you do not fully understand the material so far. The rest of the book breaks down these sentences into digestible components and gives examples that simplify the material to the point where you will be able to understand it fully.

possessory estates and future interests within each category. That analytical process probably makes no sense at this point, but the material will take you step-by-step through this process, and when you are done, you will understand how to analyze each possessory estate and future interest. In addition, practice makes perfect. The more possessory estate and future interest problems you do, the better you will be at analyzing conveyances.

Chapter 2

THE FEE SIMPLE ABSOLUTE

I. OVERVIEW

The basic combinations of possessory estates and future interests can be broken down into three core *categories* based upon the duration of the possessory estates in each category:
> (1) the fee simple absolute,
> (2) the fee simple defeasibles, and
> (3) the finite estates.

The first category, *the fee simple absolute*, is the most important and most prevalent of the possessory estates. It is so important that it is in a category all by itself.

II. THE BENCHMARK ESTATE

A. THE NATURE OF THE ESTATE

The fee simple absolute (or "fee simple" as it is also known) is the benchmark estate against which all other possessory estates are compared and analyzed.[9] You already know this estate, although you probably do not recognize it by its technical name. Return to the opening hypothetical. The material began by stating that "O owns Greenacres, ..." When you read that sentence, you probably did not even stop to think about what the material meant when it said O "owns" Greenacres. When someone *owns* a piece of property, without any qualification, what does that mean? From a possessory estate and future interest standpoint, it means the owner holds the property in fee simple absolute.

The defining characteristic of the fee simple absolute is that in theory it lasts forever – the owner has the right to possess the property forever (if he or she could live that long). There is *no future interest*. No one presently

---

[9] CORNELIUS J. MOYNIHAN, INTRODUCTION TO THE LAW OF REAL PROPERTY, 26 (1962).

has the *right* to possess the property in the future. There is *no inherent condition or restriction* limiting how the owner can use the property.[10] In addition, while the owner is alive, he or she has the right to transfer the property freely to whomever he or she wishes.[11]

Although in theory an owner has the right to possess the land forever, at some point he or she will die. Upon the owner's death, with a fee simple absolute, his or her right to possession does not end. He or she can devise the property as he or she wishes.[12] In the event the owner fails to devise the property, it (the right to possession) will pass to his or her heirs.[13] The fee simple absolute is the largest, most complete estate a person can hold.

B. THE WORDS OF PURCHASE

Having established the temporal duration of the fee simple absolute (in theory it lasts forever) and the scope of the interest (there are no conditions or limitations on an owner's right to use or transfer it), the last key is how to create (and thus recognize) a fee simple absolute.[14] Assume O

---

[10] RESTATEMENT (FIRST) OF PROPERTY §§ 14-15 (1936) [hereinafter PROPERTY RESTATEMENT].

[11] The ability to transfer property inter vivos (while the grantor is alive), either by gift or for consideration, is also known as the right to *alienate* the property.

[12] When a person dies, there are two basic ways in which the property rights which survive the decedent may be passed on to other individuals. If the decedent dies with a last will and testament ("will"), he or she is said to die "testate" and the will may direct to whom the decedent's property goes (the decedent/testator is said to "devise" the property to a devisee or beneficiary). When the decedent dies without a will (dies "intestate"), the property passes to the decedent's heirs pursuant to the state's intestate distribution scheme. The recipients (the heirs) "inherit" the property.

[13] The material just said that there is no future interest and yet now it says that upon an owner's death, the party has the right to devise it to whomever he or she wishes, and if he or she fails to devise it, his or her heirs will inherit it. Does that mean that one or the other party *must* have a future interest? No. While the owner is alive, the heirs apparent (the parties who *think* they will receive the owner's property when he or she dies) have a mere *expectancy*, but no property interest (*no* present *right* to possess the property in the future). Any expectancy the heirs have can be defeated by the owner simply executing a will which devises the property to someone else or by conveying the property *inter vivos* to someone else. Likewise, devisees under a will have no property interest until the testator dies (no present right to possess the property in the future); all they have is an expectancy. A future interest is a present *right* to possess the property in the future. Neither an heir nor a devisee has a present right while the owner is alive; hence, no future interest.

[14] As with all drafting, there is the proper terminology to create the desired end, and there is the issue of how an instrument should be construed if the drafter fails to use the proper terminology. The material will focus on, and presume, proper drafting technique based on

owns Greenacres and wants to transfer it to A in fee simple absolute. Obviously the instrument of transfer must say "to A" to indicate the party to whom the property is being transferred. These words constitute the *words of purchase*[15] – the words in the conveyance which indicate to whom the property is being transferred.[16] But inasmuch as property interests can be divided temporally, the conveyance also needs to indicate the *duration* of the property interest being transferred.

C. THE WORDS OF LIMITATION

The express words in the conveyance which indicate the duration of the estate being conveyed are called the *words of limitation*.[17] Common law was very demanding in requiring use of the appropriate words of limitation. The common law words of limitation, or "drafting language," necessary to create a fee simple absolute were "*and her heirs*."[18] Combining the words of purchase ("to A") with the words of limitation ("and her heirs"), [19] the conveyance should be expressed as follows:

---

the traditional common law approach. Later the material will cover the modern trend changes to the common law drafting principles and the default rules when improper drafting occurs. *See* discussion *infra* Ch. 2, III, and Ch. 4, III, A.

[15] Although the phrase is "words of *purchase*," there is no requirement that the grantee pay consideration. The grantee can take by gift. The phrase merely indicates *to whom* the property is being transferred via a written instrument (because of the written instrument requirement, there are no words of purchase when the property passes by inheritance, but there are when the property passes under the terms of a will). MOYNIHAN, *supra* note 9, at 28.

[16] *Id.*

[17] *Id.*

[18] Or, if the grantee were a male, "and *his* heirs." The critical word is "heirs." Other words (such as "to A and her *children*") create ambiguity as to whether a joint interest was intended for the grantee and her children, giving the children a present interest, or whether the children were intended to have a future interest after the grantee's death, or whether the children were to have no interest and the grantor intended to give the grantee a fee simple absolute. The operative word of limitation is "heirs" to indicate a fee simple absolute under the traditional common law approach.

[19] The "words of limitation" refer to the special drafting language necessary to create each possessory estate. There are special words of limitation for each possessory estate. The particular words of limitation necessary to create a fee simple absolute at common law, "and his/her heirs," are also known as the "words of general inheritance." PROPERTY RESTATEMENT, *supra* note 10, at § 27, cmt. c.

EXAMPLE 1

O →[20] To A and her heirs.

Notice the order of the words. First, the words of purchase ("to A"), which indicate to whom the property interest is being transferred, and then the words of limitation ("and her heirs"), which indicate the estate being transferred.

EXAMPLE 2

O →   To A   and her heirs.

Words of Purchase + Words of Limitation

This is the basic sequencing of the words of purchase/words of limitation of every estate, be it a possessory estate or a future interest.

D. ANALYZING THE POSSESSORY ESTATE

While the above example examines how to *draft* a fee simple absolute, from a student's perspective the norm is that you will be given a conveyance and you will be asked to *construe* the conveyance: to identify the possessory estate and future interests created. With respect to the possessory estate, the analysis is a two step process: (1) identify *who* holds the possessory estate (find the words of purchase "to X ..."), and (2) indicate *which possessory estate* the party holds (find the *words of limitation* which indicate the *duration* of the estate). That is the analytical scheme that you should apply to the possessory estate in each conveyance.

Possessory estates and future interests, and the notion of dividing property interests over time, are very abstract. For some students, it helps to

---

[20] The small arrow indicates that a property interest is being conveyed by a grantor to one or more grantees. Depending on the facts, the conveyance could take place inter vivos (typically by a deed) or testamentary (upon the owner's death). A testamentary transfer is by a will typically. (Although a will is executed inter vivos, it is not effective until the person (the testator) dies – which makes the transfers under the will testamentary transfers.) If the facts do not indicate otherwise, assume that each conveyance is an inter vivos conveyance.

visualize the material using a timeline. For example, the conveyance of a fee simple absolute from O to A can be diagrammed on a timeline as follows:

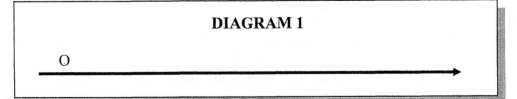

The arrow represents a timeline which stretches out to the right into the future, theoretically for eternity. For each conveyance, you should assume that the original owner ("O") holds the property in fee simple absolute unless told otherwise. Just as in theory a fee simple absolute lasts forever, so too does the timeline arrow the owner holds. If the owner were to transfer the property, the conveyance is indicated by a cross line towards the left end of the timeline:

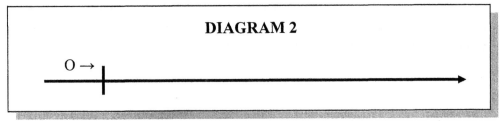

This cross line (and the smaller arrow just to the left of it) indicates the point in time when the owner conveyed the property. The part of the timeline to the right of the arrow and cross line indicates *how* the owner conveyed the property in terms of the possessory estate and future interest(s) created. If there are no other lines to the right of the "time of conveyance" cross line, just the uninterrupted timeline stretching out to the right, which indicates that the transferee/grantee[21] has the right to hold the property in theory forever – a fee simple absolute. For each property interest conveyed, to the right of the conveying cross line write: (1) the name of the grantee, and (2) the name of the property interest he or she received. For example, the complete diagram for the conveyance "To A and her heirs" is:

---

[21] These terms are synonymous for purposes of this material. They indicate to whom the property interest has been conveyed.

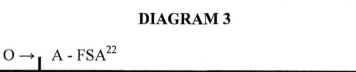

DIAGRAM 3

O → A - FSA[22]

O conveyed to A a fee simple absolute. Because a fee simple absolute lasts forever, A receives the whole, unbroken timeline.[23]

In analyzing different conveyances, the words of purchase ("to A") are relatively easy to identify and analyze. All that changes is the identity of the recipient. Accordingly, you should focus on the words immediately following the words of purchase – those words typically constitute the words of limitation (for example – "and her heirs").   The words of limitation indicate the duration of the estate created, which in turn indicate which possessory estate is being created.   To master the scheme of possessory estates and future interests you *must* memorize and master the words of limitation necessary to create the different basic estates.   The words of limitation which indicate a fee simple absolute are "and her heirs/and his heirs."

The fee simple absolute is the most complete estate a person can hold, and it is the estate against which all the other possessory estates should be compared.

III. THE MODERN TREND

The modern trend presumes that a grantor intends to convey all that he or she owns in the absence of express words of limitation indicating the

---

[22] When diagramming conveyances, you may find it easier to abbreviate the different possessory estates and future interests.

[23] For each conveyance, you need to account for the whole timeline from the time of the grant (the initial cross line) to eternity (the end of the timeline). If the owner conveys a possessory estate short of a fee simple absolute, there must be at least one future interest. In diagramming property interests, each estate which is less than a fee simple absolute must have a cross line to the *right* of the initial conveyance cross line to indicate the end of the estate and the beginning of the future interest following the estate. And at least one of the future interests must be of fee simple absolute duration to account for the whole timeline. The diagramming process will make more sense as the material demonstrates how to diagram the basic possessory estate and future interest combinations.

intent to limit the estate being conveyed.[24]   Under the modern trend, a grantor need not use the technical words of limitation "and her heirs/and her heirs" to convey a fee simple absolute (assuming that is what the grantor owned at the time of the conveyance). Any words that express the intent to convey a fee simple absolute, or what amounts to a fee simple absolute, will convey a fee simple absolute under the modern trend. Assuming the grantor owns a fee simple absolute, any conveyance that does not expressly limit the estate that is being conveyed will be presumed to convey a fee simple absolute.

The following examples demonstrate the difference between the common law and modern trend approach to the words of limitation necessary to convey a fee simple absolute:

EXAMPLE 3

O →   To A forever.

O →   To A.

O →   To A and her heirs.

Under the common law approach, only the last conveyance would transfer a fee simple absolute. Under the modern trend approach, all three conveyances would transfer a fee simple absolute. The grantor's intent is clearer under the common law approach, but the modern trend implicitly acknowledges that not all drafters/grantors know to use proper terminology. The modern trend focuses more on intent, but at a higher potential cost of administration; the common law approach takes more of a bright line/low cost of administration approach which may, on occasion, frustrate a grantor's intent.

Notice that the common law words of limitation still work under the modern trend, they are just not necessary. Where the classic words of

---

[24] PROPERTY RESTATEMENT, *supra* note 10, at §§ 39-41. For further discussion of the difference between the common law approach and the modern trend approach to the necessary words of limitation to create the different estates, *see* discussion *infra* Ch. 4, III, A.

limitation for a fee simple ("and his heirs/and her heirs") are present, the estate is a fee simple regardless of the approach. The difference between the common law approach and the modern trend approach arises when the proper words of limitation are *not* present. The common law default estate – the estate created when proper words of limitation are not used – is the life estate.[25] The modern trend default estate is the fee simple (assuming that is what the grantor held). In addition, the common law approach is very strict in requiring proper words of limitation; the modern trend focuses more on intent and does not put much emphasis on the technical words of limitation as long as the intent is present.[26]

The material will generally use, and expect you to use, the common law approach. Where the proper words of limitation are not present, you will have to fall back on whether the jurisdiction follows the common law approach or the modern trend approach. *Pay careful attention to whether your professor expects you to know only the common law approach, only the modern trend approach – or both.* The problems sets will contain problems that will remind you of the differences between the two approaches.

IV. TRANSFERABILITY, DEVISABILITY, INHERITABILITY

There are basically three ways to convey a property interest. A property interest is *transferable* if, while the owner of the interest is alive, he or she can freely transfer it to any third party. A property interest is *devisable* if, upon the owner's death, he or she can freely will it in his or her last will and testament to any third party. And a property interest is *inheritable* if the heirs of the owner of the interest can inherit the property interest if the owner dies without a valid will.[27]

The fee simple absolute is freely transferable, devisable and inheritable.[28]

---

[25] An estate measured by the life of the grantee. *See* Ch. 4, III, A.

[26] This sentence implies that (1) there are only two approaches, and (2) a jurisdiction or court must fall into one or the other. In reality it is more of a spectrum, with the traditional common law at one end and the modern trend at the other. Particularly within the common law approach there are courts and jurisdictions which take a 'loose' approach – as opposed to a strict, hard-line approach – to the necessary words of limitation. Those approaches, however, are beyond the scope of this introductory coverage.

[27] Or if the owner dies with a valid will but it does not dispose of the property interest in question.

[28] MOYNIHAN, *supra* note 9, at 26.

THE DIFFERENT CATEGORIES OF POSSESSORY ESTATES
AND THEIR FUTURE INTERESTS

CATEGORY	POSSESSORY ESTATE(S) (words of limitation)	FUTURE INTERESTS GRANTOR	THIRD PARTY
FEE SIMPLE ABSOLUTE	FEE SIMPLE ABSOLUTE (and her heirs)	NONE	NONE

CHAPTER 2 PROBLEM SET

Which of the following conveyances properly transfers a fee simple absolute to the grantee under: (a) the common law; and (b) the modern trend? (*Answers to all of the problems in the book are set forth in the back of the book in Appendix A.*)

1. O → To A and his heirs.

    (a) Common law: Fee tail

    (b) Modern trend: FSA

2. O → To A.

    (a) Common law:

    (b) Modern trend:

3. O → To A in fee simple absolute.

    (a) Common law:

    (b) Modern trend:

4.   Ollie → To the heirs of Abigail.[29]

   (a) Common law:

   (b) Modern trend:

5.   Oscar → To Beth.

   (a) Common law:

   (b) Modern trend:

6.   Olivia → All to Allison.

   (a) Common law:

   (b) Modern trend:

7.   Olivia → To Alice forever.

   (a) Common law:

   (b) Modern trend:

---

[29] Notice the introduction of first names here instead of just letters. The analysis is the same. As you progress, the material will vary how it refers to the parties.

Chapter 3

THE FEE SIMPLE DEFEASIBLES

I. OVERVIEW

The second category of possessory estates is the *fee simple defeasibles*. While the defining characteristic of the fee simple absolute is that in theory it will last forever, the defining characteristic of the fee simple defeasibles is that they *may* last forever.

II. ANALYZING THE FEE SIMPLE DEFEASIBLES

A. THE NATURE OF THE ESTATE

The following is a classic example of a fee simple defeasible:

EXAMPLE 1

O →   To A and her heirs, but if A sells alcohol on the land,
        then O has the right to re-enter and reclaim the land.

Notice the wording of the conveyance begins just like that for a fee simple absolute. The first two words, "To A," are the words of purchase which indicate to whom the property interest is being conveyed. The words immediately following the words of purchase typically are the words of limitation which help indicate which possessory estate is being conveyed. Here, the phrase immediately following the words of purchase is "and her heirs" – the classic words of limitation for the fee simple absolute. But the wording of the conveyance goes on to indicate that the fee simple being conveyed is *not* absolute but rather is qualified by a restriction or condition – here, that A not sell alcohol on the land.[30] If A sells alcohol on the land,

---

[30] Notice the condition is a condition *subsequent* – a condition which qualifies how long the right to possession may last and which applies *after* the interest becomes possessory. A condition subsequent needs to be distinguished from a condition precedent – a condition which applies to the time period *before* the interest becomes possessory and which typically *must be satisfied before* the interest *can become* possessory. As the material develops, you

O has the right to re-enter and reclaim the right to possess the land. A would lose the right to possess the property. The grantee's right to possession is not absolute, it is defeasible – subject to being terminated – if the express condition occurs.

The additional language which qualifies what would otherwise be a fee simple absolute is what distinguishes the fee simple defeasibles from the other possessory estates. The uncertain nature of the express condition subsequent or restriction (the uncertainty as to whether it will occur or not) is such that the possessory estate *may last forever* (if the condition or restriction never occurs), but the possessory estate *may end* (if the condition or restriction occurs).

If the language of a conveyance starts out like a fee simple absolute, but then there is an *express condition subsequent* after the fee simple words of limitation qualifying the fee simple, the possessory estate is one of the fee simple defeasibles. There are three fee simple defeasibles: (1) the *fee simple determinable*; (2) the *fee simple subject to a condition subsequent*; and (3) the *fee simple subject to an executory limitation*.

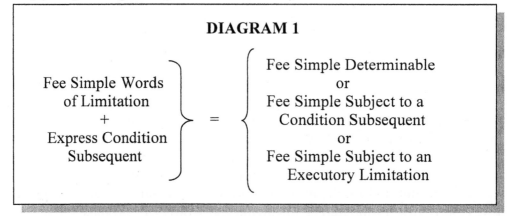

DIAGRAM 1

Fee Simple Words
of Limitation
+
Express Condition
Subsequent

=

Fee Simple Determinable
or
Fee Simple Subject to a
Condition Subsequent
or
Fee Simple Subject to an
Executory Limitation

Inasmuch as there are three different fee simple defeasibles, the next step analytically is to know how to distinguish among the three.

B. IDENTIFYING EACH FEE SIMPLE DEFEASIBLE

The features that distinguish one fee simple defeasible from another are: (1) *who holds the future interest* – the original grantor or a third party (anyone other than the grantor); and (2) *if the grantor retains the future*

---

will realize the importance of being able to distinguish between these types of conditions.

interest, how does the condition subsequent cut short the fee simple –
automatically or only upon the grantor's actions.

1. Ask "Who Holds the Future Interest?"

The first step analytically in distinguishing the fee simple defeasibles
from each other is to ask, "*Who* holds the future interest?" If the future
interest[31] is held by the grantor, the fee simple defeasible will be one of only
two possibilities: a fee simple determinable or a fee simple subject to a
condition subsequent. On the other hand, if the future interest is held by a
third party, there is only one possibility: the possessory estate is a fee simple
subject to an executory limitation:

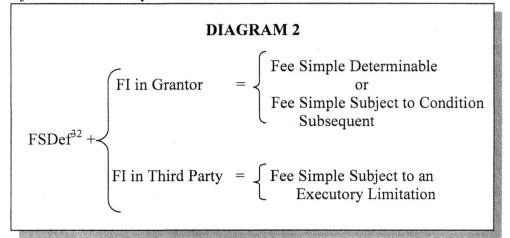

DIAGRAM 2

2. Fee Simple Determinable vs. Fee Simple Subject to a Condition Subsequent

Where the possessory estate is a fee simple defeasible, and the future
interest is held by the grantor, the possessory estate is either: (1) a *fee
simple determinable*; or (2) a *fee simple subject to a condition subsequent.*
These are the only two possibilities.

---

[31] Again, a future interest is the right to possession after the possessory estate ends
– here, after the fee simple defeasible.

[32] "FSDef" is an abbreviation for fee simple defeasible; "FI" is for future interest.

DIAGRAM 3

Fee Simple Defeasible + FI in Grantor =
$\left\{\begin{array}{c} \text{Fee Simple Determinable} \\ \text{or} \\ \text{Fee Simple Subject to a} \\ \text{Condition Subsequent} \end{array}\right.$

The key to distinguishing between these two fee simple defeasibles is *how* the condition subsequent, if it occurs, *cuts short* the fee simple: automatically or upon the grantor's actions. If the grantor's intent is to terminate the fee simple *automatically* the moment the express qualifying condition occurs, the possessory estate is a *fee simple determinable*. On the other hand, if the grantor's intent is *not* to terminate the possessory estate automatically the moment the qualifying condition occurs, but rather to give the grantor the *option to terminate* – the right to enter and reclaim the property – the possessory estate is a *fee simple subject to a condition subsequent*. (The grantor's right to re-enter is called the *right of entry*[33] or *power of termination*.[34])

While this conceptual difference may seem trivial,[35] you need to be able to distinguish these two possessory estates. Moreover, although in theory the key is the grantor's intent, the traditional common law approach focused

---

[33] Technically, under the common law approach, it is also known as a "right of entry for breach of condition/for condition broken" clause. MOYNIHAN, *supra* note 9, at 112.

[34] The modern trend prefers to call the future interest a "power to terminate." This stems from the modern trend aversion to self-help. The common law right of re-entry literally requires the grantor physically to re-enter the land to terminate the fee simple. The problem is that the party holding the possessory estate may resist the grantor's attempt at re-entry. The potential for violence, both to the parties and to innocent by-standers, has led the modern trend to repudiate self-help and to require the party (here the grantor) to use the court system to exercise his or her rights. Hence the modern trend preference to call the future interest following a fee simple subject to a condition subsequent a "power to terminate" rather than a "right of entry."

[35] The distinguishing feature of the fee simple determinable, that it terminates automatically, affects when the statute of limitations for adverse possession begins. Assuming the express condition occurs and the party who held the possessory estate does not vacate the land, with the fee simple determinable the statute of limitations begins to run immediately upon the condition occurring, whether or not the grantor knows that the condition has occurred. On the other hand, with the fee simple subject to a condition subsequent, the condition's occurrence only gives the grantor the right to re-enter and retake the property; it does not start the statute of limitations for adverse possession until the grantor tries to re-enter the property and is denied.

more on the express language used in the conveyance. The traditional common law approach created a virtual irrebuttable presumption that certain words of limitation evidenced a certain grantor's intent. Accordingly, the key to distinguishing between the two fee simple defeasibles where the future interest is held by the grantor is the words of limitation used to introduce the qualifying condition.

The classic words of limitation evidencing a fee simple determinable – the intent that the possessory estate terminate automatically the moment the qualifying condition occurs – is the phrase: "to A and her heirs *as long as/so long as* … ." Other words used less commonly but equally effective are *"until"*, *"during"*, and *"while."*[36] In contrast, the classic words of limitation evidencing a fee simple subject to a condition subsequent – the intent that the possessory estate *not* terminate automatically the moment the qualifying condition occurs, but rather continues until the grantor re-enters and re-claims the property – is the phrase "to A and her heirs, *but if* … ." Other words used less commonly but equally effective are *"however, if ..."* and *"provided that … ."*[37] Where the grantor retains the future interest, and the words of limitation cutting short the fee simple are ambiguous (unclear if the grantor intended a fee simple determinable or a fee simple subject to a condition subsequent), the courts favor construing the estate as a fee simple subject to a condition subsequent because of their distaste for forfeiture of property interests (which is inherent in the fee simple determinable).[38]

In addition, where the fee simple subject to a condition subsequent words of limitation are present, they should be coupled with an express clause (after the clause expressing the qualifying condition) which states that the grantor has the right to re-enter and re-take the right to possess the property in the event the condition occurs.[39]

EXAMPLE 2

O → To A and her heirs, but if A sells alcohol on the land,
    then O has the right to re-enter and reclaim the land.

---

[36] PROPERTY RESTATEMENT, *supra* note 10, at § 44, cmt. l.

[37] PROPERTY RESTATEMENT, *supra* note 10, at § 45, cmt. j.

[38] 1 RICHARD R. POWELL, POWELL ON REAL PROPERTY § 13.05[2] (Matthew Bender 2006).

[39] *Id.*

The express clause in the conveyance giving O the right to re-enter and retake the land is known as a *"right of entry" clause*. The presence of a right of entry clause in favor of the grantor makes it much easier to identify the fee simple subject to a condition subsequent. If the express right of entry clause is not present, its absence typically creates ambiguity over which fee simple defeasible the grantor intended. Recourse to the introductory words of limitation before the qualifying condition becomes the next best evidence of which fee simple defeasible the grantor intended. Again, where the language is ambiguous, the courts tend to favor a fee simple subject to a condition subsequent because of the judicial disfavor for forfeiture.[40]

Just as with the fee simple absolute, the fee simple defeasibles can be diagrammed on a timeline. The whole, uninterrupted arrow to the right of the initial conveyance cross line would constitute a fee simple absolute:

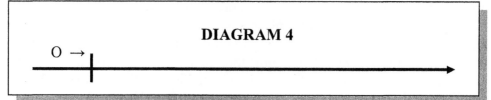

DIAGRAM 4

O →

Inasmuch as the distinguishing feature of the fee simple defeasible estates is that they *may* end at some point in the future, this possibility is indicated by a *dashed* cross line at some point on the arrow (to the right of the point in time when the fee simple defeasible estate was created):

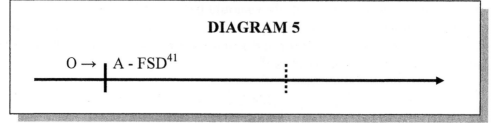

DIAGRAM 5

O → A - FSD[41]

Diagram 5 reflects that the fee simple *may* end (hence the dotted line, as opposed to a solid line) if the qualifying condition occurs. Diagram 5

---

[40] Notice that if the conveyance is construed as a fee simple determinable and the condition occurs, the effect is immediate and automatic *forfeiture* of the possessory estate; with the fee simple subject to a condition subsequent, if the condition occurs the possessory estate does not end until the grantor asserts his or her right of entry. Because of judicial disfavor for forfeiture, many courts prefer to construe ambiguous conveyances as fee simple subject to a condition subsequent. MOYNIHAN, *supra* note 9, at 109.

[41] "FSD" is an abbreviation for fee simple determinable.

depicts the fee simple determinable. *If* the qualifying condition occurs, the fee simple will end automatically the moment the condition subsequent occurs. But if the qualifying condition does not occur, the fee simple will last forever.

Diagram 5 should be modified slightly to depict the fee simple subject to a condition subsequent to reflect that if the qualifying condition occurs the estate does not end automatically. If the qualifying condition occurs, the grantor has the option to terminate the estate. The estate does not end unless, and until, the owner exercises *the right of entry/power of termination.* Graphically, the easiest way to indicate this distinguishing feature of the fee simple subject to a condition subsequent is to use a dashed cross line (to indicate that the estate *may* end) – with an arrow added to the bottom to indicate that the estate does not end unless and until the grantor re-enters and re-takes the property (exercises the power to terminate):

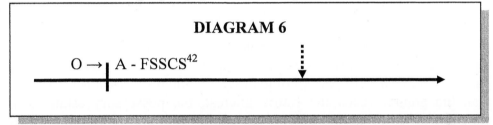

DIAGRAM 6

O → A - FSSCS[42]

The key, however, is not the difference in the diagrams. The key is the conceptual difference between the fee simple determinable and the fee simple subject to a condition subsequent which leads to the difference in their words of limitation and classifying terminology.

3. Future interest in Third Party – The Fee Simple Subject to an Executory Limitation

If the future interest following a fee simple defeasible is held by a *third party*, the fee simple defeasible is a *fee simple subject to an executory limitation.*[43] And for introductory purposes, there is one, and only one, future interest which goes with fee simple subject to an executory limitation – an *executory interest.*[44]

---

[42] "FSSCS" is an abbreviation for fee simple subject to a condition subsequent.

[43] PROPERTY RESTATEMENT, *supra* note 10, at § 46, cmt. e.

[44] There are, however, *two types* of executory interests. The executory interest can be either a *shifting* or a *springing* executory interest. This distinction is explored later in the material. *See infra* Ch. 3, II, C, 4.

Example 3 below re-drafts Example 2 to give the future interest to a third party:

EXAMPLE 3

O →   To A and her heirs, but if A sells alcohol on the land,
       then to B and his heirs.

In analyzing the conveyance in Example 3,[45] the first question is in which category of estates does the possessory estate belong – the fee simple absolute or the fee simple defeasibles? Although the first five words of the conveyance are the classic words of purchase and limitation for a fee simple absolute, the conveyance goes on to impose an express restriction on how long A's possessory estate may last (an express condition subsequent). The fee simple may end if A sells alcohol on the land. The possessory estate is a fee simple defeasible.

To determine which fee simple defeasible it is, first ask, "Who takes" the future interest following the fee simple defeasible – the grantor or a third party? Here B, a third party, holds the future interest. Because a party other than the grantor holds the future interest, the possessory estate is a fee simple subject to an executory limitation, and the future interest is an executory interest.

Where there is a fee simple defeasible and the future interest is held by the grantor, much is made of *how* the fee simple is cut short.[46] This is *not* the case if the future interest is held by a third party. Where there is a fee simple defeasible and the future interest is held by a third party, it does not matter *which language* is used to cut short the fee simple.

---

[45] Notice the generic analytical steps performed in analyzing the conveyance. First, determine who takes the possessory estate and in which category of possessory estates it falls. Once you determine which category it is, determine which possessory estate within that category it is (for the fee simple defeasibles, that requires you to ask "who takes" the future interest). Then, if the possessory estate is not a fee simple absolute, analyze the future interest(s). In analyzing each future interest, remember that there are three steps: (1) identify which future interest it is; (2) identify who holds the future interest; and (3) determine which possessory estate the future interest will be if and when it becomes possessory. This is the basic analytical process that should be performed over and over for each conveyance.

[46] If the qualifying language *automatically* cuts short the fee simple, the estate is fee simple determinable. If the qualifying language *does not* automatically cut short the fee simple but rather gives the grantor the right to re-enter and terminate the estate, the estate is a fee simple subject to a condition subsequent.

Regardless of whether fee simple determinable or fee simple subject to a condition subsequent language is used to introduce the qualifying condition, where the future interest is given to a third party, the courts have ruled that the fee simple subject to an executory limitation terminates automatically upon the occurrence of the express condition subsequent.[47]   Accordingly, where there is a fee simple defeasible, and the future interest is held by a third party, you need not worry about how the fee simple will terminate – either way the estate is a fee simple subject to an executory limitation.

III.   THE FUTURE INTERESTS WHICH FOLLOW A FEE SIMPLE DEFEASIBLE

The interests examined above – the fee simple determinable, the fee simple subject to a condition subsequent, and the fee simple subject to an executory limitation – describe the *possessory estates* in the second category of estates, the fee simple defeasibles.   Inasmuch as there is the possibility that each of these possessory estates may end, there must be a future interest which follows each of these possessory estates.   *Every possessory estate other than a fee simple absolute must be coupled with a future interest.*   Again, a future interest is the *present* right to possess the property *in the future*.   At the time the fee simple defeasible is created, because the grantor did not transfer a fee simple absolute to the party holding the possessory estate, by definition there must be a future interest. Someone must have the *present* right (at the time the possessory interest is created) to possess the property the moment the possessory estate ends at some point in the future.

A.   ANALYZING FUTURE INTERESTS

There are three steps to analyzing each future interest:[48]   (1) identify *which future interest it is* – state the name of the future interest; (2) identify *who holds* the future interest; and (3) state *the duration* of the future interest.   You will see that to some degree these steps overlap.

---

[47] LEWIS M. SIMES & ALLAN F. SMITH, THE LAW OF FUTURE INTERESTS 266 (2nd ed., West 1956); Bean v. Atkins, 89 A.2d 643 (Va. 1914).

[48] Obviously the remainder of this discussion assumes there is a future interest. If the possessory estate is a fee simple absolute, there is no future interest.   For all other possessory estates, however, there must be a future interest.

Analytically it makes the most sense to start the analysis by identifying *which* future interest it is.   After you analyze *which* future interest it is, analyzing *who holds* it and *how long it will last* is basically the same process as analyzing possessory estates – focus on the words of purchase and the words of limitation in the clause creating the future interest.

1. Identify *Which* Future Interest It Is

Analytically the first step in analyzing each future interest is to identify, by proper name, *which* future interest it is. The name of the future interest turns primarily on: (1) *which possessory estate it follows,*[49] and (2) *whether the grantor or a third party* holds the future interest.   Each possessory estate can be coupled with only a very limited number of possible future interests.[50]   If you master the limited future interest options for each possessory estate, it will make the analytical process much easier.

For purposes of this introductory coverage, the process of analyzing the respective future interests which follow the respective fee simple defeasibles is rather easy because there is only one future interest which can follow each fee simple defeasible. The *only future interest which will follow a fee simple determinable is a possibility of reverter.*[51] These two interests, the fee simple determinable and the possibility of reverter, go hand in hand. The *only future interest which will follow a fee simple subject to a condition subsequent is a right of entry/power of termination.*[52] These two interests go hand in hand. The *only future interest which will follow a fee simple subject to an executory limitation is an executory interest.*[53]   Again, these two interests go hand in hand. Although the names of the future interests help

---

[49] For some future interests, *how it terminates* the possessory estate is also a factor.

[50] This is particularly true for an introductory coverage. A more extensive coverage of possessory estates and future interests would introduce more possible combinations, but that is beyond the scope of this material.

[51] PROPERTY RESTATEMENT, *supra* note 10, at § 154, cmt. g. And conversely, in this introductory coverage, the possibility of reverter follows one, and only one, estate: a fee simple determinable. *But see* discussion *infra* Ch. 9, where the material raises the possibility of defeasible finite estates.

[52] PROPERTY RESTATEMENT, *supra* note 10, at § 155, cmt. b. And conversely, in this introductory coverage, the right of entry/power of termination follows one, and only one, estate: a fee simple subject to a condition subsequent. *But see* discussion *infra* Ch. 9, where the material raises the possibility of defeasible finite estates.

[53] PROPERTY RESTATEMENT, *supra* note 10, at § 158.

somewhat in remembering which future interest goes with which possessory estate,[54] this is where rote memorization becomes important.

2. Identify *Who Holds* the Future Interest

The easiest way to identify the holder of the future interest is to examine the express language of the conveyance to see who will receive the property if the qualifying condition occurs. Where the future interest is express, the clause creating the future interest should contain words of purchase that indicate who holds the future interest. For example:

EXAMPLE 4

O → To A and his heirs, but if A sells alcohol on the land,
then O has the right to re-enter and reclaim the land.

Although at first it looks like A has a fee simple absolute from the phrase "to A and his heirs," the additional qualifying language indicates that A must hold a fee simple defeasible. Which fee simple defeasible turns on who holds the future interest. In Example 4, the future interest is retained by the grantor, O, so the possessory estate must be either a fee simple determinable or a fee simple subject to a condition subsequent. Analyzing further, the words of limitation "but if ..." indicate a fee simple subject to a condition subsequent. The next clause (*reading comma to comma*) indicates to whom the right to possession passes in the event the condition occurs. Here, the express language indicates that O, the grantor, holds the future interest.[55] O holds a right of entry.

---

[54] Notice how the different terms for the future interests reflect the conceptual difference between the two possessory estates. With the fee simple determinable, if the condition occurs, the possessory estate automatically ends and the property automatically reverts to the grantor; hence the term *possibility of reverter*. With the fee simple subject to a condition subsequent, if the express condition occurs, the grantor has a right to re-enter and re-reclaim the property; hence the term *right of entry*. Remembering the conceptual difference between the two fee simple defeasible estates can help you remember the correct coupling of the possessory estates and future interests.

[55] Notice that the words of purchase for the future interest may not be the classic phrasing that prevails for possessory estates. For the possessory estate, the words of purchase will almost always start "To X ... ." While that often will be the case for future interest as well, it is not always – as this example demonstrates. You should, however, be comfortable enough with the concept of the words of purchase to be able to handle this slight variation.

The easiest way to determine *who holds* the future interest is to look for the *express* words of purchase in the clause introducing the future interest. That statement assumes, however, that there are express words of purchase introducing the future interest. For each *possessory* estate, there *must* be express words of purchase or there is no conveyance. But unlike possessory estates, *future interests can be created by default*. A future interest can arise by default where the grantor creates a possessory estate which is *not* a fee simple absolute, but the conveyance does *not* indicate expressly to whom the future interest is granted. Someone must have the right to possession in the event the fee simple is cut short; there must be a future interest. The common law courts reasoned that if the conveyance did not expressly indicate to whom the future interest was conveyed, the grantor must have intended to retain the interest. Thus, *if there is no express language indicating to whom the future interest is granted, the courts imply that by default the future interest is retained/held by the grantor in fee simple.*

For example, what if the conveyance read as follows:

EXAMPLE 5

O → To A and her heirs as long as she does not sell liquor
on the land.

The express words of the conveyance indicate that the grantor intended to create a fee simple defeasible, but the conveyance does not indicate who holds the future interest.[56] Because the possessory estate is a fee simple defeasible, there *must be* a future interest (because the fee simple may end, someone has to hold the present right to possession in the event it does). But the

---

[56] If the material is using proper drafting techniques, why not just make the future interest express?

> O → To A and her heirs as long as she does not sell liquor on the land,
>   *then to O and his heirs.*

At common law, the conveyance could *not* expressly create a future interest in the grantor following a fee simple determinable. Although the rule has been abolished today in many jurisdictions, the common law courts ruled that a grantor could not expressly *grant* an interest to him or herself, but he or she could retain (or "reserve") an interest. The rationale for the rule lies in the livery of seisin ceremony, which is beyond the scope of this material. But the effect of the common law rule is that you need to pay close attention to the default rule – if the grantor holds a fee simple absolute and does not convey the whole fee simple absolute, the grantor is the default holder of the future interest, because at early common law that was the only way a grantor could create a possibility of reverter (or, as you will see, a reversion) in him or herself.

conveyance does not expressly state who holds it. By default the grantor must hold the future interest. Because the future interest is held by the grantor, and the possessory estate is a fee simple defeasible, the possessory estate must be a fee simple determinable or a fee simple subject to a condition subsequent. The words of limitation introducing the qualifying condition are "as long as" so the possessory estate is a fee simple determinable. The grantor, O, holds a possibility of reverter.

3. Indicate *the Duration* of the Future Interest

After identifying *which* future interest it is (watch the terminology, you must be precise) and *who holds* it, the final step in analyzing each future interest is to indicate *the duration* of the future interest. The *name* of a future interest indicates only that the interest is a future interest – that the party who holds the interest has the right to claim actual possession of the property at some point in the future. The name of the future interest does *not* indicate how long the party will have the right to actual possession once the interest becomes possessory. How long will the right to actual possession last? The analysis with respect to the duration of a future interest is basically the same as the analysis of the duration of a possessory estate. Examine the express clause granting the future interest and look for the words of limitation which indicate the duration of the interest if and when it becomes possessory.[57] Where the future interest arises by default (i.e., there is no clause expressly granting the future interest to a party), the default taker is the grantor. The duration of a default future interest is in fee simple as a general rule.[58]

As applied to the fee simple defeasibles, because of the limited combinations of estates covered in the introductory treatment, the analysis of the future interests[59] is greatly simplified because of a number of sub-rules

---

[57] If the future interest is in fee simple absolute, then often that is the end of the analysis (as long as the interest is vested). On the other hand, if the future interest is some estate less than a fee simple absolute, then that future interest must be followed by yet another future interest until a future interest of fee simple absolute duration is identified.

[58] That statement assumes, as is the norm, that the default future interest is an "unqualified" default future interest. Later the material will introduce more complex conveyances where there is a qualified default future interest, and because the qualification is express, the default duration is not a fee simple absolute but rather a fee simple subject to an executory limitation. But do not worry about that exception to the general rule until later.

[59] First, identify the future interest (focus on what estate does the future interest follow); second, who holds the future interest (focus on the express words of purchase – "to whom?"); and third, what is the duration of the future interest (focus on the express words of limitation in the clause creating the future interest).

that emerge. First, there is one, and only one, future interest which goes with each fee simple defeasible. Once you determine the possessory estate is a *fee simple determinable, the future interest will be a possibility of reverter*; once you determine the possessory estate is a *fee simple subject to a condition subsequent, the future interest will be a right of entry/power of termination*; once you determine that the possessory estate is a *fee simple subject to an executory limitation, the future interest will be an executory interest*. Second, whichever future interest it is, the duration of the future interest will always be in fee simple absolute. This greatly facilitates analysis of the fee simple defeasibles. Once you determine that the possessory estate is a fee simple determinable, the future interest is a *possibility of reverter in fee simple absolute*. Once you determine that the possessory estate is a fee simple subject to a condition subsequent, the future interest is a *right of entry/power of termination in fee simple absolute*. Once you determine that the possessory estate is a fee simple subject to an executory limitation, the future interest is an *executory interest in fee simple absolute*.[60]

B. SHIFTING vs. SPRINGING EXECUTORY INTERESTS

Where the future interest is an executory interest, there is one further analytical step that must be performed: you must indicate *which type* of executory interest it is. There are two types of executory interests: *shifting* and *springing* executory interests. In analyzing which type it is, focus on who holds the legal right to possession immediately preceding the executory interest. Analytically ask, "*From* whom is the right to possession being taken?" An executory interest is a *shifting* executory interest if the right to possession is being taken from a third party (i.e., someone other than the grantor).[61] The executory interest is a *springing* executory interest if the right to possession is being taken from the grantor.[62] While this analysis sounds rather abstract, it is rather easy to apply.

---

[60] At about this point in the material students begin to realize that rote memorization of the different terms is an integral part of the analytical steps. If you do not know the steps in the analysis, it is difficult (if not impossible) to analyze the possessory estates and future interests created by a conveyance. But if you do not know the terminology, it is difficult (if not impossible) to analyze the possessory estates and future interests created by a conveyance. You must focus on both the terminology and the steps in the analysis.

[61] PROPERTY RESTATEMENT, *supra* note 10, at § 46, cmt. k.

[62] PROPERTY RESTATEMENT, *supra* note 10, at § 46, cmt. l. Springing executory interests are the rarer of the two executory interests. The material will examine springing executory interests in greater detail when covering the more unusual conveyances where they tend to arise. *See* discussion *infra* Ch. 7, II.

Return to Example 3:

EXAMPLE 3

O → To A and her heirs, but if A sells alcohol on the land,
then to B and his heirs.

A holds a fee simple defeasible, and the future interest is in a third party, so A holds a fee simple subject to an executory limitation. Because the future interest is held by a third party, B holds an executory interest. Is B's interest a shifting or springing executory interest? From whom is B taking the right to possession – the grantor or a third party? Here, B is taking the right to possession from A, a third party. B holds a shifting executory interest.

What is the duration of B's shifting executory interest? If and when the future interest becomes possessory, how long will B have the right to possession? Analytically this is the same as asking, "Which possessory estate does B hold?" The duration of an estate is almost always determined by the express words of limitation connected to that party's estate. Find the words of purchase with respect to that party, and then find the words of limitation (which typically immediately follow the words of purchase) that indicate the duration of the future estate if and when it becomes possessory. Here the final clause provides "then to B and her heirs." The words of purchase indicate that B holds the future interest (a shifting executory interest). The words of limitation *"and his heirs"* indicate that the duration of the future interest is in fee simple absolute.[63]

Putting it all together, the full state of the title in Example 3 is: A holds a fee simple subject to an executory limitation, and B holds a shifting executory interest in fee simple.

---

[63] Although there are a myriad of different possible combinations of possessory estates and future interests, certain generalizations apply to the introductory coverage of possessory estates and future interests. First, for each of the fee simple defeasibles, there is one, and only one, future interest which will follow it. Second, if the possessory estate is a fee simple subject to an executory limitation, the future interest will always be an executory interest – and it will always be in fee simple. The only other analytical step you will need to perform is to determine whether the executory interest is a shifting or springing executory interest. That will turn on from whom the party holding the future interest is taking the right to possession – a third party (a shifting executory interest) or the grantor (a springing executory interest).

IV. MODERN TREND

If your professor takes the modern trend approach to possessory estates and future interests, there are a few differences with respect to the fee simple defeasibles that you should note.[64] First, conceptually, there is no difference between the common law approach to fee simple defeasibles and the modern trend approach to fee simple defeasibles.   Under both approaches, the fee simple defeasibles are a fee simple which *may* be cut short. The principal difference is in the drafting/construing. Remember that under the modern trend approach, a grantor is presumed to convey all that he or she owns unless there is express language in the conveyance limiting the interest conveyed. What that means as applied to the fee simple defeasibles is that the 'fee simple' component is created differently. The conveyance does *not* need the words of limitation "and her heirs" to create a fee simple absolute. Assuming the grantor holds a fee simple, he or she is assumed to convey a fee simple to the grantee.

For example, return to Example 3:

EXAMPLE 3 – COMMON LAW

O → To A and her heirs, but if A sells alcohol on the land,
        then to B and his heirs.

That was the common law approach to drafting the conveyance. Under the modern trend, the conveyance typically would read as follows:

EXAMPLE 3 – MODERN TREND

O → To A, but if A sells alcohol on the land, then to B.

Under the common law approach, to create a fee simple (in both A and B), the words of limitation "and her/his heirs" had to be included expressly.

---

[64] If your professor is taking a common law approach to the material, you might want to skip this sub-section – it may only confuse you. It should be noted, however, that the bar examiners take the modern trend approach to the possessory estate and future interests questions on the multi-state section of the bar exam, so in the long run it is probably good to keep the modern trend approach in mind even if your professor takes the common law approach.

Under the modern trend approach, these words of limitation are assumed to be included in the words of purchase unless there are express words indicating a contrary intent.

Here are some modern trend examples of the three different fee simple defeasibles. Notice the difference in the drafting:

EXAMPLE 6 – MODERN TREND

O → To A for as long as the Golden Gate Bridge stands.

O → To A, but if A sells alcohol on the land, then O has the right to re-enter and re-take the land.

O → To A as long as he farms the land organically, then to B.

O → To A, but if she uses pesticides on the land, then to B.

Analytically the process is the same once the difference in drafting is taken into consideration. Once you see a fee simple which *may* be cut short, focus on (1) who takes the future interest – the grantor or a third party; and (2) if the grantor holds the future interest, *how* is the fee simple to be cut short – automatically or only upon the grantor's actions (re-entry).

In example 6, in the first conveyance, A holds a fee simple which may be cut short automatically, and the future interest is retained by the grantor, so A holds a fee simple determinable, and O holds a possibility of reverter in fee simple. In the second conveyance, A holds a fee simple subject to a condition subsequent, and O holds a right of entry in fee simple. In the third conveyance, A holds a fee simple subject to an executory limitation, and B holds a shifting executory interest in fee simple. In the fourth conveyance, A holds a fee simple subject to an executory limitation, and B holds a shifting executory interest in fee simple.

Some students have some trouble adjusting to the different phrasing necessary to create a fee simple under the common law versus the modern trend. To help, there will be problems scattered throughout the problem sets to remind you of the different.

Lastly, in a number of jurisdictions, legislation has been adopted which either (1) abolishes the distinction between the fee simple determinable and the fee simple subject to a condition subsequent; or (2) abolishes the respective future interests if not re-recorded periodically. Those developments, however, are beyond the scope of this coverage.

V. TRANSFERABILITY, DEVISABILITY, INHERITABILITY

The fee simple defeasibles (the fee simple determinable, the fee simple subject to a condition subsequent, and the fee simple subject to an executory interest) are freely transferable, inheritable and devisable – subject to the express condition in the conveyance. The future interests following a fee simple defeasible, however, are not as freely transferable, devisable, and inheritable. The common law rule was that a possibility of reverter and a right of entry/power of termination could be held only by the grantor. Consistent with this general rule, the common law courts ruled that the possibility of reverter and the right of entry/power of termination were not transferable or devisable, only inheritable by the grantor's heirs – thereby keeping the future interest in the grantor's bloodline.[65] Because of the uncertain nature of executory interests (they may become possessory, they may not), the common law courts reasoned that they were not transferable, but they were inheritable and devisable.[66]

Under the modern trend, the general rule is that the possibility of reverter and executory interests are freely transferable, inheritable, and devisable.[67] But as a general rule, the right of entry/power of termination is still not transferable, though it is inheritable and devisable.[68]

---

[65] Mahrenholz v. County Board of School Trustees, 417 N.E.2d 138 (Ill. App. Ct. 1981).

[66] RICHARD R. POWELL, POWELL ON REAL PROPERTY ¶ 283, at 252 (Patrick J. Rohan ed., 1979).

[67] MOYNIHAN, *supra* note 9, at 110-111, 199.

[68] *Id.* at 115-117.

RECAP

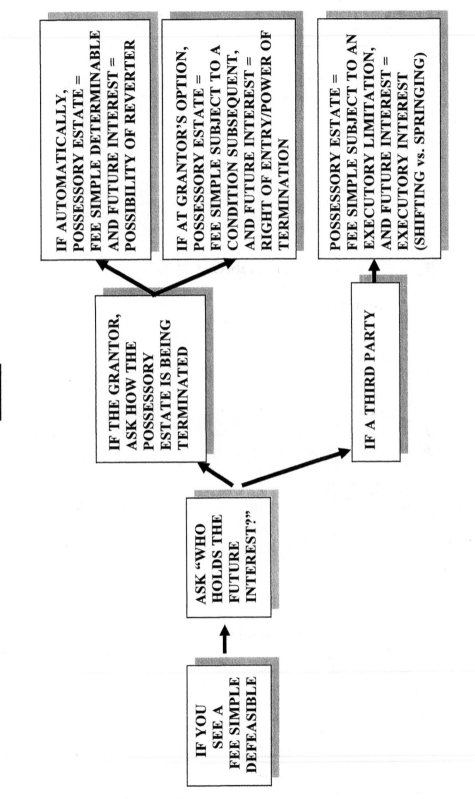

IF YOU SEE A FEE SIMPLE DEFEASIBLE

→ ASK "WHO HOLDS THE FUTURE INTEREST?"

IF THE GRANTOR, ASK HOW THE POSSESSORY ESTATE IS BEING TERMINATED

IF A THIRD PARTY

IF AUTOMATICALLY, POSSESSORY ESTATE = FEE SIMPLE DETERMINABLE AND FUTURE INTEREST = POSSIBILITY OF REVERTER

IF AT GRANTOR'S OPTION, POSSESSORY ESTATE = FEE SIMPLE SUBJECT TO A CONDITION SUBSEQUENT, AND FUTURE INTEREST = RIGHT OF ENTRY/POWER OF TERMINATION

POSSESSORY ESTATE = FEE SIMPLE SUBJECT TO AN EXECUTORY LIMITATION, AND FUTURE INTEREST = EXECUTORY INTEREST (SHIFTING vs. SPRINGING)

CATEGORY OF POSSESSORY ESTATES	POSSESSORY ESTATE(S) (words of limitation)	FUTURE INTERESTS	
		GRANTOR	THIRD PARTY
FEE SIMPLE ABSOLUTE	FEE SIMPLE ABSOLUTE (and her heirs)	NONE	NONE
FEE SIMPLE DEFEASIBLES	FEE SIMPLE DETERMINABLE (and her heirs as long as/while/until)	POSSIBILITY OF REVERTER	NONE
	FEE SIMPLE SUBJECT TO A CONDITION SUBSEQUENT (and her heirs, but if … right to enter)	RIGHT OF ENTRY/ POWER OF TERMINATION	NONE
	FEE SIMPLE SUBJECT TO AN EXECUTORY LIMITATION (and her heirs as long as/but if)	NONE	EXECUTORY INTEREST (shifting vs. springing)

CHAPTER 3 PROBLEM SET

State the title for the following conveyances. It might also help if you diagrammed the conveyances (but if not, do not force yourself; some students find this helpful, others do not).

1. O → To A and her heirs as long as she uses the land for educational purposes. ~~FSSE~~ FSD

2. O → To A and his heirs, but if he stops using the land for educational purposes, then O has the right to re-enter and re-claim the land. FSCS

3. O → To A and her heirs, but if she starts smoking, then to B and her heirs. FSSEL

4. O → To A and her heirs, but if she stops using the land for recreational purposes, then O has the right to re-enter and re-claim the property. ~~FSD~~ FSCS

O →

5.   O →   To A and her heirs as long as she farms the land organically.

FSD

O →
────────┼─────────────────────────────────────▶

6.   O →   To A and her heirs as long as she remains married to B,
         then to C and her heirs.

FSD → ~~FSSEL~~ remainder in C
A= FSSEL   → Sh EI   Int FSA

O →
────────┼─────────────────────────────────────▶

7.   O →   To A and her heirs, but if she divorces B, then O has the right to
         re-enter and re-claim the property.

A- FSSCS
O → right of reentry

8.   O →   To A and her heirs as long as she uses the land for recreational
         purposes.   *A → FSD*

9.   O →   To A and her heirs, but if she stops using the land for recreational
         purposes, then O has the right to re-enter and re-claim the
         property.   *FSSC*

10. O →   To A and her heirs, but if A stops using the land for recreational
         purposes, then to B and his heirs.

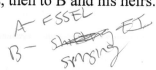

A- FSSEL
B- ~~Shifting~~ EI
*   springing*

11. O → To A and her heirs as long as she does not smoke, but if she starts
smoking, then O has the right to re-enter and re-claim the property.

FSSCS

12. O → To A and her heirs, but if she stops using the land for recreational
purposes, then O has the right to re-enter and re-claim the
property.   FSSCS

13. O → To A and her heirs as long as she uses the land to grow flowers.

FSD

14. O → To A and her heirs, but if she stops using the land for recreational
purposes, then B has the right to enter and claim the property.

FSSEL
FSS   B→EB ShiftA

15. O → To A and her heirs while she uses the land for religious purposes.

FSD

16. O → To A and her heirs, but if she uses the land for religious purposes,
O has the right to re-enter and re-take possession.

FSSCS

17. O → To A and her heirs, provided that if she stops using the land for
recreational purposes, then O has the right to re-enter and re-claim
the property.   FSSCS

18. O → To A and her heirs until B returns from Iraq, then to B and her
heirs.   FSSEL

B Shifting EI

19. O →   To A and her heirs, provided that if A gets divorced, then O has the right to re-enter and re-claim the property.

20. O →   To A and her heirs, but if she stops using the land for recreational purposes, then O has the right to re-enter and re-claim the property.

21. O →   To A and her heirs while she uses the land for charitable purposes.

22. O →   To A and her heirs, but if she stops using the land for charitable purposes, then to B and her heirs.

23. O →   To A and her heirs, but if she stops practicing law, then O has the right to re-enter and re-claim the property.

24. O →   To A and her heirs as long as she does not get a tattoo or body piercing.

25. O →   To A and her heirs, but if B gets either a tattoo or body piercing, then to B and her heirs.

26. Ollie →   To Hank and his heirs as long as he holds the record, then to Barry and his heirs.

27. Tom → To Katie and her heirs as long as she does not divorce.

28. Rooney → To Ferris and his heirs, but if he misses another day of school, then Rooney has the right to enter and re-take possession.

29. Walter → To Dude and his heirs as long as he does not smoke, then to Lebowski and his heirs.

30. Merlin → To Harry and his heirs if he graduates from witchcraft school.

> (This conveyance is different from the others. It is intended to get you thinking about the material in a different way. Give it a good faith effort, but do not spend too much time on it. The material will cover it in detail later in Chapter 6. It was intended to get you thinking about this conveyance more than to test your understanding at this point.)

Chapter 4

THE FINITE ESTATES

I. OVERVIEW

The third category of possessory estates is the finite estates. While the first category, the fee simple absolute, in theory, *will* last forever, and while the second category, the fee simple defeasibles, *may* last forever, the defining characteristic of the third category of estates is that they *must end*. The three finite estates are the *life estate*, the *fee tail*, and the *term of years*. Because they *must end*, the third category of estates may be referred to collectively as the *finite estates*.[69]

II. THE NATURE OF THE FINITE ESTATES

The distinguishing characteristic of the finite estates, that they *must end*, is reflected in the terminology. Unlike the first two categories of estates (the fee simple absolute and the fee simple defeasibles), none of the three finite possessory estates includes the phrase "fee simple" in its name. Moreover, the finite nature of the life estate, the fee tail, and the term of years is also reflected in their respective words of limitation. As you will see, none of the three includes the phrase "and her heirs/and his heirs" in its words of limitation.

Having identified the common characteristic which distinguishes the life estate, the fee tail, and term of years from the other possessory estates (that the estate *must* end), the question becomes what distinguishes these three estates from each other. The distinguishing trait, as one might expect, is in their respective *durations*. Although all of the final three possessory estates are finite, they are of different finite durations.

---

[69] To distinguish them from the fee simple defeasible estates, which may end, and the fee simple absolute, which in theory never ends.

III. DISTINGUISHING THE DIFFERENT FINITE ESTATES

A. THE LIFE ESTATE

As its name indicates, the distinguishing characteristic of the *life estate* is that it lasts for the duration of the *grantee's* life.[70] A classic example of a life estate is the following conveyance:

EXAMPLE 1

O → To A for life.

The classic words of limitation which indicate a life estate are the words "for life."

At common law, however, the life estate was also the *default estate*. The default estate is the estate which results if the grantor fails to draft properly any of the other possessory estates. Consider, for example, the following conveyance:

EXAMPLE 2

O → To A.

There are no express words of limitation indicating the duration of A's possessory estate. At common law, because the life estate was the default estate, A would be deemed to have a life estate.

At common law, the default estate also applied if the grantor failed to use the proper words of limitation, despite the clarity of the grantor's intent:

EXAMPLE 3

O → To A in fee simple absolute.

---

[70] PROPERTY RESTATEMENT, *supra* note 10, at § 18.

At common law, A would hold only a life estate. To create a fee simple absolute at common law, the grantor had to use the proper words of limitation – "and her heirs." The common law was very demanding in requiring use of the appropriate words of limitation.

The modern trend presumes that the grantor intends to convey all that he or she has – absent express words of limitation indicating the intent to limit the estate being conveyed. Thus, under the modern trend, the default estate is the fee simple absolute (assuming that is what the grantor held).[71] Accordingly, both of the above examples (2 and 3) would convey a fee simple absolute if that is what O owned at the time of the conveyance. For drafting purposes, however, you should not depend upon a rule of construction to resolve any ambiguity inherent in a conveyance. The appropriate words of limitation should be used.[72]

A grantee may transfer his or her life estate inter vivos. If a life tenant transfers his or her interest, the grantee/transferee holds a life estate *pur autre vie*: a life estate measured by the life of another (i.e., measured by the life of the original life tenant). For example, if a party holding a life estate (say "A") transfers his or her life estate to another ("B"), because one cannot transfer more than one owns, the grantee/transferee (B) would hold a life estate measured by the life of the original life tenant (A's life) – a life estate *pur autre vie*. While A is still alive, B's life estate *pur autre vie* is transferable, inheritable and devisable,[73] but upon A's death the life estate *pur autre vie* immediately expires - even if B is still alive.

B. THE FEE TAIL

The second finite estate is the fee tail. A fee tail is a series of potential life estates. A fee tail is a life estate to the immediate grantee, and upon his or her death, a life estate to his or her children, and upon each child's death, a life estate to that child's children, and so on until there are

---

[71] PROPERTY RESTATEMENT, *supra* note 10, at §§ 39-41.

[72] You should use proper drafting terminology, and thus the material will use proper drafting terminology and the common law rule of construction unless otherwise indicated. But if proper drafting language is not used, you need to pay careful attention to whether the common law or modern trend rules of construction/default rules apply.

[73] If B dies, but A, the original life tenant were still alive, B's life estate *pur autre vie* would go into B's probate estate, where B could devise it if he had a valid will; otherwise it would pass through intestacy to his heirs.

no "children" to take the fee tail.[74] The words of limitation necessary to create a fee tail are "*and the heirs of his/her body.*" For example:

EXAMPLE 4

O →   To A and the heirs of her body, then to B and the heirs of his body.

The phrase "and the heirs of her body" indicates the series of life estates, one generation after another, limited to the heirs of the body (the lineal descendants) of the identified grantee.

In essence, the fee tail is a series of life estates in a family blood line. Conceptually, this can be a bit mind boggling. On the one hand, it is conceivable that the bloodline could continue for eternity, in which case it looks something like a fee simple defeasible (possibly the reason why it is called a *fee* tail). On the other hand, it is also conceivable that the immediate grantee could die childless and the fee tail could end upon the death of the immediate grantee (i.e., as a practical matter it could last no longer than a single life estate). For analytical purposes, the latter is the better way to think about the fee tail. The common law assumed that sooner or later the family line would die out. Therefore, the analysis and future interest terminology for the fee tail are the same as for the life estate.

One additional twist to the fee tail is that the grantor can limit the eligible heirs of the body of the immediate grantee. The grantor can limit the fee tail to the male heirs of the grantee by drafting a *fee tail male*:[75]

EXAMPLE 5

O → To A and the male heirs of her body.

The grantor can limit the fee tail to the female heirs of the grantee by drafting a *fee tail female*: [76]

---

[74] PROPERTY RESTATEMENT, *supra* note 10, at § 59.
[75] PROPERTY RESTATEMENT, *supra* note 10, at § 59, cmt. e.
[76] *Id.*

EXAMPLE 6

O → To A and the female heirs of her body.

The grantor could limit the fee tail to any characteristic he or she wished. Nevertheless, such conveyances are still fee tails with the operative words of limitation "and the heirs of her body."

C.   THE TERM OF YEARS

The final finite possessory estate is the *term of years*.   The defining characteristic of a term of years estate is that the express language of the conveyance establishes a *finite duration which is calculable on the day the interest is created*[77] – *the end date must be capable of being determined on the first day the interest becomes possessory.*   Despite its name, term of *years,* the estate need not be for a year or longer.   The only requirement is that the exact term of the estate must be calculable on the first day of the term.   Although there is a plethora of different ways to express a finite time period, a couple of classic examples of term of years estates are as follows:

EXAMPLE 7

O → To A for 5 years.

O → To A from January 1, 2006 until December 31, 2010.

O → To A for 180 days starting today.

The classic words of limitation indicating a term of years possessory estate are the phrases "for (some finite time period)" or "from (a date certain) to (another date certain)."

---

[77] PROPERTY RESTATEMENT, *supra* note 10, at § 19, cmt. b.

IV. THE FUTURE INTERESTS WHICH FOLLOW A FINITE ESTATE

Inasmuch as the defining characteristic of the finite estates (the life estate, the fee tail, and the term of years) is that they *must* end, there must be a future interest following each. This point can be demonstrated by diagramming the finite estates on the timeline. Each of the finite estates can be diagrammed as a relatively short segment of the arrow with a solid cross line at the right end of the line segment indicating the estate must end at some point short of infinity. For example, the conveyance "O → To A for life" can be diagrammed as follows:

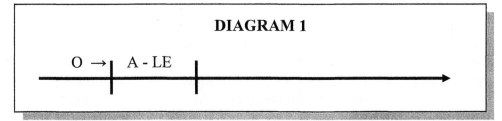

DIAGRAM 1

O → A - LE

Because the diagram does not account for the whole timeline, there must be a future interest following the finite estate. There are two possible future interests that can follow a finite estate. If the grantor holds the future interest following a life estate, a fee tail, or a term of years, the future interest is called a *reversion*;[78] if a third party (someone other than the grantor) holds the future interest following a finite estate, it is called a *remainder*.[79]

For purposes of our introductory coverage, a reversion and a remainder will follow only a finite possessory estate. A reversion will follow only a life estate, a fee tail, or a term of years. A remainder will follow only a life estate, a fee tail, or a term of years. Analytically, once you determine the possessory estate is a finite estate, then ask, "Who takes the future interest?"[80]

---

[78] PROPERTY RESTATEMENT, *supra* note 10, at § 154, cmt. d. Just as was the case with the possibility of reverter, the common law courts ruled that because of the requirements of the livery of seisin ceremony, a grantor could *not expressly* grant a reversion to him or herself. The effect of this rule is that a reversion is *reserved* by the grantor, but at common law it could *not be expressly reserved.* Under the modern trend, followed by a majority of the jurisdictions, a reversion can be created expressly. But do not worry about memorizing this rule, because it had little practical effect. If a grantor attempted to create expressly a reversion, although it would be null and void, the grantor would take the default estate: a reversion. (One of the few areas of the law where you could not do expressly what you could do by default).

[79] PROPERTY RESTATEMENT, *supra* note 10, at § 156.

[80] Be careful. When analyzing the fee simple defeasibles, the material emphasized

If the grantor holds the future interest, it is a reversion; if a third party holds the future interest, it is a remainder. Remember that possessory estates and future interests go hand in hand and should not be coupled with the wrong interests. Neither a reversion nor a remainder should follow a fee simple determinable, a fee simple subject to a condition subsequent, or a fee simple subject to an executory limitation. Reversions and remainders follow finite estates. Likewise, a finite estate must be followed by a reversion or a remainder. They go hand in hand. Coupling future interests with the appropriate preceding possessory estates greatly facilitates the analysis.

The life estate arguably is the most common, and the most important, possessory estate for estate planning purposes. The term of years estate is used primarily in leasehold conveyances these days, and any further analysis or discussion of the details of that estate is best left to landlord-tenant law. The fee tail has been abolished in all but a handful of jurisdictions and typically shows up only on Property exams these days.[81] Accordingly, the life estate is the most common finite estate. Inasmuch as the future interests following the life estate are the same as those following the fee tail and the term of years, in discussing the future interests which go hand in hand with the finite estates, the material will focus primarily on the life estate. But unless noted otherwise, any example and/or rule involving a life estate in theory applies equally well to the other two finite estates: the fee tail and the term of years.

---

that you must ask, "who takes the future interest" *before* you can determine which fee simple defeasible it is. With the finite estates, you should ask the question, "who holds the future interest" *after* you have determined which finite possessory estate it is. With the finite estates, you can and should determine which finite estate it is (based on the express words of limitation) *before* you ask, "who takes the future interest?"

[81] There is some disagreement over how the fee tail words of limitation are treated today. One authority asserts that there are at least six different approaches to the language. POWELL, *supra* note 35, at § 14.01. Some jurisdictions still recognize the estate, some have abolished it all together, and other give a modified construction to it. A number of sources claim that a majority of the states construe the language as creating a fee simple absolute. Many state statutes deem "to A and the heirs of her body" as creating a fee simple absolute *if* A dies survived by issue. If A dies without surviving issue, however, and if there is an express gift over to a third party (someone other than grantor), then such gift over will be given effect. (In essence these states construe A's interest as a fee simple determinable – determinable if A dies without issue and there is an express gift over to a third party.) A few state statutes deem "to A and the heirs of her body" as creating a life estate in A, and A's issue take a remainder in fee simple. MOYNIHAN, *supra* note 9, at 37-38. If your professor takes the modern trend approach to the fee tail, pay close attention to which approach he or she emphasizes.

V. MODERN TREND

If your professor takes the modern trend approach to the material, there are a number of modern trend revisions which should be noted. The first, and most important, is the default estate. As noted above,[82] the common law default is the life estate, while the modern trend default is the fee simple absolute. Accordingly, under the modern trend, if the grantor wants to convey only a life estate, he or she has to expressly indicate that intent. The classic way to do so is to include the "for life" words of limitation. Otherwise, the modern trend approach to drafting the different finite estates is the same as the common law approach – although the common law is more intent based so there is not the same need to be precise in the use of the words of limitation as long as the intent is ascertainable.

The modern trend also revises the finite estate classifications. Under the modern trend, a majority of jurisdictions have abolished the fee tail as a distinct estate and have instead construed it as creating one of the other common law estates – which one in particular depends on the jurisdiction. Depending on the jurisdiction, there are a number of different possible modern trend constructions of the fee tail words of limitation, but those details are beyond the scope of this introductory material. This material will assume that even if the professor takes a modern trend approach to the *drafting/construction* of the different possessory estates and future interests, that he or she still recognizes the common law classifications and combinations of possessory estates and future interests (i.e., that he or she still recognizes the fee tail). If that is not the case for your professor, take your cues from him or her.

VI. TRANSFERABILITY, DEVISABILITY, INHERITABILITY

1. The Finite Possessory Estates

In discussing the transferability, devisability, and inheritability of the finite estates,[83] the starting point is the nature of each estate. As a general rule, one cannot transfer, devise, or pass through intestacy more than one has. That principle greatly affects the transferability, devisability, and inheritability of the finite estates.

---

[82] *See* Ch. 2, III.

[83] For a statement of what each of these terms mean, *see* discussion *supra* Ch. 2, IV.

A life estate, by its nature, is not devisable or inheritable. The interest terminates upon the death of the life estate holder, so there is nothing to devise or pass through intestacy. The only question is whether it is transferable inter vivos. A life estate is transferable, but again one cannot transfer more than one owns as a general rule. If a party holding a life estate transfers that interest, the recipient receives the transferor's life estate: a life estate measured by the life of the transferor – a life estate *pur autre vie*. For example, where O grants A a life estate, and A transfers it to B, B holds a life estate measured by A's life, not B's.

Inasmuch as a fee tail is nothing more than a series of life estates, each holder of an interest under a fee tail holds nothing more than a life estate. Each party's interest will terminate upon his or her death, so it is neither devisable nor inheritable.[84] It is, however, transferable while the party is alive. But the party can transfer no more than he or she owns. The transferee would take a life estate *pur autre vie* measured by the life of the party who transferred the life estate.[85]

Absent express conditions in the conveyance creating a term of years, it is freely transferable, devisable and inheritable. For example, if O conveys a term of years for 25 years to A, A can transfer that interest during his or her lifetime, and if he or she were to die before the term were up, he or she could devise the remaining term to whomever he or she wished, and if A were to die intestate (without a will), A's heirs would inherit the remaining term.

2. The Future Interests

Because reversions are vested interests, they are freely transferable, devisable, and inheritable.[86] The transferability, devisability and inheritability of remainders, on the other hand, depend upon whether they are vested or contingent – the topic of the next chapter.

---

[84] MOYNIHAN, *supra* note 9, at 44-45.
[85] *Id.*
[86] *Id.* at 105.

RECAP

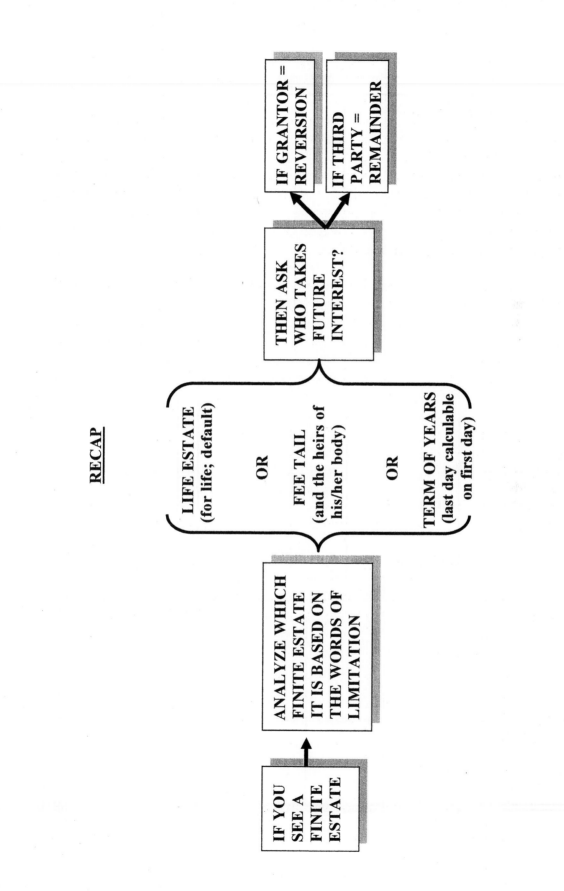

IF YOU SEE A FINITE ESTATE → **ANALYZE WHICH FINITE ESTATE IT IS BASED ON THE WORDS OF LIMITATION**

- **LIFE ESTATE** (for life; default)

OR

- **FEE TAIL** (and the heirs of his/her body)

OR

- **TERM OF YEARS** (last day calculable on first day)

THEN ASK WHO TAKES FUTURE INTEREST?

- **IF GRANTOR = REVERSION**
- **IF THIRD PARTY = REMAINDER**

See if you can complete the following chart (use abbreviations for the different names if necessary):

CATEGORIES OF POSSESSORY ESTATES	POSSESSORY ESTATES (words of limitation)	FUTURE INTERESTS	
		GRANTOR	THIRD PARTY
1ST : _____	(_____	_____	_____
2nd : _____	(_____ (_____ (_____	_____ _____ _____	_____ _____ _____
3rd: _____	(_____ (_____ (_____	_____ _____ _____	_____ _____ _____

Before you can master the analytical steps inherent in possessory estates and future interest, you *must* have *complete command* of this chart. You must be able to quickly recite the different possible possessory estates and future interests without recourse to the chart.

CATEGORIES OF POSSESSORY ESTATES	POSSESSORY ESTATES (words of limitation)	FUTURE INTERESTS	
		GRANTOR	THIRD PARTY
FEE SIMPLE ABSOLUTE	FEE SIMPLE ABSOLUTE (and her heirs)	NONE	NONE
FEE SIMPLE DEFEASIBLES	FEE SIMPLE DETERMINABLE (and her heirs as long as/while/until)	POSSIBILITY OF REVERTER	NONE
	FEE SIMPLE SUBJECT TO A CONDITION SUBEQUENT (and her heirs, but if … right to enter)	RIGHT OF ENTRY/ POWER TO TERMINATE	NONE
	FEE SIMPLE SUBJECT TO AN EXECUTORY LIMITATION (and her heirs as long as/but if)	NONE	EXECUTORY INTEREST (shifting vs. springing)
FINITE ESTATES	LIFE ESTATE (for life; default)	REVERSION	REMAINDER
	FEE TAIL (and the heirs of his/her body)	REVERSION	REMAINDER
	TERM OF YEARS (first & last day calculable first day)	REVERSION	REMAINDER

CHAPTER 4 PROBLEM SET

State the title for each of the following conveyances.

1. O →   To A for life, then to B and her heirs.

2. O →   To A and the heirs of her body, then to B for life.

3. O →   To A, then to B, then to C and his heirs.

4. O →   To A for life, the to B and her heirs as long as she does not smoke, but if she starts smoking, then O has the right to re-enter and re-claim the property.

5. O →   To A and the heirs of her body, then to B and her heirs, but if she grows marijuana on the land, then to C and her heirs.

6. O →   To A and the heirs of her body, then to O and her heirs.

7. O →   To A for life, then to B and her heirs as long as she farms the land organically.

8. O →   To A for ten years, then to B and her heirs as long as she remains married to C, then C and her heirs.

9. O →   To A for life, then to B and the heirs of her body, then to C for ten years.

10. O →   To A and the heirs of his body, then to B and her heirs, but if she fails to maintain the wetlands on the property then O has the right to re-enter and re-claim the property.

11. O →   To A for 5 days, then to B for life, then to C and the heirs of her body, then to D and her heirs.

12. O →   To A and the heirs of her body, then to B for life, then to C and her heirs, but if she stops using the land for charitable purposes, then O has the right to re-enter and re-claim the property.

13. O →   To A for 5 years, then to B, then to C for life, then to D and her heirs.

14. O →   To A for life, then to B and her heirs, but if she stops using the land for recreational purposes, then to C and her heirs.

15. O →   To A for life, then to B for life, then to C.

16. Olivia →   To Bert for life, then to Ernie and his heirs.

17. George → To Mary for life.

18. Olivia →   To Gonzo and the heirs of his body, then to Ralph and his heirs.

19. Olivia →   To Rizzo and the heirs of his body.

20. Olivia →   To Bird and his heirs as long as he farms the land organically.

21. Olivia →To Groucho, then to Harpo, and then to Zeppo and his heirs.

22. Olivia →   To Hannibal for 99 years.

23. Olivia →   To Oscar and his heirs, then to Felix and his heirs.

24. Mutt →   To Jeff in fee simple.

25. Ozzie →   To Harriette.

26. Romeo → To Juliette for ever and ever.

27. George → To Dick and his heirs, but if Dick ever goes hunting again on the land, then to Howard and his heirs.

28. Donald → To Rosie for life, then to Barbara and her heirs.
    (a) State the title as written.

    (b) Thereafter, Rosie transfers her interest to Ellen.

29. Olivia → To Bill and his heirs as long as he remains married, then to Hillary and her heirs.

30. Oliver → To Simon and his heirs as long as he stays out of England.

Chapter 5

REMAINDERS:
VESTED vs. CONTINGENT

I. OVERVIEW

Just as there are two types of executory interests – shifting and springing – there are two types of remainders: *vested* and *contingent*.[87] A remainder is the future interest which follows a finite estate – a life estate, fee tail, or term of years – if the future interest is held by a third party (someone other than the grantor).[88] Once you determine that a future interest is a remainder, you must determine whether it is vested or contingent. A remainder is contingent unless it qualifies as vested.

II. THE TEST FOR VESTED REMAINDERS

A remainder is vested if (1) the remainderman (the party who holds the remainder) is:

(a) *born and*
(b) *ascertainable* (i.e., you can identify the party by his or her personal name), *and*
(2) there is *no express condition precedent, in the same clause creating the remainder or the preceding clause.*[89] (A condition precedent is one which typically must be satisfied *before* the remainderman can take actual possession.)

---

[87] The Restatement uses the term "remainder subject to condition precedent," but that terminology has not been widely adopted and will not be used in this material. PROPERTY RESTATEMENT, *supra* note 10, at § 157.

[88] If the future interest is held by a third party, but it follows a fee simple defeasible, it is an executory interest. Any time a future interest is held by a third party, there is an additional step in the analysis. It is not enough to give the basic name of the future interest. You must also give the particular subset of that future interest: shifting vs. springing; vested vs. contingent.

[89] If the express condition precedent is set forth in *a subsequent clause*, the remainder is a vested remainder subject to divestment. *See* discussion *infra* Ch. 7, III.

The remainder must satisfy all three requirements or it is a contingent remainder. In applying the test, *analyze the express words* creating the remainder, *reading comma to comma*, in light of the facts at the time of the conveyance.[90]

A. BORN AND ASCERTAINABLE

The first two requirements, that the remainderman must be born and ascertainable, would appear to overlap, and to a large degree they do. If the grantee is not born, he or she is not ascertainable. But they are not identical. One can be born but not ascertainable. For example:

EXAMPLE 1

O → To A for ten years, then to whomever is then President of the United States of America.

State the title. First, the possessory estate is a finite estate. It looks like a term of years, though if the term is not calculable, the default is a life estate. Is the exact term calculable on the first day? Whatever the first day is, once the first day is determined then the last day can be calculated – it is ten years later. A holds a term of years. Who holds the future interest? Whoever is "*then*[91] President of the United States ..." – *then* being at the end of the ten year term. What interest does the President hold? Because the interest is a future interest following a term of years, and the interest is held by a third party, it is a remainder. What kind of remainder – contingent or vested? Although the person who will be President then must be alive when the conveyance is created, at the time of the conveyance one cannot identify the person by his or her personal name. Therefore, the party is not ascertainable, and the remainder is a contingent remainder. So while the first two prongs of the test for a vested remainder, that the holder be *born* and *ascertainable*, overlap to a large degree, they are separate tests.

---

[90] And/or at the time of analysis (if later than the time of creation), taking into consideration any change in facts between the time of conveyance and the time of analysis.

[91] Read all conveyances very, very carefully – comma to comma.

B. NO EXPRESS CONDITION PRECEDENT

The third prong of the vested/contingent remainder analysis is that there must be *no express condition precedent, in the same clause creating the remainder or the preceding clause,*[92] which must be satisfied before the remainder can become possessory. If there is such an express condition precedent, the remainder is contingent until the condition is satisfied. Notice the fee simple defeasibles involved a condition *subsequent*, while the contingent remainders involve a condition *precedent*. The difference between a condition *precedent* and a condition *subsequent* is somewhat abstract, but it is critical to develop a comfort level with these terms and concepts if you are to master possessory estates and future interests.

1. Qualifying Condition must be a *Condition Precedent*

A condition *precedent* is a condition that applies to an interest *before* it becomes possessory. With respect to remainders, the condition precedent typically is one that *must be satisfied* before the remainderman has the right to claim actual possession. In contrast, a condition subsequent is a condition which applies *after* the interest becomes possessory. The condition subsequent typically qualifies *how long* the possessory interest may last.

The difference between a condition precedent and a condition subsequent is an abstract, conceptual analysis that requires careful reading of the express language of the conveyance from a *temporal* perspective. Focus on *when* the property interest in question is to become possessory – the point in time when the party holding the interest has the right to take *actual* possession. Examine the express condition relative to *that* point in time. Ask whether the express condition is one which applies *before* the interest can become possessory or one which applies *after* the interest becomes possessory (in which case it typically qualifies how long the interest may remain possessory). Where the express condition is one which applies *before* the point in time when the interest is to become possessory (a condition which

---

[92] *Where* in the conveyance the express condition precedent is located, which clause it is in, is critical. As the material notes, if the express condition precedent is in the same clause as the clause creating the remainder, or the preceding clause, the remainder typically is a contingent remainder. If, however, the condition precedent is located in the clause after the clause creating the remainder, and it applies to that remainder, the property interest typically will be a vested remainder subject to divestment. *See infra* Ch. 7, III.

could occur or which *must be satisfied before* the interest can become possessory), the condition is a condition precedent. Where the express condition is one which applies to the time period *after* the interest becomes possessory (a condition which qualifies how long the possession may last), the condition is a condition subsequent.[93]

There are different types of conditions *precedent*, but the most common example of a conveyance containing a condition precedent is the contingent remainder. For example:

EXAMPLE 2

O → To A for life, then to B and his heirs if he gets married.

State the title. A holds a term of years, and B holds a remainder in fee simple. Is the remainder vested or contingent? B is born and ascertainable, but there is an express condition in the same clause creating the remainder. Is it a condition precedent or a condition subsequent? To B and his heirs "if he gets married." The logical assumption is that at the time of the conveyance, B is not married yet. B gets the possessory interest (the right to take actual possession) if, and only if, he gets married. That express condition must occur *before* B's right can become possessory. It is a condition precedent – so B holds a contingent remainder.

Similarly, there are different types of conditions *subsequent*. The most common example of a conveyance containing a condition subsequent is a fee simple defeasible. In a fee simple defeasible, the express condition is always a condition subsequent. It applies to the interest *after* it becomes possessory and qualifies how long the party's right to possession may last. For example:

---

[93] This discussion implies that an express condition must be *either* an express condition precedent or an express condition subsequent, but later the material will introduce express condition which can be *both*. Do not worry about those for now, but the rule is that as long as it is possible that the express condition may occur *before* the interest becomes possessory, it is an express condition precedent even if it can also occur *after* it becomes possessory.

EXAMPLE 3

O →   To A for life, then to B and her heirs as long as she farms the land organically.

State the title. A holds a life estate, and B holds a remainder. Is the remainder vested or contingent? Notice there is an express condition in the same clause as the clause creating the remainder, but the issue is whether the condition is a condition precedent or a condition subsequent. If the condition is a condition precedent, B will hold a contingent remainder in fee simple absolute; if the condition is a condition subsequent, B will hold a vested remainder in fee simple determinable. The express condition, "as long as she farms the land organically," applies to her use of the land which inherently applies *after* she takes actual possession – after her interest becomes possessory. It is a condition subsequent; B holds a vested remainder in fee simple determinable.

In performing the abstract temporal analysis inherent in determining whether an express condition is a condition precedent or a condition subsequent, some guidance may be gained from focusing on the words which introduce the qualifying condition. While it is dangerous to generalize too much when discussing drafting language, the word "*if*" typically introduces a condition precedent. Notice in Example 2 above, "To A for life, then to B and his heirs *if* he gets married," the qualifying clause was introduced by the word "*if* ... ." Where the qualifying clause is introduced by the word "if" there is a high probability the condition is a condition precedent. On the other hand, where the express condition is introduced by the words "as long as" or "while" or "until" – it is almost always a condition subsequent. But be careful, where the express condition is introduced by the words "but if" – it can be *either* a condition precedent or a condition subsequent – or both.[94]

2. Qualifying Condition must be express

In analyzing whether there is a condition precedent which must be satisfied before a remainder can become possessory, remember that the qualifying condition precedent must be *express*. There must be a condition

---

[94] *See infra* Ch. 7, III, D.

set forth in *the express words of the conveyance* which must be satisfied before the holder can claim the right to possess the property. For example:

EXAMPLE 4

O →   To A for life, then to B and his heirs.

O →   To A for life, then to B and his heirs if B survives A.

O →   To A for life, then to B for life.

State the titles. In all three conveyances, A has a life estate. Because the future interest following the life estate is held by a third party, B, in all three conveyances the future interest is a remainder. Is it a vested or contingent remainder? B is an abbreviation for a person's full name, so we assume B is alive and ascertainable.[95] The question is whether there is an *express* condition precedent in the language of the conveyance, in either the same clause creating the remainder or a preceding clause, which must be satisfied before B can claim actual possession of the property.

In the first conveyance, "To A for life, then to B and her heirs," there is no express condition precedent. B holds a vested remainder. While it is true that B has to survive A if B *personally* is to take actual possession of the property, because B holds a *vested* remainder in *fee simple absolute* (as opposed to a life estate) B does not have to survive A to have the right to take possession of the property when A's life estate ends. Even if B were to predecease A, the vested remainder in fee simple absolute is still B's property and would pass to B's devisees or heirs (depending on whether B dies testate, with a will, or intestate, without a will). Because B holds a vested remainder in fee simple, B's death would not affect B's right to possess the property at the end of A's life estate.[96]

In the second conveyance, "To A for life, then to B and his heirs if B survives A," there is an express condition precedent - an express condition that must be satisfied *before* B can take possession of the property. The

---

[95] Always assume that a person identified by a first name or letter is alive unless the facts of the problem tell you otherwise. *See* discussion *supra* fn. 1.

[96] If the grantor wanted the future interest in B to be contingent on B surviving A, the grantor could do so fairly easily. The key would be to make the condition precedent express – as the second conveyance demonstrates.

conveyance expressly provides that B is to have the right to possess the land only if B survives A. There is an express condition which must be satisfied before, or at the moment, the preceding finite estate ends. The nature of the condition, if B survives A, is one which intrinsically cannot be satisfied before the preceding finite estate ends. It can only be satisfied, if at all, *at the moment* the finite estate ends. Thus, as long as A is alive, B holds a contingent remainder in fee simple.

In the third conveyance, "To A for life, then to B for life," B holds a remainder in life estate. For B's life estate to be worth anything, as a practical matter, B must survive A. Does that make B's life estate contingent? No. The condition precedent must be an *express* condition, not one implicit in the nature of the estate. There is no express condition precedent in this conveyance, just an express life estate. B holds a vested remainder in life estate.

3. Qualifying Condition must be in Same Clause or Preceding Clause

If there is an express condition precedent, it must be in the *same clause* as the clause creating the remainder or *the preceding clause* for the remainder to be contingent. This requirement is derived from the historical evolution of possessory estates and future interests. Prior to the Statute of Uses in 1536, the common law rule was that if a party held a vested remainder, the party could not lose the right to possession before taking actual possession. Pre-1536, if the conveyance contained an express condition precedent, but the condition precedent was in the clause *after* the clause creating the remainder, the remainder was deemed vested and the express condition was null and void. Therefore, to indicate clearly that the remainder's right to take possession was conditioned on the occurrence of the express condition precedent, the express condition precedent had to be in the same clause creating the remainder or the preceding clause.

Today, if the express condition precedent is in a clause subsequent to the clause creating the remainder, the condition is not null and void, but it creates a new combination of estates which the material will examine later.[97]

---

[97] The material will cover this combination of estates later, but for now remember that if the express condition precedent is in the *subsequent* clause (reading comma to comma, the clause *after* the clause creating the remainder) it makes the remainder a vested remainder subject to divestment. *See* discussion *infra* Ch. 7, III.

For now, remember that to make a remainder contingent, the express condition precedent must be set forth in the same clause creating the remainder or the preceding clause.

4. Recap

By default, all remainders are contingent remainders unless they meet the test for vested. A remainder is vested if (1) the party holding the remainder is (a) born and (b) ascertainable, and (2) *there is no* express condition precedent in the same clause creating the remainder or the preceding clause. If any of these requirements is not satisfied, the remainder is contingent.

III. DESTRUCTIBILITY OF CONTINGENT REMAINDERS

The distinction between the vested and contingent remainder is important for several reasons. The most important is the common law rule of destructibility of contingent remainders: a contingent remainder *must vest prior to, or at the moment, the preceding finite estate ends, or the contingent remainder is destroyed by operation of law.* The following example demonstrates the significance of the destructibility of contingent remainder rule:

EXAMPLE 5

O →   To A for life, then to B and her heirs if B graduates
      from law school.

State the title. A holds a finite estate, a life estate. The future interest is in B, a third party, so it must be a remainder. The words of limitation "and her heirs" indicate that the remainder is in fee simple. Is the remainder vested or contingent? There is an express condition in the same clause as the clause creating the remainder, so the issue is whether it is a condition precedent or subsequent? It is introduced by the word "if" and requires B to graduate from law school before B's interest can become possessory. The condition is a condition precedent. B holds a contingent remainder.

Under the common law destructibility of contingent remainders, the remainder must vest prior to, or at the moment, the preceding finite estate ends, or the contingent remainder is destroyed. Here, B holds a contingent remainder in fee simple, contingent on B graduating from law school. Assume A dies before B graduates from law school. Under the common law destructibility of contingent remainders, B's contingent remainder is destroyed. Even if B were to graduate later, *after* A died, it would be too late. B's interest was destroyed the moment A died. B lost all interest in the property. But if B's interest was destroyed the moment A died, who takes the property?

Anytime there is a contingent remainder in fee simple, there must be someone to take the property in the event the contingent remainder fails to vest in time. Where there is no express party to take in case the contingent remainder fails to vest, the *default taker is the original grantor*.[98] Because the grantor (O) would take the property after the finite possessory estate (A's life estate), the grantor holds a future interest. Because the future interest follows a finite estate and the grantor holds it, it is a reversion (and because it is a "default"[99] reversion, it is in fee simple absolute). Returning to example 5 for a moment, the full state of the title is:

EXAMPLE 5 – STATE OF THE TITLE

O →   To A for life, then to B and her heirs if B graduates from law school.

        A has a life estate;
        B has a contingent remainder in fee simple, and
        O has a reversion in fee simple.

If the express condition precedent is not satisfied either prior to or at the moment the finite estate ends, the contingent remainder is destroyed by operation of law under the common law rule of destructibility of

---

[98] MOYNIHAN, *supra* note 9, at 133-134.

[99] It is a default reversion in the sense that it is not express. The term "default" reversion is not a recognized term of art under the common law terminology. Nevertheless, many students find it helpful to call it a default reversion, and technically there should be nothing wrong with calling it a default reversion because the term "default" describes how it is created. But technically a default reversion is just a reversion, and when stating the title should be called just a reversion.

contingent remainders. If B fails to graduate from law school before A's life estate ends, the moment A's life estate ends B's contingent remainder is destroyed, and O's reversion becomes possessory. O would hold the property in fee simple absolute.

The analysis changes dramatically, however, if the contingent remainder *does vest before* the end of the preceding finite estate. Assume B graduates from law school while A is still alive. Now the express condition precedent has been satisfied. B is born, ascertainable, and the express condition precedent has been satisfied. The remainder vests the moment B graduates. Assuming the contingent remainder was *in fee simple*, the norm, once it vests there is no need for the default reversion in the grantor, O. The default reversion is extinguished. The state of the title would be: A has a life estate, and B has a vested remainder in fee simple. Notice remainders should be analyzed not only in light of the facts at the time the conveyance was created, but also in light of subsequent factual developments – all the way up to the point in time when the analysis is being performed. As long as the remainder vests *before or at the moment* the preceding finite estate ends (assuming the remainder is in fee simple), the default reversion in the grantor is extinguished.[100]

Contingent remainders can be diagrammed. First, return to Example 5 as it was originally drafted: "O → To A for life, then to B and her heirs if B graduates from law school." What is the state of the title at the time of the conveyance? A has a life estate, B has a contingent remainder in fee simple, and O has a reversion in fee simple. First, diagram A's life estate:

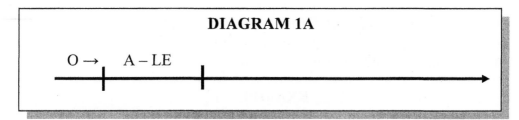

DIAGRAM 1A

O → A – LE

What about the contingent remainder and the default reversion? Although there are several possible ways to diagram the relationship between these estates, the diagram should reflect the key characteristics of the estates.

---

[100] So is O's reversion called a *contingent* reversion, or *a possibility of* reversion, to reflect the fact that it may not become possessory? No – neither. This point is implicitly reflected in the fact that it is a default reversion following a contingent remainder. It is still a reversion and has all the other characteristics of a reversion (in particular, it is transferable).

First, because the remainder is *contingent*, it should be depicted as a dashed line[101] parallel to the timeline.   Second, because of the destructibility of contingent remainders, the contingent remainder exists only as long as there is a supporting finite estate.   Thus, for purposes of diagramming the contingent remainder, the cross line which indicates the end of the preceding finite estate becomes something of a vertical beam (or "crane") supporting the contingent remainder:

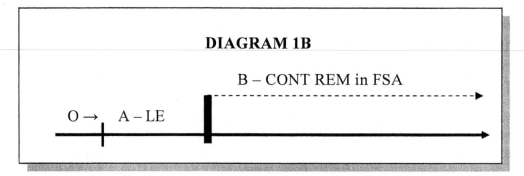

DIAGRAM 1B

B – CONT REM in FSA

O →   A – LE

As always, the reversion is depicted on the timeline as a solid line[102] following the finite estate:

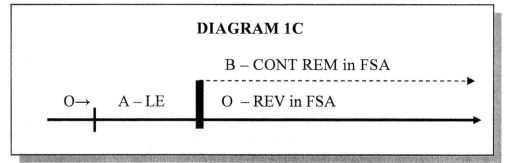

DIAGRAM 1C

B – CONT REM in FSA

O→   A – LE   O – REV in FSA

What if the contingent remainder vests prior to the end of the supporting finite estate? Return to Example 5:

EXAMPLE 5

O →   To A for life, then to B and her heirs if she
graduates from law school.

---

[101] The dashed line is used to show the tenuous, "iffy" nature of the interest. Remember the dashed line was also used to depict the possibility that the fee simple *may* end in the fee simple defeasible graphs.

[102] All reversions are vested interests.   LEWIS M. SIMES, SIMES ON FUTURE INTERESTS 25 (West Publishing 1951).

State the title first as written. A has a life estate, B has a contingent remainder in fee simple, and O has a reversion in fee simple. Diagram the title as written:

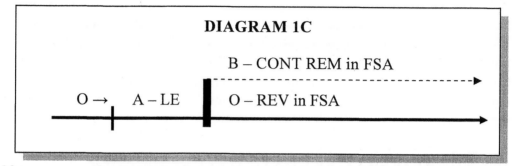

Now assume the facts go on to state that while A is alive, B graduates from law school. The moment B graduates the express condition precedent is satisfied. B is born, ascertainable, and there is no longer an express condition precedent to B's interest becoming possessory. If the contingent remainder vests prior to the end of the supporting finite estate (or the moment it ends), the moment the remainder vests it is lowered down the "crane" onto the arrow, displacing the reversion. Because the remainder has vested, it no longer is a dashed line. It is on the solid timeline:

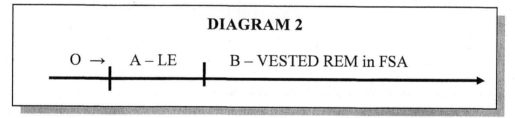

If, on the other hand, the life estate ends prior to the contingent remainder vesting, the contingent remainder no longer has a supporting finite estate. The vertical beam which supported finite estate is extinguished when the finite estate ends, and if the contingent remainder has not vested by then, it comes crashing down and is destroyed pursuant to the destructibility of contingent remainders. In Example 5 above, assume the facts went on to state the A died before B graduated from law school. The express contingent precedent was not satisfied before, or at the moment, the preceding finite estate ended. B's contingent remainder comes crashing down and is destroyed pursuant to the destructibility of contingent remainders. O's reversion would then become possessory, and she would hold the property in fee simple absolute:

DIAGRAM 3

O – FSA

Notice O would not hold a *reversion* in fee simple absolute because the moment A died and B's contingent remainder had not vested, O's reversion became possessory. It is no longer is a future interest. O holds the property in fee simple absolute.

IV. THE ALTERNATIVE CONTINGENT REMAINDER

A. INTRODUCTION

The final twist on contingent remainders concerns the *alternative contingent remainder*. An alternative contingent remainder arises where the conveyance sets forth two contingent remainders, with the second expressly contingent on the first failing to vest. For example:

EXAMPLE 6

O → To A for life, then to B and her heirs if she graduates from law school, but if she fails to graduate from law school, then to C and his heirs.

State the title. A has a life estate. The future interest is in B, a third party, so B has a remainder. The words of limitation "and her heirs" indicates that B holds a remainder in fee simple. The express condition precedent in the same clause as the clause creating the remainder indicates that B's interest is a contingent remainder in fee simple.

C's interest is a future interest which, if it were to become possessory, would follow A's life estate.[103] Thus, C's interest must also be a remainder (a future interest following a finite estate – A's life estate – held by a third party – C). The express words of limitation "and his heirs"

---

[103] C's interest will become possessory only if B's contingent remainder does not vest. Thus, C will take possession, if at all, following A's life estate.

indicates that it is a remainder in fee simple absolute. The more difficult question is whether it is vested or contingent. The language of the conveyance expressly provides that C's interest is to become possessory *only* if B's interest fails ("if B fails to graduate from law school"). That constitutes an express condition precedent which must occur before C's interest can become possessory. The express condition precedent is in the clause *before* the clause creating the remainder. C has a *contingent remainder* in fee simple absolute. It is an *alternative* contingent remainder because it will become possessory only if another contingent remainder fails to vest. Where there is an alternative contingent remainder, is there a need for a default reversion in the grantor?

The key to analyzing whether alternative contingent remainders in fee simple need a default reversion is to diagram the state of the title. A's life estate is easy enough, for it is the first segment on the timeline - it is a vested interest:

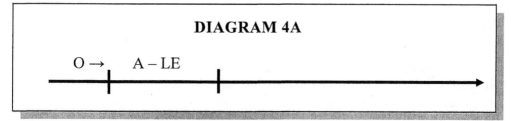

DIAGRAM 4A

O →   A – LE

B's interest, because it is a contingent remainder, is depicted as a dotted line secured to the top of the bolded cross line depicting the end of A's life estate:

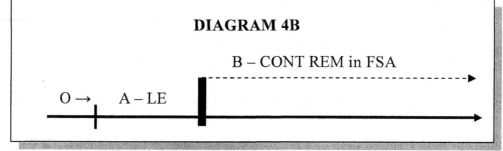

DIAGRAM 4B

B – CONT REM in FSA

O →   A – LE

C's interest, because it is an alternative contingent remainder, is likewise depicted as a dotted line secured to the bolded cross line depicting the end of the life estate:

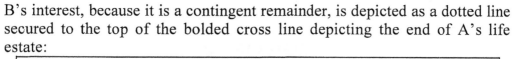

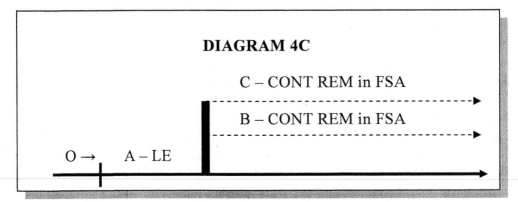

The problem is that the state of the title does not account for the whole timeline. It fails to account for the rest of the timeline following the life estate (until one of the contingent remainders vests). The default taker is always the grantor – O. Because it is a future interest held by the grantor following a life estate, it is a reversion; and because it is the rest of the timeline, and it is a default reversion, it is in fee simple absolute.

That accounts for the whole timeline. The full state of the title is: A has a life estate, B has a contingent remainder in fee simple, C has an alternative contingent remainder in fee simple, and O holds a reversion in fee simple. The full state of the title can be depicted on the timeline as follows:

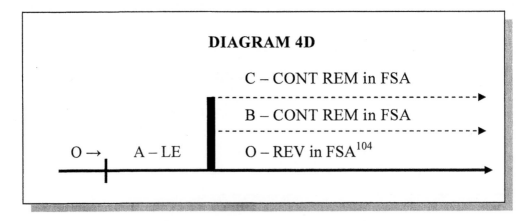

---

[104] You might be wondering why O has a default reversion. Logically it appears as though either B's contingent remainder will become possessory or C's contingent remainder will become possessory – there is no need for O to have a default reversion. Patience. The material in a couple of pages will explain why O must have a default reversion. *See infra* section V.

B. ALTERNATIVE PHRASING

There are two ways to phrase alternative contingent remainders. The first is the wording used in example 6 above (restated in Example 7 below) where the alternative contingent remainder is preceded by an *express* clause stating that the alternative remainder is contingent upon the first remainder not meeting its express condition precedent. There is, however, a more subtle way of stating the same condition precedent. For example:

EXAMPLE 7

O →   To A for life, then to B and her heirs if she graduates from law school, but if B fails to graduate from law school, then to C and his heirs.

O →   To A for life, then to B and her heirs if B graduates from law school, *otherwise* to C and his heirs.

In the second conveyance, the word "otherwise" serves the same function as the express clause in the first conveyance stating that the alternative remainder is contingent upon the first remainder not meeting its express condition precedent. Watch for either form of phrasing alternative contingent remainders.

V. PREMATURE TERMINATION OF FINITE ESTATE

A. METHODS BY WHICH FINITE ESTATE MAY END PREMATURELY

The analysis of the destructibility of contingent remainders is rather simple and straightforward where the supporting finite estate[105] ends naturally (i.e., typically upon the death of the life estate holder). For example, in the conveyance "O → To A for life, then to B and her heirs if she graduates from law school," A holds a life estate, B holds a contingent remainder in fee simple, and O holds a (default) reversion in fee simple. If A were to die

---

[105] Typically the supporting finite estate is a life estate. The discussion will assume that the underlying finite estate is a life estate, but it need not be.

before B graduates from law school, B's contingent remainder would be destroyed, and O's reversion would become possessory.

While a finite estate may end naturally, it may also end *prematurely*. There are three ways a finite estate may end prematurely: *forfeiture*, *renunciation*, and *merger*. Moreover, the common law destructibility of contingent remainders (that the contingent remainder must vest at or prior to the end of the preceding estate or it is deemed destroyed by operation of law), applies with equal force whether the finite estate end naturally or prematurely.

1. Forfeiture

At common law, if a life tenant[106] committed certain crimes, the punishment could include *forfeiture*. Forfeiture terminated the life tenant's life estate interest in the property. If the contingent remainder had not vested prior to or at the moment of forfeiture, the contingent remainder was destroyed, and the grantor's reversion would become possessory. This method of prematurely terminating a finite estate, however, is extremely rare today because society no longer recognizes forfeiture to the same degree as it did at common law.[107]

2. Renunciation

A life tenant can voluntarily *renounce* their interest in the life estate at any time during the life estate. The effect of a renunciation is to terminate the party's interest in the property as of the moment of the renunciation. If there is a contingent remainder and it has not vested by the time of, or at the moment of, renunciation, the contingent remainder will be destroyed under the rule of the destructibility of contingent remainders.

3. Merger

The third and final way a life estate[108] can end prematurely is by *merger*. The doctrine of merger provides that if the same party holds successive vested interests, the interests should be merged and re-identified

---

[106] The holder of the life estate.

[107] Although some jurisdictions still use forfeiture in connection with certain crimes, for example drug dealing.

[108] Or fee tail or terms of years, as the case may be.

based upon the largest estate created by the merger (the smaller estate mergers into the larger estate). There are, however, a couple of points to note about the merger doctrine. First, merger applies *only* to vested interests.[109] Second, for the merger doctrine to apply the vested interests must be *successive* and *held by the same party*.

The timeline diagram facilitates understanding the merger doctrine. First, an example:

EXAMPLE 8

O → To A for life, then to B and her heirs.

State the title. A has a life estate, B has a vested remainder in fee simple. Diagram the title:

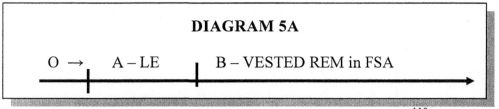

DIAGRAM 5A

O →   A – LE   B – VESTED REM in FSA

What if while A was alive, A transferred his life estate to B?[110] B would now hold the life estate (*pur autre vie*) and the vested remainder in fee simple absolute.

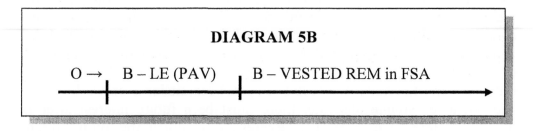

DIAGRAM 5B

O →   B – LE (PAV)   B – VESTED REM in FSA

B would now hold the possessory interest and the only future interest. B holds the whole timeline. If one owns the whole timeline, one holds a fee

---

[109] All possessory estates are vested, but only reversions and vested remainders are vested. Vested interests are those depicted on the timeline diagram *on* the timeline.

[110] Merger typically comes into play when a finite estate is transferred. Merger may also apply, however, if a fee simple defeasible is transferred back to the grantor. But this scenario is much less common than the transfer of a finite estate.

simple absolute. Therefore, under the doctrine of merger, the life estate would merge into the remainder (two successive vested interests held by the same party) to create a fee simple absolute in B:

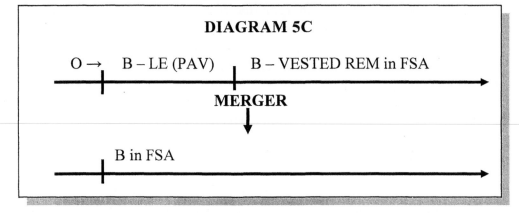

For merger to apply, however, the vested interests must be successive. There cannot be another vested interest in between them. For example:

EXAMPLE 9

O → To A for life, then to B for life, then to C and her heirs.

State the title. A has a life estate. The future interest is in a third party, B, so B holds a remainder. The express words of limitation, "for life," indicate that B's remainder is in life estate. Is the remainder vested or contingent? Reading comma to comma, B is born, ascertainable, and there is no express condition precedent in the same clause creating the remainder or the preceding clause, so the remainder is vested. B holds a vested remainder in life estate. Because B's vested remainder is only a life estate, and not a fee simple absolute, there must be a future interest after B's interest. Here, that interest is express – C holds the future interest following B's life estate. Because B's possessory interest is a life estate, the future interest following it must be a reversion or a remainder. Because C holds the future interest following B's interest, it must be a remainder. The express words of limitation describing C's interest, "and her heirs," indicate that C's remainder is in fee simple absolute. Is it vested or contingent? Reading comma to comma (or in this clause, comma to the end of the conveyance), C is born, ascertainable, and there is no express condition precedent in the same clause creating the remainder or the preceding clause, so the remainder is vested. C holds a vested remainder in fee simple absolute.[111]

The state of the title can be diagrammed:

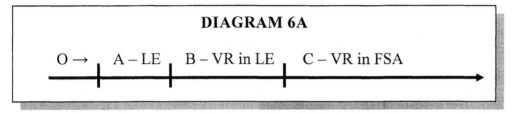

DIAGRAM 6A

O →   A – LE   B – VR in LE   C – VR in FSA

Now assume A transfers her life estate to C. Does the merger doctrine apply?

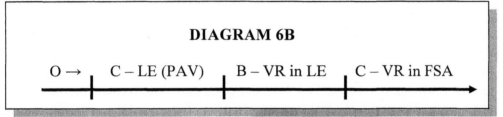

DIAGRAM 6B

O →   C – LE (PAV)   B – VR in LE   C – VR in FSA

Merger does not apply. The merger doctrine permits lesser estates to be merged into a greater estate if the same party holds successive vested interests. Although C holds two vested interests (a vested remainder in fee simple absolute and a life estate *pur autre vie*), the interests are not successive. B's vested remainder in life estate is in between.

Merger is relevant to contingent remainders because the effect of merger is to terminate the lesser estate, typically a life estate.[112] Coupling the merger doctrine with the common law destructibility of contingent remainders, when a supporting life estate ends prematurely through merger, if the contingent remainder has not vested prior to or at the moment the life estate ends, the contingent remainder is destroyed. For example, return to Example 5:

---

[111] Olivia, the original grantor, holds nothing. There is no need for a default reversion as Olivia has transferred all that she owned.

[112] Or other finite estate, as the case may be.

EXAMPLE 5

O →   To A for life, then to B and her heirs if she
graduates from law school.

State the title. A has a life estate. The future interest must be a reversion
or a remainder. Because B, a third party holds it, the future interest must
be a remainder. The words of limitation "and her heirs" indicate that B
holds a remainder in fee simple. Is it a fee simple defeasible? There is
qualifying language *after* the fee simple words of limitation. But here the
qualifying language introduces an express condition *precedent* – "*if* B
graduates from law school." For the estate to be fee simple defeasible,
the qualifying language has to introduce an express condition *subsequent*.
So B holds a remainder in fee simple. But is the remainder vested or
contingent? As just mentioned, there is an express condition precedent in
the same clause creating the remainder, so B holds a contingent
remainder in fee simple. Because B's remainder is contingent, there must
be a default taker in case B's interest does not vest before the end of the
preceding life estate. O holds a reversion in fee simple.

The state of the title can be diagrammed:

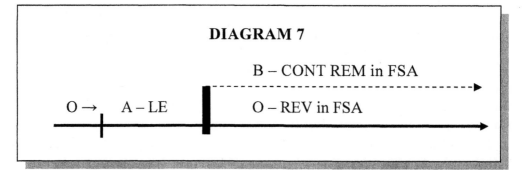

DIAGRAM 7

B – CONT REM in FSA

O →   A – LE   O – REV in FSA

Now assume the problem went on to tell you that while A was still alive
and before B graduated from law school, A transferred her life estate to O
(or, conversely, O transferred her reversion in fee simple to A). One party
would hold successive vested interests so the merger doctrine would apply
to create a fee simple absolute. If either of those transfers were to occur,
because the contingent remainder had not vested prior to, or the moment,
the life estate ends, it would be destroyed by the combined effect of the

merger doctrine and the destructibility of contingent remainders. (On the other hand, if the problem had told you that while A was still alive, B graduated from law school, the remainder would vest and the default reversion in O would be extinguished.)

Anytime there is a contingent remainder in fee simple, there should be a default reversion in the grantor. Anytime one party transfers his or her interest to another party who already holds an interest, analyze whether the merger applies.

B. APPLICATION TO THE ALTERNATIVE CONTINGENT REMAINDER

The twist on the alternative contingent remainder is that as long as the first contingent remainder has not vested, both contingent remainders are subject to the rule of destructibility of contingent remainders through either merger, renunciation or forfeiture. Assuming a standard alternative contingent remainder state of the title (life estate, contingent remainder in fee simple, alternative remainder in fee simple, and reversion in fee simple),[113] if the life tenant transfers her life estate to the grantor, or if the grantor transfers her reversion in fee simple to the life tenant, the resulting fee simple absolute (through merger) would destroy *both* contingent remainders. Moreover, if the life tenant were to renounce her interest, the result would be the same, both contingent remainders would be destroyed – as they would be if the life tenant committed a crime which carried the punishment of forfeiture. Premature termination of the underlying finite estate often has harsh consequences in the alternative contingent remainder setting.

The key then to analyzing alternative contingent remainders is to focus on how the preceding finite estate ends. Anytime there are alternative contingent remainders, if the preceding finite estate ends *prematurely (through merger, renunciation or forfeiture), only the reversion or the first possessory estate can become possessory*. If the first contingent remainder has not vested prior to or at the moment the finite estate ends prematurely, *both* of the contingent remainders are destroyed and the

---

[113] For example: "To A for life, then to B and her heirs if she graduates from law school, but if B fails to graduate from law school, then to C and her heirs."

reversion becomes possessory. If, on the other hand, the first contingent remainder *has* vested by the premature termination of the preceding finite estate, upon the vesting of the first contingent remainder, the alternative contingent remainder and the reversion are destroyed.

If, however, there are alternative contingent remainders and the preceding finite estate ends *naturally*, there is no chance that the default reversion will become possessory. The only issue is whether the first contingent remainder has vested. If the first contingent remainder has vested prior to or at the moment the finite estate ends naturally, the first finite estate will become possessory and the alternative contingent remainder and the reversion in the grantor are destroyed. On the other hand, if the preceding finite estate ends naturally and the first contingent remainder has *not* vested prior to or at the moment the finite estate ends naturally, the first contingent remainder will fail (and will be destroyed under the destructibility of contingent remainders) and the alternative contingent remainder will become possessory. Notice, if the preceding finite estate ends naturally, one of the two alternative contingent remainders will become possessory and the reversion will be destroyed. Which of the two contingent remainders will become possessory depends upon whether the first contingent remainder vests prior to or at the moment of the natural expiration of the preceding finite estate.

VI.   ALTERNATIVE CONTINGENT REMAINDER LOOK-ALIKE

One more conveyance should be noted. Up until now, all of our contingent remainder examples have involved contingent remainders *in fee simple*. Where the first contingent remainder is *not* in fee simple, there can be an express gift over to a third party in fee simple which eliminates any need for a default reversion in the grantor. For example:

EXAMPLE 10

O →   To A for life, then to B for *life* if she graduates from
         law school, but if B fails to graduate from law school,
         then to C and her heirs.

State the title. At first blush the conveyance looks like a set of classic alternative contingent remainders, but upon closer analysis it is not. A has a life estate. B has a contingent remainder – but *only in life estate*, not in fee simple. If that were all the conveyance expressly provided for, O would have a default reversion whether B's contingent remainder became possessory or not. But in Example 10 above, the conveyance grants an express future interest to C. C's interest will follow either A or B's life estate, so it is a remainder. The express words of limitation "and her heirs" indicate it is a remainder in fee simple. And there is no express condition precedent qualifying C's right to take possession so it is vested. Because there is a vested remainder in fee simple, there is no need for a default reversion in the grantor.

The conveyance can be diagrammed as follows:

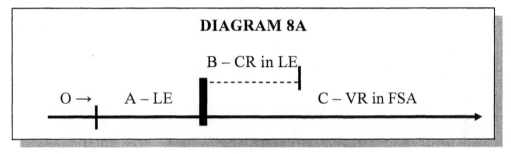

B's remainder is of finite duration so it is a short line segment with a definite end point. B's remainder is contingent so it is a dotted line segment. Again, because it is contingent, it is secured to and dependent upon the supporting life estate in A. If the facts went on to state that during A's lifetime B graduated from law school, B's remainder would vest. Schematically, the life estate would be lowered down the supporting crane and inserted on the timeline between the two vested interests (A's life estate and C's vested remainder in fee simple). Because B's interest is only a finite estate, it would not displace any interest:

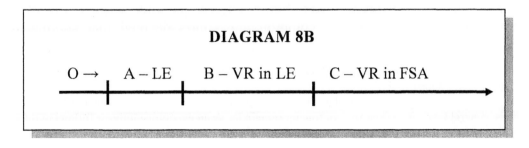

If, on the other hand, A were to die *before* B graduated from law school, the destructibility of contingent remainders would apply and B's contingent remainder would be destroyed. C's vested remainder in fee simple would become possessory.

So where the conveyance transfers a contingent remainder of a finite estate *and* a vested remainder in fee simple, there is no alternative contingent remainder and thus there is no default reversion.

VII. MODERN TREND

The modern trend is to repudiate, either statutorily or judicially, the destructibility of contingent remainders.[114] These developments, and their consequences, are beyond the scope of this introductory coverage for the most part.[115]

VIII. TRANSFERABILITY, DEVISABILITY AND INHERITABILITY

Vested remainders are freely transferable, devisable, and inheritable to the extent permitted by the express terms of the conveyance and/or the nature of the possessory duration of the future interest.[116] For example, if O conveyed the property "To A for life, then to B for life, then to C and his heirs," B holds a vested remainder in life estate. Although in theory B's vested remainder is freely transferable, devisable, and inheritable, because it is a vested remainder in life estate, if B were to die before A, the interest would terminate upon B's death – thereby making it not devisable or inheritable. But because C's vested remainder is in fee simple, it is freely transferable, devisable, and inheritable, even if C were to die before the interest becomes possessory.

On the other hand, the common law courts viewed contingent remainders with disfavor. The future interest is, after all, *contingent* – uncertain. Accordingly, the common law courts decreed that contingent

---

[114] 3 THOMPSON ON REAL PROPERTY § 23.23(b) Second Thomas Edition (David A. Thomas, ed., 2006).

[115] If your professor teaches the modern trend on this point, the practical effect, at a very general level, is to treat the contingent remainder as an executory interest following the point in time when it otherwise would have been destroyed. *See infra* Ch. 7, II & Ch. 10, III.

[116] MOYNIHAN, *supra* note 9, at 139.

remainders were not transferable.[117]   But contingent remainders were devisable and inheritable to the extent the nature of the express condition precedent and the duration of the future interest permitted.[118] For example, if O were to convey the property "To A for life, then to B and her heirs if A graduates from law school," if B were to die, the future interest would not terminate upon A's death. If A were to graduate from law school after B's death, the remainder would vest. And because B's contingent remainder is in fee simple, the interest still has value after B's death. B's contingent remainder is not transferable while she is alive, but it is devisable and inheritable upon her death. On the other hand, if O's conveyance read "To A for life, then to B for life if A graduates from law school," upon B's death her interest would terminate because it was only a life estate measured by B's life. In addition, if O's conveyance read "To A for life, then to B and her heirs if B survives A," although B's contingent remainder is in fee simple, because the express condition is that B must survive A, upon B's death before A, the interest would be destroyed under the destructibility of contingent remainders and would not be devisable or inheritable.

In summary, at common law all possessory estates and future interests were transferable, devisable, and inheritable to the extent permitted by the nature of the estate (i.e., its duration), with the exception of (1) the possibility of reverter and right of entry/power of termination, which were not transferable or devisable, and (2) the contingent remainders and executory interests,[119] which were not transferable.[120]

---

[117] *Id.*

[118] *Id.* at 140.

[119] Executory interests were non-transferable until the end of the sixteenth century. POWELL, *supra* note 57, ¶ 283 at 252.

[120] If is very important that you practice analyzing as many conveyances as possible. There are two problem sets after the next chapter. The next chapter is a short chapter designed primarily to help with the mechanics of how to analyze a conveyance. If you feel you are ready, you can try to analyze the conveyances in Problem Sets 4 and 5 at this point.

ALTERNATIVE APPROACH TO ANALYZING CONVEYANCES: LEAD WITH THE PARTIES

I. OVERVIEW

Although the analysis of the basic possessory estates and future interests started out simply enough, by now the material has conveyed a sense of the complexity and myriad of combinations which are possible. Remember the process of stating the title is a multiple step process.

First, analyze the possessory interest. For the possessory estate: (1) identify *who* holds the possessory interest (focus on the *words of purchase*); and (2) identify *which possessory estate* the party holds (first identify which *category* of possessory estates it is in and then focus on the *words of limitation* in the clause creating the possessory estate to determine which possessory estate it is).

For each future interest, the analysis is a three step process: (1) identify *which future interest* it is; (2) identify *who* holds the future interest (focus on the *words of purchase* at the beginning of the future interest clause); and (3) state the *duration* of the future interest (focus on the *words of limitation* in the clause creating the future interest).

II. ALTERNATIVE APPROACH: LEAD WITH THE PARTIES

A slightly different approach is to identify all of the parties named in the conveyance who could have a property interest in the conveyance (including the grantor) and list them. For example, start with the following conveyance:

EXAMPLE 1

O → To A for life, then to B for life, then to C and the
heirs of his body.

There are four parties who could possibly hold an interest:

EXAMPLE 2

A:
B:
C:
& O:

Having listed all of the parties who *may* have a property interest, the task is simply to identify the property interest of each, if any.

In identifying the property interest of each, remember that the first party, the party holding the possessory interest,[121] will have only one phrase describing his or her property interest (because the name of the possessory estate and its duration are one and the same). In contrast, all the other parties who hold a property interest must have two phrases describing their property interest: first, the name of the future interest (which depends on the possessory estate it follows), and second, the duration of the future interest (which turns on the express words of limitation in the clause creating that future interest):

EXAMPLE 3

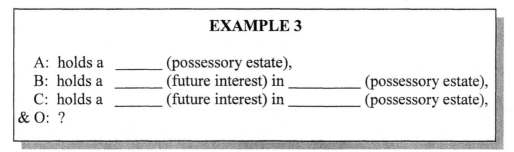

A: holds a _____ (possessory estate),
B: holds a _____ (future interest) in _____ (possessory estate),
C: holds a _____ (future interest) in _____ (possessory estate),
& O: ?

---

[121] There is one situation in which the first party named in the conveyance will not hold the possessory estate – but that estate combination is to come. *See* discussion *infra* Ch. 7, II, A.

O may or may not hold a future interest depending on whether the last express grantee holds a vested future interest in fee simple. In our example, if C holds a vested future interest in fee simple, O will hold nothing. But if C does not, O is the default taker of the remaining future interest in fee simple absolute.

Now, looking at the express language of the conveyance ("To A for life, then to B for life, then to C and the heirs of his body"), the words of limitation "for life" after the words of purchase "to A" indicate that A has a life estate:

EXAMPLE 4

A: holds a <u>life estate</u>,
B: holds a _____ (future interest) in _____ (possessory estate),
C: holds a _____ (future interest) in _____ (possessory estate),
& O: ?

Inasmuch as A holds a life estate, the future interest following it must be either a reversion or a remainder. Because B holds it, the future interest must be a remainder. Of what duration? The express words of limitation in the clause creating B's remainder are "for life," so B holds a remainder in life estate. Is B's remainder vested or contingent? B is born, ascertainable, and there is no express condition precedent, so it is vested:

EXAMPLE 5

A: holds a <u>life estate</u>,
B: holds a <u>vested remainder</u> in <u>life estate</u>,
C: holds a _____ (future interest) in _____ (possessory estate),
& O: ?

Inasmuch as B holds a life estate, the future interest following it must be either a reversion or a remainder. Because C holds it, it must be a remainder. Of what duration? The express words of limitation in the clause creating C's remainder are "and the heirs of his body," so C holds a remainder in fee tail. Is C's remainder vested or contingent? C is born, ascertainable and there is no express condition precedent, so it is vested:

EXAMPLE 6

A: holds a life estate,
B: holds a vested remainder in life estate,
C: holds a vested remainder in fee tail,
& O: ?

Does O hold any interest? If we were to diagram the conveyance, have we accounted for the whole timeline? :

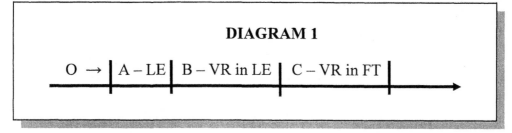

DIAGRAM 1

No, C's remainder in fee tail does not account for the end of the timeline.

Another way to think about whether O has a default interest without diagramming the conveyance is to ask whether the last express future interest is in fee simple absolute? If the answer is "no," then you have not accounted for the whole timeline, and O must hold a reversion in fee simple absolute. If the answer is yes, but the future interest is a *contingent* remainder in fee simple, you still have to give O a default reversion in fee simple. Returning to our example, because C holds a vested remainder but only in fee tail, not fee simple absolute, the state of the title so far has not accounted for the whole timeline. The courts will imply that O reserved a reversion in fee simple absolute:

EXAMPLE 7

A: holds a life estate,
B: holds a vested remainder in life estate,
C: holds a vested remainder in fee tail,
& O: holds a reversion in fee simple absolute.

By including the grantor in each of your lists of potential takers it will force you to think about whether you have accounted for the *whole* fee simple absolute in stating the title to the conveyance.

One last point that should help you analyze each conveyance. Notice that with the finite possessory estates, there can be, and often are, more than one future interest. Future interests following a finite estate can be combined (or "stacked") in all sorts of different combinations. In contrast, with the fee simple defeasibles (the fee simple determinable, the fee simple subject to a condition subsequent, and the fee simple subject to an executory limitation), for our introductory purposes only one future interest will follow the fee simple defeasible possessory estates (and it will be in fee simple duration).

CHAPTER 6 PROBLEM SET

State the complete title for the following problems.

1. O → To A for life, then to B and his heirs if he graduates from law school.

A has a _____ ,

B has a _____ in _____ ,

O has? _____ in _____ .

2. O → To A, then to B and the heirs of her body, then to C for ten
   years.

A has a _____ ,

B has a _____ in _____ ,

C has a _____ in _____ ,

O has? _____ in _____ .

3. O → To A and the heirs of his body, then to B and her heirs if she
   graduates from law school, otherwise, to C and her heirs.

A has a _____ ,

B has a _____ in _____ ,

C has a _____ in _____ ,

O has? _____ in _____ .

4. O → To A for life, then to B, then to C and her heirs if she quits smoking.

O has a _____ ,

B has a _____ in _____ ,

C has a _____ in _____ ,

O has? _____ in _____ .

5. O →   To A for 2 years, then to B and the heirs of her body, then
to C and her heirs as long as she does not smoke.

A has a _____ ,

B has a _____ in _____ ,

C has a _____ in _____ ,

O has? _____ in _____ .

6. O → To A for life, then to B and her heirs if she is married when A
dies.

A has a _____ ,

B has a _____ in _____ ,

O has? _____ in _____ .

7. O → To A, then to B, then to C for life if she is still alive.

A has a _____ ,

B has a _____ in _____ ,

C has a _____ in _____ ,

O has? _____ in _____ .

8. O → To A for life, then to B and her heirs if she farms the land organically, but if she does not, then to C and his heirs.

A has a _____ ,

B has a _____ in _____ ,

C has a _____ in _____ ,

O has?   _____ in _____ .

9. Gollum → To for Bilbo for life, then to Frodo and his heirs.

Bilbo has a _____ ,

Frodo has a _____ in _____ ,

Gollum has? _____ in _____ .

10. Deagol → To Smeagol for life, then to Bilbo and the heirs of his body, then to Frodo and his heirs.

Smeagol has a _____ ,

Bilbo has a _____ in _____ ,

Frodo has a _____ in _____ ,

Deagol has? _____ in _____ .

11. Paul → To John and the heirs of his body, then to George for life, then to Ringo and his heirs as long as he maintains the strawberry fields on the property.

John has a _____ ,

George has a _____ in _____ ,

Ringo has a _____ in _____ ,

Paul has?   _____ in _____ .

12. Bernini →To Raphael for life, then to Donatello for life, then to
     Michelangelo for life.

Raphael has a _____ ,

Donatello has a _____ in _____ ,

Michelangelo has a _____ in _____ ,

Bernini has?_____ in _____ .

13. Bob → To Ted for 10 years, then to Carol and the heirs of her
     body, then to Alice for life.

Ted has a _____ ,

Carol has a _____ in _____ ,

Alice has a _____ in _____ ,

Bob has? _____ in _____ .

14. Goldie → To Kate for life, then to Goldie and her heirs.

Kate has a _____ ,

Goldie has a _____ .

15. Ross → To Chandler and the heirs of his body, then to Monica
     and the heirs of her body, then to Joey and his heirs,
     but if Joey opens an acting school on the property, then
     Ross has the right to re-enter and reclaim the property.

Chandler has a _____ ,

Monica has a _____ in _____ ,

Joey has a _____ in _____ ,

Ross has? _____ in _____ .

REVIEW PROBLEM SET 1

State the title to the following problems.

1. O → To A for life, then to B.

2. O → To A and the heirs of her body, then to B for life if she graduates from law school.

3. O → To A, then to B and the heirs of her body, then to C and his heirs as long as C does not sell alcohol on the land.

4. O → To A for life, then to B and her heirs, but if she drains the wetlands on the property, then O has the right to re-enter and re-claim the property.

5. O → To A for 5 years, then to B and his heirs if he becomes Dean of the Law School, otherwise to C and her heirs.

6. O → To A, then to B his heirs as long as does not hunt on the land.

7. O → To A for life, then to B if he is married.

8. O → To A and her heirs as long as she remains married, then B and her heirs.

9. O →   To A for life, then to B and her heirs if she marries C, otherwise to C and her heirs.

10. O →   To A and her heirs, but if she fails to maintain the gardens on the property then O has the right to re-enter and re-claim the property.

11. O →   To A, then to B for life, then to C and the heirs if she returns from London.

12. O →   To A for life, then to B for life, then to C and her heirs but if she stops using the land for charitable purposes, then O has the right to re-enter and re-claim the property.

13. O →   To A, then to B for 10 years, then to C for life, then to D and her heirs if he attends medical school.

14. O →   To A for life, then to B and her heirs if she attends law school, otherwise to C and her heirs.

15. O →   To A for life, then to B and the heirs of her body, then to C.

16. O →   To A for 3 years, then to B and her heirs, but if B ever uses chemical pesticides on the property then to C and her heirs.

17. O →   To A and her heirs as long as she votes Democratic.

18. O →   To A and her heirs, but if she ever votes Democratic, then O has the right to re-enter and re-claim the property.

19. O →   To A for life, then to B and her heirs, but if she ever commits a crime on the property then to C and her heirs.

20. O →   To A for life, then if B is out of jail, to B and her heirs.

21. Rocky → To Adrian.

22. Rocky → To Adrian and her heirs.

23. Rocky → To Adrian for life.

24. Oprah → To Nelson and his heirs as long as the land is used for educational purposes.

25. Ray →   To Shoeless and his heirs, but if Shoeless stops using the land as a baseball field, then Ray and his heirs shall have the right to reenter and reclaim the land.

26. Joe →   To Marilyn and the heirs of her body.

27.   Oprah → To Nelson and his heirs as long as Nelson uses the land for educational purposes, then to Stedman and his heirs.

28. Britney → To Paris and her heirs, but if Paris ever goes to college, then to Nicole and her heirs.

29. Britney → To Paris and the heirs of her body, then to Nicole and her heirs.

30. Oprah → To Barbara and the heirs of her body, then if Rosie is still living, to Rosie and her heirs.

31. Oprah → To Tom and his children.

32. Karl → To Fidel for life, then to Hugo and his heirs.

33. Simon → To Randy for life, then to Ryan and his heirs if he is married, and if Ryan he is not married, then to Paula and her heirs.

34. Paula → To Randy for life, then to Simon and his heirs if he moves back to England.

35. Kingsfield → To Susan for life, then to whomever is then Dean of the Law School and his or her heirs.

36. Joe → To Ali for life, then to Leon for life, then to Oscar's heirs and their heirs. (Assume Oscar is still alive.)

37. Thoreau → To Ralph for life, then to Horace and his heirs as long as Walden is not developed.

38. Thoreau → To Ralph for life, then if Horace has agreed not to develop Walden, to Horace and his heirs.

39. Elizabeth → To William for life, then to Harry and his heirs if Harry marries Chelsy.

40. Babe → To Hank for life, then to Barry and his heirs if he breaks the record.

Chapter 7

VARIATIONS ON THE EXECUTORY INTEREST

I. OVERVIEW

A. REVIEW

The analytical scheme developed so far is based upon three categories of possessory estates: the fee simple absolute, the fee simple defeasibles, and the finite estates. There are three fee simple defeasibles: the fee simple determinable, the fee simple subject to a condition subsequent, and a fee simple subject to an executory limitation. The future interest following the fee simple subject to an executory limitation is an executory interest.

B. HISTORICAL BACKGROUND

From a historical perspective, the fee simple subject to an executory limitation is "the new kid on the block." Pre-1536, if a fee simple were to be cut short, the future interest *had to be* in the grantor. Only the fee simple determinable ("To A and her heirs as long as she does not sell alcohol on the land") and the fee simple subject to condition subsequent ("To A and her heirs, but if she sells alcohol on the land, then the grantor has the right to re-enter and reclaim the land") were permitted. Notice both of these estates implicitly assume and require that the underlying fee simple defeasible is held by a third party, and the future interest is in the grantor.

In 1536, however, the Statute of Uses was adopted. The common law courts construed it as permitting a fee simple to be cut short with the future interest in a third party. To acknowledge this new combination, the courts gave the estates in the combination a new name: the fee simple subject to an executory limitation and the executory interest. The defining characteristic of this combination is that the future interest following a fee simple defeasible is held by a third party, not a grantor ("To A and her heirs, but if she sells alcohol on the land, to B and her heirs"). But inasmuch as the future interest is held by a third party, that opened up the possibility that the *underlying fee simple defeasible* could be held either by a third party *or the grantor*.

C. SHIFTING vs. SPRINGING EXECUTORY INTERESTS

The most common fee simple defeasible scenario is for a third party to hold the possessory estate. Under that scenario, the fee simple defeasible looks just like a fee simple determinable or a fee simple subject to a condition subsequent, except the future interest is held by a third party ("To A and her heirs as long as she farms the land organically, then to B and her heirs" or "To A and his heirs, but if he sells alcohol on the land, then to B and his heirs"). Because the future interest is held by a third party, the underlying fee simple defeasible is a fee simple subject to an executory limitation and the future interest held by third party is a *shifting* executory interest[122] (in fee simple).

Where, however, the underlying fee simple defeasible is *held by the grantor*, the future interest is called a *springing* executory interest. While the shifting executory interest is the more common executory interest, you need to be familiar with, and able to recognize, springing executory interests. Admittedly it is not as easy intuitively to envision a conveyance involving a springing executory interest. When springing executory interests do occur, they usually occur in one of two types of conveyances:[123] (1) the "future interest only" conveyance, or (2) the "gap" scenario conveyance.

II. SPRINGING EXECUTORY INTERESTS

A. THE "FUTURE INTEREST ONLY" CONVEYANCE

In all of the conveyances examined so far, the grantor has conveyed a possessory estate to the grantee identified first. For example, in the conveyances "O → To A for life, then to B and her heirs" and "O → To A and her heirs," in both conveyances the moment the conveyance is effective, A holds the possessory estate.[124] But it is possible to draft a conveyance where the grantee identified first takes a future interest, not a possessory estate. For example:

---

[122] The right to possession is being *shifted* from one third party to another.

[123] These scenarios were not permitted before the Statute of Uses was adopted in 1536. To reflect that these estate combinations are "new," the common law courts adopted new terminology to describe the estates.

[124] In fact, prior to 1536, for a conveyance to be valid, the grantee *had* to receive a possessory estate.

EXAMPLE 1

O → To A and his heirs if A is married.

Based on the wording of the conveyance, the logical assumption is that A is *not* married at the time of the conveyance. Assuming A is not married, he does not have the right to claim actual possession immediately after the conveyance. There is an express condition precedent which must be satisfied *before* he can claim the right to actual possession.

The presence of an express condition precedent which must be satisfied *before* the party's interest can become possessory makes the interest look a bit like, and sound a bit like, a *contingent* remainder. But here the interest cannot be a contingent remainder because it is not a remainder. There is no preceding finite estate. The express condition precedent is in the same clause as the clause which *appears* to be conveying a possessory interest to the grantee. It is not a possessory interest, however, due to the express condition precedent. The grantee is taking a future interest, not a possessory estate. The conveyance is a "*future interest only*" conveyance.

Because the grantee is taking a future interest only, the grantor retains the right to possession until the express condition precedent occurs – if it ever occurs. The assumption is that the grantor held a fee simple absolute before the conveyance. Where the conveyance is of a future interest only, the grantor's fee simple *may be* cut short if the express condition precedent occurs. Accordingly, after the conveyance, the grantor holds a fee simple defeasible. Because the future interest is held by a third party, the grantor must hold a fee simple subject to an executory limitation and the third party must hold an executory interest (in fee simple). Because the right to possession will be *taken from the grantor* if the possessory estate is cut short, the third party holds a *springing* executory interest in fee simple.

Anytime there is a "future interest only" conveyance (there is an express condition precedent that must be satisfied before the grantee has the right to claim actual possession under the conveyance), after the conveyance the grantor holds a fee simple subject to an executory limitation,[125] and the grantee holds a springing executory interest in fee simple.

---

[125] Assuming the grantor held a fee simple absolute before the conveyance.

B. THE "GAP" SCENARIO

The "gap" scenario arises when there is what appears to be a contingent remainder, but the express condition precedent is one which by its nature cannot be satisfied before the end of the preceding finite estate. For example, compare the future interest in the following two conveyances:

EXAMPLE 2

O →   To A for life, then to B and his heirs if B marries A.

O →   To A for life, then to B and his heirs if B attends A's funeral.

State the title. In both conveyances A has a life estate, and the express future interest is in B, a third party, so in both conveyances the future interest looks like a remainder. The words of limitation "and his heirs" in both conveyances indicate that the future interest is in fee simple. Is the future interest contingent or vested? In both conveyances the future interest looks like a contingent remainder because there is an express condition precedent in the same clause as the clause creating the future interest which must be satisfied before the interest can become possessory. In both conveyances the future interest looks like a contingent remainder.

But upon closer inspection of the express condition precedent in the respective conveyances, it becomes apparent that there is a difference. In the first conveyance ("To A for life, then to B and his heirs if B marries A"), the express condition precedent is one which by its nature is capable of occurring (being satisfied) during or at the moment the preceding finite estate ends. B will either marry A or not during A's life estate. Because the express condition precedent has a chance of occurring during the preceding finite estate, the future interest is a contingent remainder.

In the second conveyance ("To A for life, then to B and his heirs if B attends A's funeral"), however, the express condition precedent is one which by its nature *cannot* be fulfilled during the preceding finite estate. Temporally there is a "gap" between the end of the preceding finite estate and the point in time when the express condition precedent could occur. The express condition precedent is that B must attend A's funeral. B cannot attend A's funeral until *after* A dies. The express condition precedent cannot be satisfied before, or at the moment, the preceding finite estate ends; the express condition precedent is such that it cannot be satisfied until *after* the preceding finite estate ends. There is, implicitly, a temporal "gap" between the end of the finite estate and the point in time when the express condition precedent may be satisfied.

Because the conveyance did not expressly provide for who had the right to possession during the "gap," by default the grantor retained the future interest following the finite estate – the grantor held a reversion in fee simple. That meant that the express clause granting the future interest to the third party if the condition were to occur would have to cut short the grantor's fee simple with the future interest in a third party. Pre-1536, if a fee simple were to be cut short, the future interest had to be in the grantor. Thus, pre-1536, the future interest following the "gap" type conveyance was null and void.

Post-1536, however, the "gap" type conveyance is just a variation on the fee simple subject to an executory limitation with a *springing* executory interest combination. In the "gap" type conveyance, the grantor's reversion in fee simple might be cut short by the express condition precedent which could not, by nature, occur during the preceding finite estate. Inasmuch as the grantor's reversion in fee simple might be cut short, the grantor holds a fee simple defeasible. In the "gap" scenario, the future interest will be held by a third party. The grantor holds a fee simple subject to an executory limitation, and the third party holds a springing executory interest in fee simple.

The "gap" scenario is fairly easy to identify as long as the conveyance is read carefully. Watch for a conveyance which appears to create a contingent remainder because of the presence of an express condition precedent, except the express condition precedent, by nature, cannot be fulfilled during the preceding finite estate. Whenever that is the case, there is a "gap" scenario. Whenever there is a "gap" scenario, the grantor will hold a reversion in fee simple subject to an executory limitation to cover the gap, and the third party will hold an executory interest in fee simple. Because the executory interest, if it is to become possessory, will take the right to possession from the grantor and give it to a third party, it is a *springing* executory interest in fee simple.[126]

---

[126] The preceding finite estate is almost always a life estate, but in theory it can be any of the finite estates. It is difficult to imagine, however, a "gap" scenario where the preceding finite estate is a fee tail. The norm is for the preceding finite estate to be a life estate, though occasionally it will be a term of years.

III.   THE VESTED REMAINDER SUBJECT TO DIVESTMENT

The common law courts also construed the Statute of Uses as permitting another "new" conveyance – one in which a party who held a vested remainder could *lose* the right to possession *before* he or she ever took possession of the property.   Again, that statement is so abstract a couple of examples should help.   Compare the wording in the following conveyances:

EXAMPLE 3

O →   To A for life, then to B and her heirs, but if *B* stops
        farming the land, then to C and her heirs.

O →   To A for life, then to B and her heirs, but if *A* stops
        farming the land, then to C and her heirs.

State the titles.   In both conveyances, A has a life estate.   In both conveyances, because the future interest is in B, she holds a remainder.   In both conveyances, the words of limitation "and her heirs" indicate that B's interest is in fee simple.   Moreover, in both conveyances B's remainder is vested.   The party holding the remainder, B, is born, ascertainable, and reading comma to comma, there is no express condition precedent in the same clause creating the remainder or the preceding clause.   But in both conveyances the fee simple is not a fee simple absolute because there is additional language which qualifies B's fee simple.   At first blush, it would appear that B has a fee simple defeasible – a fee simple which might be cut short by an express condition subsequent.

That is the case in the first conveyance, but not in the second.   In the first conveyance ("To A for life, then to B and her heirs, but if *B* stops farming the land, then to C and her heirs"), the express condition that may terminate B's interest is "if *B* stops farming the land … ."   That condition applies to and qualifies B's right to possession *after* B takes actual possession.   It is an express condition subsequent.   B holds a vested remainder in fee simple subject to an executory limitation, and C holds a shifting executory interest in fee simple.

But in the second conveyance ("To A for life, then to B and her heirs, but if *A* stops farming the land, then to C and her heirs"), the express condition that may affect B's interest is "if *A* stops farming the land, ..." Relative to B's interest, that event must occur, if at all, *during* A's life estate – *before* B's interest becomes possessory. It is an express condition precedent relative to B's future interest becoming possessory. It is not an express condition precedent which must be satisfied before B's interest can become possessory, rather it is an express condition precedent which, if it occurs, will shift the right to possession from A to C, thereby destroying (or "divesting") B's vested remainder.

Pre-1536, once a vested remainder vested, the right to possession could not be taken away from the party before it became possessory. But after the Statute of Uses in 1536, the common law courts construed the statute as permitting the right to possession under a vested remainder to be taken away before it became possessory. Because this was a "new" combination of estates, the courts again created new terminology to acknowledge this "new" development. The vested remainder is said to be "subject to divestment" and the future interest following a vested remainder subject to divestment is an "executory interest."[127]

Returning to the second conveyance above, the title is that A has a life estate, B holds a vested remainder in fee simple subject to divestment, and C holds an executory interest in fee simple. Which type of executory interest, springing or shifting? Because the right to possession would be taken from one third party and "shifted" to another third party if the condition were to occur, C's executory interest is a shifting executory interest.

Notice, in analyzing any *remainder* which has an express condition qualifying it, there are two key variables. First, is the express condition a condition precedent or a condition subsequent? If the condition is a condition subsequent, and the remainder is in fee simple, the estate is one of the fee simple defeasibles. Second, if the express condition is a condition precedent, the key is *where* in the conveyance is the condition expressed? If the condition precedent is in the same clause as the clause creating the remainder, or the preceding clause, the remainder is a contingent remainder. If the condition precedent is in a clause subsequent to the clause creating the

---

[127] Notice the term "executory interest" is used to describe the future interest in all the "new" estate combinations permitted after the Statute of Uses; and all of them are held by a third party. You should never use the term "executory interest" to describe a future interest retained by the grantor.

remainder, the remainder is a vested remainder subject to divestment, and the future interest following it will be a shifting executory interest in fee simple.

Although a vested remainder subject to divestment looks rather straightforward in isolation, when contrasted with other conveyances some students have difficultly distinguishing it. It should help you identify the vested remainder subject to divestment if you pay close attention to the subtle requirements which are implicit in the analysis of the vested remainder subject to divestment. The material will examine those requirements in greater detail.

A. THE REQUIREMENT OF A VESTED REMAINDER

Before there can be a vested remainder subject to divestment, there must be a vested remainder. There is no chance that an estate is a vested remainder subject to divestment unless (1) there is a remainder, and (2) it is a vested remainder. That means that the preceding estate in the conveyance must be a finite possessory estate (typically a life estate). If there is no preceding finite possessory estate, the express condition cannot be one which could occur *before* the party takes possession. For example:

EXAMPLE 4

O → To B and his heirs, but if B sells alcohol on the land, then to C and her heirs.

O → To A for life, then to B and his heirs, but if A sells alcohol on the land, then to C and her heirs.

Notice in the first conveyance, there is no finite estate. The qualifying condition which could affect the party's right to possession ("but if *B* sells alcohol on the land") is a condition subsequent. B holds a fee simple defeasible. Because the future interest is held by C, a third party, B holds a fee simple subject to an executory limitation, and C holds a shifting executory interest in fee simple. In contrast, in the second conveyance, there is a preceding finite estate. A holds a life estate, B holds a vested remainder, and the express condition is a condition precedent – it must occur, if at all, during the finite estate preceding the vested remainder ("but if *A* sells alcohol on the land"). Because the condition is one which must occur, if at all, prior to B's remainder becoming possessory, the remainder is a vested remainder subject to divestment.[128]

B. THE EXPRESS CONDITION PRECEDENT REQUIREMENT

Another point which is implicit in the discussion of the vested remainder subject to divestment is that the condition must be an express condition *precedent* – not a condition subsequent. For example:

EXAMPLE 5

O → To A and her heirs as long as she maintains the wetlands on the property.

O → To A and her heirs, but if she fails to maintain the wetlands on the property, then O has the right to re-enter and reclaim the property.

O → To A and her heirs as long as she maintains the wetlands on the property, then to B and his heirs.

O → To A and her heirs, but if she fails to maintain the wetlands on the property, then to B and his heirs.

O → To G for life, then to A and her heirs as long as she maintains the wetlands on the property, then to B and his heirs.

O → To G for life, then to A and her heirs, but if A fails to maintain the wetlands on the property, then to B and his heirs.

In all of the conveyances the express condition is a condition subsequent. In the first four conveyances, there is no preceding finite estate, so the possessory estate is one of the fee simple defeasibles. In the last two, there is

---

[128] Notice the words "but if" introduce the qualifying condition in both conveyances. In the firsts conveyance, the words introduce a condition precedent; in the second a condition subsequent. The words "but if" can introduce *either* type of condition, so the temporal nature of the condition must be analyzed carefully.

a preceding finite estate, but the express condition qualifying the remainder is still a condition subsequent (applies subsequent to the remainder becoming possessory), so the remainder in each of the last two conveyances is a vested remainder in fee simple defeasible, not subject to divestment.

There must be a vested remainder and an express condition *precedent* in the clause subsequent to the remainder before the remainder can be a vested remainder subject to divestment.

EXAMPLE 6

O → To X for life, then to A and her heirs, but if A fails to maintain the wetlands on the property, then to B and his heirs.

O → To X for life, then to A and her heirs, but if X fails to maintain the wetlands on the property, then to B and his heirs.

In the first conveyance there is a vested remainder, and the express condition qualifying it ("but if A fails to maintain the wetlands") is a condition subsequent. The express condition is one which by its nature applies, if at all, after A's remainder becomes possessory. A holds a vested remainder in fee simple subject to an executory limitation.

In the second conveyance there is a vested remainder, and the express condition qualifying it ("but if X fails to maintain the wetlands") is a condition precedent. The express condition is one which by its nature applies *before* A's remainder becomes possessory. It must occur, if at all, during the preceding finite estate. Because A's vested remainder is qualified by an express condition *precedent* in the clause *subsequent* to the clause creating the remainder, A holds a vested remainder in fee simple subject to divestment, and B holds a shifting executory interest in fee simple.

The next point which is implicit in the analysis of vested remainders is a relatively minor point - the condition precedent must be express. The "subject to divestment" component of the analysis must be the result of an express condition in the conveyance, not because of the nature of the remainder. For example:

EXAMPLE 7

O →   To A for life, then to B for life, then to C and her heirs.

O →   To A for life, then to B and his heirs, but if B dies
          before A, then to C and her heirs.

State the title. In the first conveyance, A has a life estate, B has a vested remainder in life estate, and C has a vested remainder in fee simple. But if B dies before A, B will lose his right to possession before his remainder becomes possessory. Does that mean that the remainder is subject to divestment? No. That is the nature of a life estate – there is no express condition precedent. The vested remainder is subject to divestment only if there is an express condition in the subsequent clause which could occur prior to the vested remainder becoming possessory. That is not the case in the first conveyance.

In the second conveyance, there is an express condition precedent: "but if B dies before A" (that condition must occur, if at all, during A's life estate, so it constitutes an express condition precedent). It is in the clause subsequent to the clause creating the remainder. The state of the title is A holds a life estate, B holds a vested remainder in fee simple subject to divestment, and C holds a shifting executory interest in fee simple.

C. THE CONDITION PRECEDENT MUST BE IN THE SUBSEQUENT CLAUSE

Related to the points made above is that the express condition precedent must be in a clause *subsequent* to the clause creating the remainder. If the express condition precedent is in the same clause as the clause creating the remainder or a preceding clause, then the condition precedent makes the remainder a contingent remainder. Where there is an express condition precedent, the remainder will either be a contingent remainder or a vested remainder subject to divestment – there will *not* be a *contingent* remainder subject to *divestment*.[129]

---

[129] At least not in your typical introductory coverage of possessory estates and future interests.

EXAMPLE 8

O → To A for life, then if A restores the wetlands on the property, to B and her heirs.

O → To A for life, then to B and her heirs if A restores the wetlands on the property.

O → To A for life, then to B and her heirs, but if A fails to restore the wetlands on the property, then to C and her heirs.

O → To A for life, then if A restores the wetlands on the property, to B and her heirs, but if A fails to restore the wetlands on the property, then to C and her heirs.

In all four conveyances, A holds a life estate, and because B holds the future interest, B holds a remainder in fee simple. In all four conveyances, B's remainder is qualified by an express condition precedent relating to A restoring the wetlands on the property. In the first two conveyances, the express condition precedent is in the *same* clause creating the remainder or the *preceding* clause, so B's remainder is a contingent remainder is fee simple. There is no express taker in the event the express condition precedent is not satisfied, so the grantor, O, holds a default reversion in fee simple.

In the third conveyance, A holds a life estate, B holds a remainder in fee simple, and the express condition precedent is in the clause *after* the clause creating the remainder. B's remainder is a vested remainder in fee simple subject to divestment, and C holds a shifting executory interest in fee simple. The location of the express condition precedent in the conveyance is critical to the analysis.

In the fourth conveyance, A holds a life estate and B holds a remainder in fee simple. Because the express condition precedent is in the same clause as the clause creating the remainder, B holds a contingent remainder in fee simple. What about the clause which restates the express condition precedent in the clause subsequent to the clause creating the remainder? That is just re-stating the express condition precedent which also qualifies C's interest. This is just another example of an alternative contingent remainder. B holds a contingent remainder in fee simple, and C holds an alternative contingent remainder in fee simple – contingent on A failing to maintain the wetlands. B's *contingent* remainder is *not subject to divestment*. B holds a contingent remainder in fee simple, and C holds an alternative contingent remainder in fee simple. There must be a vested remainder before there can be a vested remainder subject to divestment. To complete the state of the title, the grantor, O, holds a default reversion in fee simple (in the event the preceding finite estate ends prematurely and the first contingent remainder has not vested).

D. EXPRESS CONDITION WHICH CAN BE *EITHER* A CONDITION PRECEDENT OR CONDITION SUBSEQUENT

The material so far has discussed the express condition precedent and the express condition subsequent separately, thereby creating the impression that the same condition could not be both. It is possible, however, to have an express condition that can be both – a condition which could occur before the remainder becomes possessory and which could also occur after the remainder becomes possessory. This is particularly true where the express condition is not tied to the use of the land or the life of the party holding the preceding finite estate. For example:

EXAMPLE 9

O → To A for life, then to B and her heirs, but if A sells alcohol on the property, then to C and her heirs.

O → To A for life, then to B and her heirs, but if B sells alcohol on the property, to C and her heirs.

O → To A for life, then to B and her heirs, but if A marries C, then to C and her heirs.

O → To A for life, then to B and her heirs, but if P marries G, then to C and her heirs.

In all four conveyances, A holds a life estate. In all four conveyances, because a third party holds the future interest, B holds a remainder. In all four conveyances, because B is born, ascertainable, and there is no express condition in the clause creating the remainder or the preceding clause, B holds a vested remainder (in fee simple because of the express words of limitation "and her heirs"). But there is express language qualifying the remainder in all four conveyances in the clause after the clause creating the remainder. What type of vested remainder does B hold in each?

In the first conveyance, "To A for life, then to B and her heirs, but if A sells alcohol on the property, then to C and her heirs," the condition qualifying the remainder is an express condition precedent which must occur, if at all, during the preceding finite estate (either A will or will not sell alcohol on the land during his lifetime). B holds a vested remainder in fee simple subject to divestment, and C holds a shifting executory interest in fee simple.

In the second conveyance, "To A for life, then to B and her heirs, but if B sells alcohol on the property, to C and her heirs," the condition qualifying the remainder is an express condition subsequent which must occur, it at all, during the time that the remainder is possessory (either B will or will not sell alcohol on the land *after* she takes possession of the land).[130] Because the condition is a condition subsequent, B holds a vested remainder in fee simple subject to an executory limitation, and C holds a shifting executory interest in fee simple.

In the third conveyance, "To A for life, then to B and her heirs, but if A marries C, then to C and her heirs," the condition qualifying the remainder is one which is not tied to the land, rather it is tied to the life tenant, and because it is tied to the life tenant, it must occur, if at all, during the preceding finite estate. Either A will get married or not during his lifetime. The express condition "if A marries C" is an express condition precedent relative to B's remainder. B holds a vested remainder in fee simple subject to divestment, and C holds a shifting executory interest in fee simple.

In the fourth conveyance, "To A for life, then to B and her heirs, but if P marries G, then to C and her heirs," the express condition qualifying the remainder is not tied to the property or to the life tenant. The express condition is one which *could* occur *before* the remainder becomes possessory, but it *could* also occur *after* the remainder becomes possessory. As long as the condition is one which could occur before the remainder becomes possessory, the remainder is a vested remainder subject to divestment. At the

---

[130] Assume that B does not have access to the land during the preceding finite estate. That is the norm and the logical assumption.

time of the conveyance, and up until the remainder becomes possessory, B's vested remainder in fee simple is subject to divestment. If the preceding finite estate ends, and the express condition has not occurred but is of the nature that it could still occur, the remainder becomes the possessory estate – but the estate could still be cut short if the condition were to occur. For example, assume the fourth conveyance went on to tell you that A died. B's remainder would become possessory the moment the finite estate ends, so it no longer is a remainder. B holds the property in fee simple. But because the express condition qualifying B's estate could still occur even after she takes possession (P could still marry G), B's fee simple could be cut short. The express condition is only a condition subsequent now. B holds a fee simple defeasible. If B's right to possession were cut short, the right to possession would go to C – a third party. That means that B would hold a fee simple subject to an executory limitation, and C would hold a shifting executory interest in fee simple.[131] The analysis of the possessory estate and future interests created by a conveyance can change over time.

E. EFFECT UPON THE PRECEDING FINITE ESTATE

One final point about divesting conditions is that there is almost always an inherent ambiguity with respect to what effect, if any, the divesting condition should have upon the preceding finite estate. If the divesting condition occurs during the course of the preceding finite estate, does it only divest the vested remainder or should it also cut short the preceding finite estate (i.e., immediately terminate the preceding finite estate)? For example:

EXAMPLE 10

O →   To A for life, then to B and her heirs, but if A fails to graduate from law school, then to C and her heirs.

---

[131] Technically one could argue that before B's vested remainder became possessory the proper state of the title should have been that B held a vested remainder, subject to divestment, in fee simple, subject to an executory limitation. This accurately reflects that B's remainder is, at that point in time, subject to both (1) the possibility of divestment before becoming possessory, and (2) subject to being cut short after becoming possessory. This level of detail, however, is usually more than is necessary in the introductory coverage.

State the title. A has a life estate, B has a vested remainder in fee simple subject to divestment, and C has a shifting executory interest in fee simple. Assume that the facts go on to state that A dies without having graduated from law school. The divesting condition has occurred, and B's vested remainder in fee simple is divested. B loses her right to possession before it ever becomes possessory. Notice that the nature of the divesting condition is such that it is not tested until the end of the preceding finite estate, so by its nature, it has no effect upon the preceding finite estate.

Often, however, the express divesting condition is one which may occur during the preceding finite estate, and if it does, a question which may arise is whether the divesting condition should also cut short the preceding finite estate. For example:

EXAMPLE 11

O →   To A for life, then to B and her heirs, but if A marries L, then to C and her heirs.

State the title. A has a life estate, B has a vested remainder in fee simple subject to divestment, and C has a shifting executory interest in fee simple. Now assume the problem goes on to state that after the conveyance, A marries L. How does A's marriage to L affect the state of the title?

A's marriage to L constitutes the divesting condition, so at a minimum B's vested remainder is divested. B loses her right to possession before it ever became possessory. But has A also lost his right to possession? Should the divesting condition be construed not only to divest the remainder, but also to cut short the preceding finite estate?

Ultimately that is a question of the grantor's intent. There is an inherent ambiguity in the phrasing of the conveyance. Does the word "then" in the clause "*then* to C and her heirs" describe the moment the divesting condition occurs or the moment the preceding finite estate ends? If the grantor intended the word "*then*" to refer to the moment the divesting condition occurred, then the divesting condition would also cut short the preceding finite estate. If that is the intended effect, that intent needs to be reflected in the state of the title. The phrase "subject to an executory limitation" should be added to the name of the preceding finite estate. With respect to the example above, if the grantor intended that if A married L that event should not only divest B's vested remainder but also cut short A's life estate, the proper state of the title would be: A holds a life estate subject to an executory limitation, B holds a vested remainder subject to divestment, and C holds a shifting executory limitation in fee simple.

Whether the divesting condition should be construed as only divesting the vested remainder or whether it should be construed as also cutting short the preceding finite estate is beyond the scope of this introductory coverage. It would require a subtle analysis of the grantor's intent based on the nature of the condition and the express words used that would require more time than it is worth in the introductory coverage. *This material will assume that the divesting condition only divests the vested remainder and does not affect the underlying finite estate.* In answering the problems in this book, assume that the divesting condition *never* cuts short the preceding finite estate. If your professor decides to cover this issue, listen carefully to him or her for guidance as to when the language of the conveyance should be construed as not only divesting the remainder but also cutting short the finite estate.

IV. RECAP

The most common executory interest is the shifting executory interest which follows a fee simple subject to an executory limitation. But it is also possible to have a springing executory interest (the "future interest only" conveyance or the "gap" scenario) which follows a fee simple subject to an executory limitation; and where a vested remainder has an express condition precedent in the clause subsequent to the clause creating the remainder, the vested remainder is subject to divestment and the future interest is a shifting executory interest in fee simple.

When there is a vested remainder in fee simple, followed by an express qualifying condition and the future interest is in a third party, the key is *when* the qualifying condition may occur. If the qualifying condition *may occur prior* to the vested remainder becoming possessory, the vested remainder is subject to divestment and the future interest in the third party is a shifting executory interest in fee simple. If the qualifying condition *can occur only after* the vested remainder has become possessory, the remainder is a vested remainder in fee simple subject to an executory limitation, and the future interest is a shifting executory interest in fee simple.

CHAPTER 7 PROBLEM SET

1. O →   To A for life, then to B and her heirs, but if A gets married, then to C and her heirs.

2. O →   To A for and the heirs of her body, then to B and her heirs, but if B stops farming the land, then O has the right to re-enter and re-claim the property.

3. O →   To A, then to B and her heirs, but if B sells alcohol on the land, then to C and her heirs.

4. O →   To A and her heirs if she graduates from law school.

5. O →   To A for 5 years, then to B and his heirs as long as she uses the property for grazing purposes, then to C and her heirs.

6. O →   To A, then to B his heirs, but if B gets a body piercing, then to C and her heirs.

7. O →   To A for life, then to B and her heirs as long as she remains single.

8. O →   To A and her heirs as long as she remains married, then B and her heirs.

9. O →   To A for life, then to B and her heirs, but if A starts to cut down the redwoods on the land, the C has the right to re-enter and reclaim the property.

10. O →   To A and her heirs, but if she fails to maintain the gardens on the property then to B and her heirs.

11. Spock →   To Scottie for life, then to Kirk and his heirs if he distributes Scottie's ashes in space.

12. Walter →   To Dude and his heirs if he recovers his rug.

13. George →To Mary for life, then to Zuzu and her heirs as long as she grows flowers on the property.

14. Spock →   To Sulu for life, then to Uhura and her heirs, but if she marries, then to McCoy and his heirs.

15. Michael →   To Scottie for life, then to Shaq and his heirs if he becomes a police officer.

16. Pierre →   To Lance for life, then to Floyd and his heirs as long as he permits people to bicycle across the property.

17. Akeem → To Shaq for life, then to Kobe and his heirs, but if Shaq is ever traded, then to Nash and his heirs.

18. Goose → To Jack for life, then to Jill and her heirs as long as the land is farmed.

19. Goose → To Jack for life, then to Jill and her heirs, but if Jill stops farming the land, then Goose can re-enter and reclaim the land.

20. Goose → To Jack for life, then to Jill and her heirs as long as the land is farmed, then to Bo and her heirs.

21. Goose → To Jack for life, then to Jill and her heirs, but if Jill stops farming the land, then to Bo and her heirs.

22. Walt → To Hewey for life, then to Dewey and his heirs, then to Louie and his heirs.

23. Mother → To Jill for life, then to Bo and her heirs, but if Bo grazes sheep on the land, then to Alice and his heirs.

    (a) Assume Jill, Bo and Alice are alive.

    (b) Assume Jill dies and Bo and Alice are alive.

24. Andy → To Woody for life, then to Buzz and his heirs if he graduates from the astronaut training program.

25. Buzz → To Woody and his heirs if marries Jessie.

REVIEW PROBLEM SET 2

State the title to the conveyances as written unless told otherwise.

1. O → To A and her heirs.

2. O → To A and her heirs, but if she stops farming the land, O has the right to re-enter and reclaim the property.

3. O → To A and her heirs as long as she farms the land.

4. O → To A and her heirs as long as she farms the land, then to B and her heirs.

5. O → To A and her heirs if she graduates from medical school.

6. O → To A for life.

7. O → To A for life. (Assume A transfers her interest to B).

8. O → To A and the heirs of his body.

9. O → To A for life, then to B if she becomes CEO.

10. O → To A for life, then to B and her heirs as long as she farms the land.

11. O → To A for life, then to B and her heirs if she graduates from medical school.

12. O → To A for life, then if B graduates from medical school, to B and her heirs.

13. O → To A for life, then to A's first child and his or her heirs. (Assume A has no children.)

14. O → To A for life, then to the next President of the United States and his or her heirs.

15. O → To A for life, then to the then President of the United States and his or her heirs.

16. O → To A for life, then if A graduates from medical school, to B and her heirs.

17. O → To A for life, then to B and her heirs if she graduates from medical school, but if she does not graduate from medical school, to C and her heirs.

18. O → To A for life, then to B and her heirs if she graduates from medical school, otherwise to C and her heirs.

19. O →   To A for life, then to B and her heirs if she graduates from medical school, but if she does not graduate from medical school, to C and her heirs.

    (a) Assume A transfers her interest to O.

20. O →   To A for life, then to B and her heirs if she attends A's funeral.

21. O →   To A for life, then to B and her heirs as long as she does not sell alcohol on the land, but if she does, then to C and her heirs.

22. O →   To A for life, then to B and her heirs as long as A does not sell alcohol on the land, but if A does, then to C and her heirs.

23. O →   To A for life, then to B and her heirs, but if B marries X, then to C and her heirs.

24. O →   To A for life, then to B and her heirs, but if B marries X, then to C and her heirs.

    (a) Assume A dies; restate the title:

25. Mother → To Jack for life, then to Bo and her heirs as long as the land is used to graze sheep.

26. Mother → To Jack for life, then to Bo and her heirs, but if Bo stops grazing sheep on the land, then Mother can re-enter and reclaim the land.

27. Hedley → To Mongo for life, then to Bart and his heirs as long as the land is farmed, then to Waco and her heirs.

28. Ben → To Little Joe for life, then to Hoss and his heirs, but if Hoss stops farming the land, then to Adam and his heirs.

29. Ben → To Little Joe for life, then to Hoss and his heirs, but if Little Joe stops farming the land, then to Adam and his heirs.

30. Elizabeth → To Charles for life, then to William and his heirs, but if William marries Kate, then to Harry and his heirs.

     (a) Assume Charles, William, Kate, and Harry are alive.

     (b) Assume Charles dies, and William, Kate, and Harry are alive.

31. Veronica → To Archie for life, then to Jughead and his heirs if Jughead graduates from high school.

     Assume Archie and Jughead are both alive and Jughead has not graduated from high school yet.

32. Hanna → To Elmer for life, then to Bugs and his heirs, but if Elmer goes hunting without a license, then to Yosemite and his heirs.

33. White → To Doc for life, then to Sleepy and his heirs if Doc graduates from medical school, but if Doc fails to graduate from medical school, then to Dopey and his heirs.

34. Hook → To Wendy for life, then to Peter and his heirs as long as he never leaves Neverland.

35. Thurston → To Ginger for life, then to MaryAnne and her heirs, but if Gilligan returns, then to Gilligan and his heirs.

Chapter 8

DISTINGUISHING CONDITION PRECEDENT FROM CONDITION SUBSEQUENT FROM DIVESTING CONDITION

I. OVERVIEW

Presented individually, the basic scheme of possessory estates and future interests is not that difficult. But when faced with a batch of problems which mix the different estates in different combinations, many students fall into the Bermuda Triangle of possessory estates and future interests: they have difficulty distinguishing a condition precedent, from a condition subsequent, from a divesting condition; and thus confuse contingent remainders, vested remainders subject to divestment, and fee simple defeasibles. This chapter's material will review these estates, starting with the basic and moving to the more complicated.

II. REVISITING THE CONDITION SUBSEQUENT

The first condition the material presented, and in many respects the easiest to understand and recognize, was the condition subsequent. A condition subsequent is a condition which affects a grantee's *right to retain possession* of the property *after* the grantee has taken possession. The condition subsequent is the defining characteristic of the fee simple defeasibles: the fee simple determinable, the fee simple subject to a condition subsequent, and the fee simple subject to an executory limitation. The only difference between (1) the fee simple determinable and fee simple subject to a condition subsequent on the one hand, and (2) the fee simple subject to an executory limitation on the other hand, is who holds the future interest following the estate: the grantor (the first two estates) or a third party (in which case the estate is a fee simple subject to an executory limitation). The only difference between the fee simple determinable and the fee simple subject to a condition subsequent is whether the condition subsequent automatically terminates the estate (in which case it is a fee simple determinable) or whether the condition subsequent gives the grantor the option – the right to re-enter and terminate the estate (in which case it is a fee simple subject to a condition subsequent). In all of the fee simple defeasibles, the express condition is a condition subsequent.

The differences and similarities between and among the three condition subsequent estates are evident in the following conveyances:

EXAMPLE 1

O →   To A and her heirs as long as she does not sell alcohol on the land.

O →   To A and her heirs, but if she sells alcohol on the land, O has the right to re-claim the land.

O →   To A and her heirs as long as she does not sell alcohol on the land, then to B and her heirs.

O →   To A and her heirs, but if she sells alcohol on the land, then to B and her heirs.

The first conveyance is a classic example of a fee simple determinable. The second conveyance is a classic example of a fee simple subject to a condition subsequent. The third and fourth conveyances are classic examples of a fee simple subject to an executory limitation. In all four conveyances, the condition concerning the sale of alcohol is a condition subsequent in that it affects the grantee's (A's) *right to retain possession* of the property *after* the grantee has taken possession. The words of limitation which typically[132] introduce a condition subsequent are "as long as/so long as ... ." But be careful. The words *"but if/however/provided that ..."* can introduce either a condition subsequent *or a condition precedent*. Where these latter words are used to introduce a condition qualifying a remainder, a careful analysis of the temporal nature of the express condition is necessary. In all four of the conveyances above, reading comma to comma, the condition subsequent is either in the same clause creating the estate or in the subsequent clause.

---

[132] Be particularly careful to note that these observations are *generally* true but cannot be taken as hard and fast absolute rules.

III. REVISITING THE CONDITION PRECEDENT

A. REVISITING CONTINGENT REMAINDERS

The second type of condition analyzed, and one which is also fairly easy to understand and recognize, is the condition precedent. A condition precedent is a condition which affects a grantee's right to *take* possession of the property *before* the grantee has taken possession of the property. The condition precedent is the defining characteristic of the contingent remainder.

EXAMPLE 2

O → To A for life, then to B and his heirs if he graduates from law school.

O → To A for life, then if B graduates from law school, to B and his heirs.

Both of these conveyances are classic examples of contingent remainders. In both, the condition concerning B's graduating from law school is a condition precedent in that it affects the grantee's (B's) right to *take* possession of the property *before* B has taken possession of the property. It is a condition which must be satisfied *before* the grantee can take possession of the property. With respect to contingent remainders, the qualifying word "*if*" is the classic drafting word of limitation which typically[133] introduces the condition precedent. Reading comma to comma, the condition precedent introducing a contingent remainder is either in the same clause creating the estate or in the immediately preceding clause.

B. REVISITING THE DIVESTING CONDITION

The divesting condition is where the water suddenly turns murky. The reason is that the divesting condition looks a lot like *both* of the other types of express conditions. For example:

---

[133] Be particularly careful to note that these observations are *generally* true but cannot be taken as hard and fast absolute rules.

EXAMPLE 3

O → To A for life, then to B and his heirs, but if A fails to graduate from law school, then to C and her heirs.

This conveyance is a classic example of a vested remainder subject to divestment. The divesting condition is a condition precedent: B's right to take possession is dependent upon whether A graduates from law school, an event which must occur (or not occur, as the case may be) during the A's life estate. If A fails to graduate from law school, B's vested right to take possession of the property will be divested. The divesting condition is a condition precedent because it affects the grantee's right to take possession of the property *before* the grantee has taken possession of the property.

That statement, however, appears to be the same definition used to define the condition precedent for purposes of a contingent remainder. What is the difference? The difference is in the wording and structure of the conveyance. In the contingent remainder, the condition precedent is in the *same* clause creating the remainder or the *preceding* clause and is typically[134] introduced by the word "*if.*" In contrast, in the vested remainder subject to divestment, the condition precedent is in the clause *immediately following* the clause creating the remainder and is typically introduced by the words "*but if.*" For example:

EXAMPLE 4

O → To A for life, then to B and his heirs if A graduates from law school.

O → To A for life, then if A graduates from law school, to B and his heirs.

O → To A for life, then to B and her heirs, but if A fails to graduate from law school, then to C and her heirs.

---

[134] Be particularly careful to note that these observations are *generally* true but cannot be taken as hard and fast absolute rules.

In all three of the above conveyances, the condition precedent to B taking possession of the property is that A must graduate from law school. The key is in which clause the condition is expressed. In the first two conveyances – the contingent remainder conveyances – the condition precedent is either in the same clause creating the remainder or the preceding clause and it is introduced by the word "*if.*" In the third conveyance – the conveyance creating the vested remainder subject to divestment – the condition precedent is in clause subsequent to the clause creating the remainder and the condition precedent is introduced by the words "*but if.*"

Notice the potential confusion that can arise if you automatically assume too much about the use of the words "*but if ...*" to introduce the express condition. The phrase "*but if ...*" are the words of limitation which typically introduce the *condition subsequent* in the fee simple subject to a condition subsequent and the fee simple subject to an executory limitation. But the phrase "*but if ...*" are also the words of limitation typically used to introduce a *condition precedent* for purposes of the vested remainder subject to divestment. That is one of the reasons why the divesting condition is sometimes confused with the condition subsequent. Return to the first set of conveyances:

EXAMPLE 5

O →   To A and her heirs as long as she does not sell alcohol on the land.

O →   To A and her heirs, but if she sells alcohol on the land, O has the right to re-enter and re-claim the land.

O →   To A and her heirs as long as she does not sell alcohol on the land, then to B and his heirs.

O →   To A and her heirs, but if she sells alcohol on the land, then to B and her heirs.

It is unlikely that anyone would mistake these conveyances for a vested remainder subject to divestment because there is no vested remainder in any of the conveyances. While that is true, it is easy to throw a life estate at the front to show the difficulty distinguishing (1) the vested remainder subject to a condition subsequent and vested remainder subject to an executory limitation from (2) the vested remainder subject to divestment.

EXAMPLE 6

O →   To A for life, then to B and her heirs, but if B sells alcohol on the land, then O has the right to re-enter and re-claim the property.

O →   To A for life, then to B and her heirs, but if B sells alcohol on the land, then to C and his heirs.

O →   To A for life, then to B and her heirs, but if A sells alcohol on the land, then to C and his heirs.

In all three of the conveyances, the words of limitation introducing the condition are the phrase "*but if ... .*" Obviously no hard and fast rule about the characterization of an estate can be derived simply from the use of that phrase. In the first conveyance, the vested remainder subject to a condition subsequent is somewhat easy to identify because of the express clause giving the grantor, O, the right to re-enter and re-claim the property following the occurrence of the condition subsequent. But distinguishing the vested remainder subject to an executory limitation from the vested remainder subject to divestment is much more difficult and much more subtle.

C. ANALYTICAL KEYS

The key to distinguishing the vested remainder subject to an executory limitation from the vested remainder subject to divestment is *when* the qualifying condition may occur: if the condition may occur *before* the remainder becomes possessory, the estate is *a vested remainder subject to divestment; if* the condition may occur only *after* the remainder becomes possessory, the estate is *a vested remainder subject to an executory limitation.* Looking at the second and third conveyances, there is only one difference in the express wording of the conveyances. In the second conveyance, the condition must occur, if at all, while B has possession of the property. Because the condition can only occur, if at all, *after* B's remainder becomes possessory, the condition is a condition subsequent – and thus the estate is a vested remainder subject to an executory limitation. In contrast, in the third conveyance, the condition must occur, if at all, while A has possession of the property. Because the condition can only occur, if at all, *before* B's remainder becomes possessory, the condition is a condition precedent and hence the estate is a vested remainder subject to divestment.

What if the condition is one which could occur *either before or after* the remainder becomes possessory? For example:

EXAMPLE 7

O →   To A for life, then to B and her heirs, but if C
graduates from law school, then to C and her heirs.

First of all, in stating the title you should be able to narrow the choices concerning which estate B has. A has a life estate, so B's interest must be a remainder. Is it a vested remainder or a contingent remainder? Is the condition: (1) in the same clause creating the remainder or the preceding clause, or (2) in the immediately following clause? The latter, so it is not a contingent remainder but rather a vested remainder. Because there is additional qualifying language, it cannot be a vested remainder in fee simple absolute; and because the future interest is in a third party, the vested remainder cannot be in fee simple determinable or a fee simple subject to a condition subsequent. *Where the conveyance creates a vested remainder and there is a qualifying condition in the clause subsequent to the clause creating the remainder, and the future interest is in a third party, the remainder is either a vested remainder subject to an executory limitation or a vested remainder subject to divestment.*

The key is whether the condition is one which *could* occur prior to the remainder becoming possessory. Is it conceivable that C could graduate from law school while A is still alive? Certainly. Therefore, while A is still alive, B holds a vested remainder subject to divestment. But what if the facts told you that thereafter A died, but B and C were still alive. Restate the title. Following these factual developments, the conveyance in essence would read as follows:

EXAMPLE 8

O →   To B and her heirs, but if C graduates from law
         school, then to C and her heirs.

B's interest has become possessory, so it is no longer a remainder, but it is
still subject to the possibility that C may graduate from law school. But now
that condition can only occur, if at all, *after* the estate which it qualifies has
become possessory. B would hold a fee simple subject to an executory
limitation, and C would hold a shifting executory interest in fee simple. To
distinguish the vested remainder in fee simple subject to an executory
limitation from a vested remainder in fee simple subject to divestment, the
key is the express condition and whether it is a condition subsequent or a
condition precedent.

As if that were not enough murkiness, the "*but if* ..." words can also
appear in the express words of a contingent remainder, thus completing the
Bermuda triangle.

EXAMPLE 9

O →   To A for life, then to B and his heirs, *but if* A sells
       alcohol on the land, then to C and his heirs.

O →   To A for life, then to B and his heirs, *but if* B sells
       alcohol on the land, then to C and his heirs.

O →   To A for life, then if B agrees in writing not to sell
       alcohol on the land, to B and his heirs, *but if* B refuses
       to agree not to sell alcohol on the land, then to C and
       his heirs.

The key to analyzing these complex conveyances is to read comma to
comma, clause to clause. In the first two conveyances, the second clause
creates a vested remainder in B in fee simple of some sort, and because the
future interest is in a third party, the only question is whether the vested
remainder is a vested remainder subject to an executory limitation or a

vested remainder subject to divestment. As discussed in the prior paragraph, the focus is on whether the condition can occur before or after the remainder becomes possessory: if before, the vested remainder is subject to divestment; if after, the vested remainder is subject to a limitation. In the second conveyance, the express condition can only occur after B's right to possession becomes possessory, so the remainder is a vested remainder subject to an executory limitation.

In the third conveyance ("To A for life, then if B agrees in writing not to sell alcohol on the land, to B and his heirs, but if B refuses to agree not to sell alcohol on the land, then to C and his heirs"), reading comma to comma, in the second clause we find an express condition precedent introduced by the word *if*. Thus the remainder is a contingent remainder; but what about the "*but if* ..." clause? It simply states the opposite of the condition precedent and thus serves to introduce an alternative contingent remainder. You can always spot when the "*but if* ..." phrase is being used to introduce an alternative contingent remainder because (1) it will immediately follow a clause creating a contingent remainder, and (2) you can strike the whole "*but if...*" clause and simply insert the word "*otherwise, ...*"

As you should have discerned by now, do not put too much weight on the introductory words "*but if ... .*" That clause can introduce *either* a condition precedent or a condition subsequent. You must analyze the temporal nature of the qualifying condition very carefully. In and of themselves, the words "*but if*" do not help you very much in analyzing which estate a conveyance creates.

Having now navigated through the potentially choppy and murky waters of the Bermuda Triangle of possessory estate and future interests, you are in store for some smooth sailing (at least until the Rule against Perpetuities!).

IV. RECAP

The distinguishing characteristic of the *fee simple defeasibles* (the fee simple determinable, the fee simple subject to a condition subsequent, and the fee simple subject to an executory limitation) is that there is a *condition subsequent* which affects the grantee's right to retain possession of the property *after* the grantee has taken possession of the property.

The distinguishing characteristic of the *contingent remainder* is that there is a *condition precedent* which affects the grantee's right to take possession of the property *before* the grantee has taken possession of the property. The condition precedent should be in the same clause as the clause creating the remainder or in a preceding clause.

The distinguishing characteristic of the *vested remainder subject to divestment* is that the grantee's right to take possession is subject to a *condition precedent* which is expressed in a *clause immediately following* the clause creating the remainder.

In distinguishing the vested remainder subject to an executory limitation and the vested remainder subject to divestment, the key is whether the qualifying condition expressed in the clause immediately following the clause creating the remainder is one which *may occur before* the remainder becomes possessory (in which case the remainder is a vested remainder subject to divestment) or if the condition is *one which can occur, if at all, only after* the remainder becomes possessory (in which case the remainder is a vested remainder subject to an executory limitation).

CHAPTER 8 PROBLEM SET

State the title to the following conveyances *as written* first, and then if the problem goes on to give you additional facts, in light of those developments.

1. O → To A and the heirs of her body, then to A's first child and his or her heirs. (A has no children.)

2. O → To A for life, then to B and her heirs if B graduates from medical school.

3. O → To A for life, then to B and her heirs if she graduates from medical school, but if she does not, then to C and her heirs.

4. O → To A for life, then to B and her heirs, but if A fails to graduate from medical school, then to C and her heirs.

5. O → To A and the heirs of her body, then to B and her heirs as long as no alcohol is consumed on the land, then to C and her heirs.

6. O → To A and her heirs if she graduates from law school.

7. O → To A for life, then to B and her heirs if B attends A's funeral.

8. O → To A for life, then to B and her heirs as long as no alcohol is sold on the land.

9. O → To A for life, then to B and her heirs, but if B sells alcohol on the land, then to C and her heirs.

10. O → To A for life, then to B and her heirs, but if A sells alcohol on the land, then to C and her heirs.

11. Bill → To Harry for life, then to Jack and his heirs if Jack buries Harry's ashes under home plate in Wrigley Field.

12. Neil → To Felix for life, then to Oscar and his heirs if Oscar is married.

    (a) Assume Felix and Oscar are alive, and Oscar is not married.

    (b) Assume Felix dies, and Oscar is not married.

13. Fezzik → To Westley and his heirs as long as the land is farmed, then to Buttercup and her heirs.

14. Max → To Joni and her heirs, but if the land is used for commercial purposes, then to Jimi and his heirs.

15. Obi   →   To Luke and his heirs if he graduates from Jedi School.

16. Oracle →   To Neo for life, then after Neo's funeral, to Trinity and her heirs.

17. Glinda → To Dorothy for life, then to Tinman and his heirs, but if Tinman stops growing poppies on the land, then to Scarecrow and his heirs.

18. Glinda → To Dorothy for life, then to Tinman and his heirs, but if Dorothy stops growing poppies on the field, then to Scarecrow and his heirs.

19. Peter → To my lovely wife Gerri for life, then to my daughter Carolyn and her heirs, but if she ever dates Matt again, then to my son Paul and his heirs.

20. George → To Dr. Brown for life, then to Marty and his heirs if he gets back from the future, otherwise to Biff and his heirs.

ONE LAST SET OF ESTATES:
LIFE ESTATE DEFEASIBLES

I. OVERVIEW

There is one last set of estates that you should be familiar with that does not fit neatly into the above scheme: the estates created when a life estate is cut short.[135]

The material has already analyzed "cutting short" an estate when it looked at the fee simple defeasibles: the fee simple determinable, fee simple subject to a condition subsequent, and fee simple subject to an executory limitation. In all three of those scenarios, the estate being cut short is a fee simple. Notice that analysis had to deal with only one contingency: if the fee simple was going to be cut short, who took the right to possession (i.e., who held the future interest). In contrast, because a life estate by definition *must* end, if a life estate may also be cut short, there are *two* contingencies that must be dealt with: (1) who is going to get the right to possession *if the life estate ends naturally*; and (2) who is going to get the right to possession *if the life estate is cut short - if it ends prematurely*?

This point can be better understood by diagramming the concept of cutting short a life estate. First, an example of a life estate being cut short:

EXAMPLE 1

O → To A for life, but if A marries B, then to C and her
      heirs.

---

[135] Theoretically, fee tails and term of years can also be cut short. But the fee tail has been abolished for all practical purposes, and the term of years is best left for landlord-tenant law. If a finite estate is to be cut short, the norm is for the estate to be a life estate. The life estate discussion, however, in theory applies equally to the fee tail and the term of years. Just as we had fee simple defeasibles, we have finite estate defeasibles.

In the "life estate being cut short" scenario there are two points in time when we have to account for the possibility that the right to possession may transfer hands from one party to another. First, if the condition cutting short the life estate occurs (indicated by the dashed cross line); and second, if the condition cutting short the life estate does not occur but the life estate ends naturally (indicated by the hard cross line):

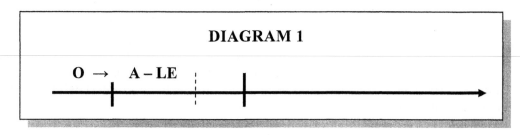

The analysis is not as bad as it looks. The key is to determine if the express words of limitation cutting short the life estate are *determinable* words of limitation or *condition subsequent* words of limitation.

II.   THE LIFE ESTATE CUT SHORT BY DETERMINABLE WORDS OF LIMITATION.

If determinable words of limitation are used to cut short the life estate, the courts assumed that the grantor intended for the *same party to hold the future interest whether the condition occurs or not*. For example:

EXAMPLE 2

O → To A for life as long as she remains unmarried.

State the title. A has a life estate which may be cut short if she gets married. Because her life estate would be cut short if she marries, there are two possible points where the future interest could become possessory: (1) if the life estates ends naturally (without A marrying), and (2) if the life estate ends prematurely because A marries. Where the 'determinable' words of limitation are used to introduce the condition which would cut short the life estate,[136] the courts construed that language as indicating that the same party

---

[136] The classic determinable words of limitation again are "*as long as* ... ." These words of limitation come from the fee simple determinable words of limitation: "*as long as/so*

held the future interest whether the condition occurs or not (i.e., the party holds the future interest for *both* possible scenarios – the life estate ending naturally or prematurely). Hence there is minimal change in the terminology for the state of the title. All that is added is the word "determinable" to the life estate to indicate that it could end prematurely, but no change is made in the wording for the future interest. So in the example above, "To A for life as long as she remains unmarried," A would hold a life estate determinable, and the grantor, O, would hold a reversion in fee simple absolute.

Similarly, if the express words of limitation "*as long as*" are used to cut short the life estate and there is an express reference to a *third party holding the future interest*, the courts construed the determinable language as indicating that the third party was to receive the future interest whether the condition occurred or not:

EXAMPLE 3

O → To A for life as long as she remains unmarried, then
to B and his heirs.

There is minimal change in the terminology for the state of the title. The only change is to add the word "determinable" to the life estate to reflect that it could be cut short. A holds a *life estate determinable*. B holds a *vested remainder in fee simple absolute*. The term "remainder" following a life estate determinable indicates that the third party holds the future interest whether the life estate is cut short or not.

As long as the future interest is held by the same party (whether the condition cutting short the life estate occurs or not), the basic reversion/remainder terminology applies except the word "determinable" is added to the life estate to reflect that it may be cut short.

---

long as/while/until/during ... ." Although the phrase "*as long as*" is the most commonly used of these possible words of limitation for cutting short a life estate, if any of such words are used, the assumption is that the same party holds the future interest whether the condition occurs or not.

III. THE LIFE ESTATE CUT SHORT BY CONDITION SUBSEQUENT WORDS OF LIMITATION.

If the express words of limitation introducing the condition which may cut short the life estate are the 'subject to condition subsequent' phrases ("but if ..." being the most common), the analysis is a bit more complicated. Where the 'condition subsequent' phrasing is used to cut short a life estate, the key becomes who holds the future interest.

If 'condition subsequent' words of limitation are used to cut short the life estate, *and the future interest is held by the grantor,*[137] there is again minimal change in the terminology for the state of the title. The grantor is deemed to hold the future interest whether the life estate ends naturally or prematurely (i.e., whether the condition occurs or not). The only change in the state of the title is to add the phrase 'subject to a condition subsequent' to the life estate to reflect that it may be cut short. There is no change to the future interest. The possessory estate is called a *life estate subject to a condition subsequent* (to indicate that it may be cut short), and the grantor holds a *reversion* in fee simple. For example:

EXAMPLE 4

O → To A for life, but if he marries, then the life estate ends.

O → To A for life, but if he marries, then to O and his heirs.

In both conveyances, A has a life estate subject to a condition subsequent, and the grantor, O, has a reversion in fee simple.

If, however, the *condition subsequent words of limitation* are used (typically "but if ...") *and the express future interest is held by a third party*, a completely different analysis is performed. The courts construed this combination as indicating that the third party was to take the future interest **only** if the life estate was cut short, and if it ended naturally, the grantor retained the future interest. For example, the 'condition subsequent' words of limitation are used in the following conveyance with an express future interest in a third party:

---

[137] Either expressly or by default

EXAMPLE 5

O → To A for life, but if he marries, then to B and his heirs.

State the title. Because the courts construed the condition subsequent qualifying language coupled with an express future interest in a third party as indicating that the third party took the future interest *only* if the life estate was cut short, the state of the title needs to account for both possible contingencies. The life estate is called a *life estate subject to an executory limitation* to indicate that it may be cut short in favor of a third party; the third party holds a *shifting executory interest* (typically in fee simple); and because the grantor will take possession of the property if the condition subsequent does *not* occur, the grantor will take possession *only* if the life estate ends naturally – the grantor holds a *reversion* in fee simple.[138] The state of the title is: A has a *life estate subject to an executory limitation*; B has a *shifting executory interest* in fee simple; and O has a *reversion* in fee simple absolute.

IV. RECAP

The keys to analyzing the life estate which may be cut short are: (1) whether *determinable* or *condition subsequent* words of limitation are used to cut short the life estate, and (2) whether the future interest is held by the same party whether or not the condition occurs.

If the express condition which might cut short the life estate is introduced by the determinable words of limitation (typically "as long as"), the same party is deemed to hold the future interest whether the condition occurs or not. If the future interest is expressly given to a third party, the life estate is a life estate determinable and the third party holds a remainder in fee simple. If there is no express taker for the future interest, or if it is expressly reserved by the original grantor, the life estate is a life estate determinable and the future interest is a reversion in the grantor.

---

[138] If the condition occurs, the life estate ends prematurely (immediately upon the condition occurring) and the right to possess the property passes to the express third party taker. If the condition does not occur, however, upon the natural end of the life estate the future interest falls to our default taker, the original grantor, O.

If the express condition is introduced by the condition subsequent words of limitation (typically "but if ...") and the future interest is held, either expressly or implicitly, by the grantor, the life estate is a life estate subject to a condition subsequent and the future interest is a reversion in the grantor. If, however, the condition subsequent words of limitation are used and the future interest is expressly given to a third party, then the common law deemed that the third party received the right to possession only if the condition occurred; and if it did not, the grantor received the right to possession upon the natural end of the life estate. The life tenant held a life estate subject to an executory limitation, the third party held a shifting executory interest in fee simple, and the grantor held a reversion in fee simple.

CHAPTER 9 PROBLEM SET

State the title to the following problems as written:

1. O → To A as long as A farms the land.

2. O → To A for life, but if A stops farming the land, then to O and her heirs.

3. O → To A for life as long as A farms the land.

4. O → To A for life, then to B for life, but if B stops farming the land, then to C and her heirs.

5. O → To A for life as long as A farms the land, then to B and her heirs.

6. O → To A for life, but if A stops farming the land, then to B and her heirs.

7. O → To A for life, then to B as long as B farms the land.

8. O → To A for life, then to B for life, but if B hunts on the land, then to C and her heirs.

9. O → To A for life, then to B for life, but if B sells alcohol on the land, then O has the right to re-enter and re-claim the property.

10. O → To A for life, then to B for life as long as she lives on the land.

11. O → To A for life, then to B for life, but if B uses pesticides on the land, then to C and her heirs.

12. O → To A for life, then to B as long as she remains married.

13. O → To A for life, then to B, but if B gets divorced, then to C and her heirs.

14. Dad → To Carolyn for life as long as she does not date Matt, then to Paul and his heirs.

15. Morocco → To Rick as long as he operates a café on the property, then to Victor and his heirs.

16. The King → To Priscilla for life, but if she fails to maintain Graceland, then to Lisa Marie and her heirs.

17. Jonathon → To Clark and his heirs as long as he farms the land, then to Martha and her heirs.

18. Jonathon →   To Clark as long as he farms the land, then to Martha and her heirs.

19. Homer → To Bart for life as long as he does not skateboard.

20. Jonathon →   To Clark, but if he marries Lois instead of Lana, Jonathon has the right to terminate Clark's right to possession.

Chapter 10

MISCELLANEOUS COMMON LAW RULES REGULATING CONVEYANCES

I. OVERVIEW

Although we take for granted the right to inherit property, in early common law there was no such right. The king owned all the land, and grants were only in life estate. In time, however, grantees negotiated for the right to inherit (the right[139] for the property to pass to their heirs); but if the property did pass by inheritance, the heirs had to pay what amounted to an inheritance tax.[140] The inheritance tax applied, however, *only* if a party *inherited* the property. With time, grantors and their lawyers began to manipulate the scheme of possessory estates and future interests in an attempt to avoid the inheritance tax. There were two conveyances in particular which grantors used in an attempt to avoid the dreaded inheritance tax. The common law courts, however, responded to these efforts by creating special rules that countered, and defeated, these attempts at avoiding the inheritance tax.

II. RULES FURTHERING THE COMMON LAW INHERITANCE TAX

A. THE RULE IN SHELLEY'S CASE

Assume O owns a piece of property that he want to give to A, with the expectation that upon A's death the property will go to A's heirs. O could simply convey it to A in fee simple absolute:

EXAMPLE 1

O → To A and her heirs.

---

[139] But not the obligation – hence the heirs take *no* property interest while the grantee *is* alive, only the expectation of the right to take the property upon the grantee's death if he or she does not transfer it *inter vivos* or devise it to another.

[140] Technically it is called a "relief."

But then upon A's death, the property would be inherited by A's heirs who would have to pay the dreaded inheritance tax. What if, however, O conveyed only a life estate to A, and a remainder to the heirs of A?

EXAMPLE 2

O → To A for life, then to the heirs of A and their heirs.

The heirs of A would *not* take through inheritance but rather through the express conveyance. Thus the grantor arguably could avoid the feudal inheritance tax.

The common law courts saw through this conveyance, however, and adopted what came to be known as the Rule in Shelley's Case to close this loophole. Under the Rule in Shelley's Case, if a *life estate* is given to a grantee, and in the *same instrument* a *remainder* is given to the *life tenant's heirs*, give the remainder to the life tenant (and check for merger).[141] The best way to apply the Rule in Shelley's Case is always to state the title of each conveyance as written. Returning to the example above, the state of the title as drafted is:

EXAMPLE 2 – THE STATE OF THE TITLE

O → To A for life, then to the heirs of A and their heirs.

A has a life estate;
A's heirs have a contingent remainder[142] in fee simple; and
O has a reversion in fee simple.

The life tenant is A, and the conveyance attempts to give a remainder to the heirs of A, the life tenant. The conveyance is a classic example of a conveyance falling within the scope of the Rule in Shelley's Case. Applying

---

[141] Shelley's Case, 1 Co. Rep. 93b (1581); PROPERTY RESTATEMENT, *supra* note 10, at §§ 312-13. The parenthetical to check for merger is *not* a part of the Rule in Shelley's Case, but it is such a frequent by-product of the Rule that you should be sure to couple these two rules together for analytical purposes.

[142] The remainder is contingent because to qualify as an heir, the party must survive the decedent. As long as a person is alive, he or she has only heirs apparent, no heirs, because it cannot be determined who survived the party until he or she dies.

the Rule, give the remainder to the life tenant, A. Because A is born, ascertainable, and there is no express condition precedent, the remainder in A is vested. Because the vested remainder is in fee simple, O's default reversion is destroyed. Pursuant to the Rule in Shelley's Case, A now holds the life estate and a vested remainder in fee simple. Because A now holds two successive vested interests, the merger doctrine applies, and the life estate merges with the vested remainder in fee simple to give A a fee simple absolute. (Remember, merger is *not* part of the Rule in Shelley's case, but it often applies in conjunction with the Rule in Shelley's case.)

The scope of the Rule in Shelley's Case is fairly narrow, however. First, the Rule applies only if the remainder is given to the heirs of the life tenant *in the same instrument* as the instrument creating the life estate. For example, in the above scenario, if the grantor gave A a life estate, and then – in another instrument/conveyance – conveyed the reversion to the apparent heirs of A, they would *not* be taking in the same instrument. The Rule in Shelley's Case would not apply.[143]

A second, and arguably more important, limitation on the scope of the Rule in Shelley's Case is that it applies only if a *remainder* is given to a life tenant's heirs. The Rule does not apply if an executory interest is given to a life tenant's heirs:

EXAMPLE 3

O → To A for life, then one day after A's death, to A's heirs and their heirs.

This conveyance presents the classic "gap" scenario. A has a life estate. O holds a reversion in fee simple subject to an executory limitation. And A's heirs hold a springing executory interest in fee simple. Because there is no remainder, the Rule in Shelley's Case does not apply.

The third limitation on the Rule in Shelley's Case is that the life tenant's *heirs* must hold the remainder. If other relatives or individuals hold the remainder, the Rule does not apply. Accordingly, if the conveyance provides:

---

[143] Under this scenario, the apparent heirs of A would not be taking by inheritance, but rather by separate conveyance from the grantor.

EXAMPLE 4

O → To A for life, then to A's children and their heirs.

The Rule in Shelley's Case would not apply. The remainder is held by A's children, not A's heirs. The Rule's application is limited to remainders held by a life tenant's *heirs*.

Lastly, if the Rule in Shelley's Case does apply, the merger doctrine *often* applies, but not always. For example:

EXAMPLE 5

O → To A for life, then to B for life, then to A's heirs and their heirs.

State the title:

EXAMPLE 5 – TITLE AS WRITTEN

A: has a life estate,
B: has a vested remainder in life estate,
A's heirs: have a contingent remainder in fee simple, and
O: has a reversion in fee simple.

Because the heirs of one of the life tenants, A, are taking a remainder, give the remainder to the life tenant. Restate the title:

EXAMPLE 5 – TITLE UNDER RULE IN SHELLEY'S CASE

A: has a life estate,
B: has a vested remainder in life estate,
A: has a vested remainder in fee simple.[144]

---

[144] Because the remainder is vested in A, there no longer is a default reversion in the grantor, O.

Now check to see if the merger doctrine applies. A holds a life estate and a vested remainder in fee simple, but B's intervening vested remainder in life estate prevents merger. Merger is not an official part of the Rule in Shelley's Case, and although it often applies following the effect of the Rule in Shelley's Case, it does not always.

In conclusion, according to the Rule in Shelley's Case, if there is a *remainder* in the heirs of a *life tenant*, give the remainder to the life tenant (and check to see if merger applies).

B. THE DOCTRINE OF WORTHIER TITLE

Assume O, the owner of the property, wants to convey a life estate to A. The logical conveyance would be "O → To A for life." If A is younger than O (which is the norm for these types of conveyances), the likely result is that O will die before A. When O dies, O's reversion will pass to O's heirs, but at early common law the reversionary interest would pass to O's heirs subject to the common law inheritance tax. If that were the likely scenario, O could try to avoid the inheritance tax by expressly conveying the future interest directly to O's heirs:

EXAMPLE 6

O → To A for life, then to the heirs of O and their heirs.

State the title to the conveyance as written:

EXAMPLE 6 – STATE OF THE TITLE

A: has a life estate,
O's heirs: have a contingent remainder in fee simple,[145] and
O: has a reversion in fee simple.

---

[145] As written, the remainder is contingent because a party has no heirs while he or she is alive, only heirs apparent. The assumption is that O is still alive.

Thus O's heirs would not take the property through inheritance but rather through the words of purchase in the conveyance, thereby avoiding the feudal "inheritance tax" if this type of conveyance were permitted.

The common law courts, however, were fairly protective of the feudal inheritance tax. They closed this loophole by developing the Doctrine of Worthier Title.[146] The *Doctrine of Worthier Title* is conceptually similar to the Rule in Shelley's Case, only the Doctrine of Worthier Title applies to any future interest (remainder or executory interest) given to the grantor's heirs. *Under the Doctrine of Worthier Title, if an instrument conveys a possessory interest to a third party and the same instrument purports to give a remainder or executory interest to the grantor's heirs, give that future interest to the grantor* (and check for merger).[147] In the example above, if we give the future interest to O, then it no longer is a contingent remainder but rather becomes a reversion in O in fee simple. If O were to die before A, and O did not dispose of the reversion by transfer or devise, the heirs of O would end up receiving the future interest – but through their right of inheritance, subjecting them to the feudal inheritance tax.

Although there is some ambiguity as to the full scope of the Doctrine of Worthier Title, the better view appears to be that the doctrine applies not only to remainders but also to executory interests. Assume the conveyance were as follows:

EXAMPLE 7

O →   To A for life, then one day after A's death, to O's
      heirs and their heirs.

This conveyance presents the classic "gap" scenario. As written, A has a life estate; O holds a reversion in fee simple subject to an executory limitation; and O's heirs hold a springing executory interest in fee simple.

---

[146] Technically, the Doctrine of Worthier Title is a rule of construction, not a rule of law. The significance of that difference, however, is beyond the scope of this coverage.

[147] The parenthetical "and check for merger" is *not* a part of the Doctrine of Worthier Title, but merger is such a frequent by-product of the Doctrine that you should be sure analytically to couple these two rules together.

Because the Doctrine of Worthier Title applies not only to remainders but also to executory interests, it applies. O would then hold the reversion in fee simple subject to an executory limitation *and* the springing executory interest in fee simple absolute. The springing executory interest and the reversion would merge. Thus, the title would be A holds a life estate, and O holds a reversion in fee simple absolute. If O dies without transferring or devising the interest, the practical effect will be the same as if the Doctrine were not applied. O's heirs would receive the future interest, but subject to the inheritance tax because they take by inheritance under the Doctrine, not as grantees under the words of purchase in the conveyance.

The Doctrine of Worthier Title applies only if the party who holds the future interest is the original grantor's *heirs* (in that sense it is similar to the Rule in Shelley's Case.) The Doctrine does not apply if the conveyance expressly gives the future interest to the grantor's "children," "nieces and nephews," or any other relatives or friends. Like the Rule in Shelley's Case, the Doctrine also applies only where the avoidance is attempted in a single conveyance. If O conveys a life estate to A, and thereafter in a different *inter vivos* instrument O transfers the reversion to O's heirs apparent, the Doctrine would not apply.

In conclusion, according to the Doctrine of Worthier Title, where a conveyance purports to convey *a future interest (remainder or executory interest)* to the *heirs of the grantor*, give the future interest to the grantor (and check to see if merger applies).

III. THE RULE IN PUREFOY'S CASE

An inherent characteristic of executory interests is that unlike contingent remainders, they are not subject to the common law destructibility of contingent remainders doctrine. A by-product of this difference was that at common law, a grantee of a future interest would prefer to have the interest construed as an executory interest rather than a contingent remainder – thereby avoiding the risk of the interest being destroyed if it did not vest in time.

For example:

EXAMPLE 8

O → To A for life, then to B and his heirs if B
graduates from law school.

State the title. A has a life estate. What about B? Does B have a contingent remainder in fee simple, in which case O would have a reversion in fee simple; or does B have a springing executory interest in fee simple, in which case O would have a reversion in fee simple subject to an executory limitation? In the event A's life estate ends before B graduates from law school, this distinction would make all the difference in the world to B. Contingent remainders were subject to the destructibility of contingent remainders, but executory interests were not.[148] The *Rule in Purefoy's Case* established that if an interest could be characterized as either a contingent remainder or an executory interest (because the condition was such that it could occur during the prior finite estate or it could occur after), the interest is deemed a contingent remainder subject to the destructibility of contingent remainders. The rationale behind the Rule in Purefoy's Case is that favoring the contingent remainder construction would mean that there was a chance that the interest would be destroyed, thereby cleaning up the state of the title and promoting the productive use of the land and its marketability.

Today, many jurisdictions have abolished the common law destructibility of contingent remainder. In those jurisdictions, the contingent remainder is functionally indistinguishable from an executory interest for our purposes and the issue underlying the Rule in Purefoy's Case is moot.

In conclusion, according to the Rule in Purefoy's Case, where an *interest can be construed as either a contingent remainder or an executory interest, construe it as a contingent remainder.*

---

[148] If the interest were construed as a contingent remainder and A's life estate ended before B graduated from law school, B's contingent remainder would be destroyed and B would be out of luck. On the other hand, if the interest were construed as an executory interest, it would not matter whether A's life estate was still possessory or not. All B had to do was graduate from law school for the interest to become possessory.

IV. MODERN TREND

A. THE RULE IN SHELLEY'S CASE

The Rule in Shelley's Case has been abrogated, either statutorily or by judicial decision, in all but a handful of jurisdictions.[149] Its abrogation, however, typically is only prospectively (does not apply to documents executed before its abrogation), so the exact scope of the modern trend varies from jurisdiction to jurisdiction. In part for that reason, this material will take the common law approach to the Rule in Shelley's Case and will assume that it still applies.

B. THE DOCTRINE OF WORTHIER TITLE

Similarly, under the modern trend the Doctrine of Worthier Title has been highly criticized and repudiated by a number of jurisdictions – either statutorily or by judicial decision.[150] Again, the detailed scope of these developments, and the consequences which follow, are beyond the scope of this introductory coverage.

C. THE RULE IN PUREFOY'S CASE

The modern trend looks with disfavor upon the Rule in Purefoy's Case as well. The purpose of the Rule was to favor construing future interests as contingent remainder over executory interests to subject the interest to the destructibility of contingent remainders. Inasmuch as the modern trend favors abolishing the doctrine of the destructibility of contingent remainders, there is not much purpose for the Rule in Purefoy's Case; hence its limited relevance under the modern trend. But yet again, this introductory coverage will take the common law approach to the doctrine.

You may have surmised by now that the easiest way for a professor to take the modern trend approach to the material in this chapter is to skip this chapter entirely so that students will analyze the material without the benefit/burden of the material in this chapter.

---

[149] 3 RICHARD R. POWELL, POWELL ON REAL PROPERTY § 31.07[3] (Matthew Bender 2006).

[150] 3 THOMPSON ON REAL PROPERTY § 22.05 Second Thomas Edition (David A. Thomas, ed., 2006).

RECAP CHART

CATEGORY	POSSESSORY ESTATE	FUTURE INTEREST GRANTOR	THIRD PARTY
FEE SIMPLE	FEE SIMPLE ABSOLUTE	NONE	NONE
FEE SIMPLE DEFEASIBLES	FEE SIMPLE DETERMINABLE	POSS REV	--
	FEE SIMPLE SUBJECT TO CONDITION SUBSEQUENT	RT of ENTRY/ POWER TERM	--
	FEE SIMPLE SUBJ TO EXEC LIM	--	EXEC INT
FINITE ESTATES	LIFE ESTATE	REVERSION	REMAINDER
	FEE TAIL	REVERSION	REMAINDER
	TERM OF YEARS	REVERSION	REMAINDER

1. Contingent rem: Must vest prior to, or at, the exp (incl merger/forfeiture/renun) of prec poss estate or it is destroyed
2. Alt cont rem: 1st cont rem must vest prior to merger/forfeiture/renun or both are destroyed
3. Vested rem: remainder must be 1) born, 2) ascertainable, and 3) no express condition precedent (same/prec clause)
4. Vested rem subj to divestmt: vested rem w/ express condition prec in clause subsequent to clause creating remainder
5. Executory interests: shifting (3rd party to 3rd party) vs. springing (grantor to 3rd party: "gap"/future interest only)
6. Rule in Shelley's Case: If rem in heirs of life tenant, give rem to life tenant (check for merger)
7. Doc Worthier Title: If future int (rem or exec int) in heirs of grantor, give future int to grantor (check for merger)
8. Rule in Purefoy's Case: If conveyance can be construed as cont rem or exec int, construe as cont rem

CHAPTER 10 PROBLEM SET

First, state the title to the following problems as written, and then apply any rules regulating the conveyance which may apply, and if necessary, restate the title:

1. O → To A for life, then to A's heirs and their heirs.

2. O → To A for life, then to A's heirs who attend A's funeral and their heirs.

3. O → To A for life, then to A's children and their heirs. (A has no children yet.)

4. O → To A for life, then to O's heirs and their heirs.

5. O → To A for life, then to O's heirs who attend O's funeral and their heirs.

6. O → To A for life, then to O's children and their heirs. (O has no children yet.)

7. O → To A for life, then to B and his heirs when he gets married.

8. O → To A for life, then to B and his heirs if B is appointed executor of A's probate estate.

9. O → To A for life, then to A's heirs and their heirs who spread A's ashes across the pacific ocean.

10. O → To A for life, then to B and her heirs if she graduates from law school. (Thereafter, O transfers O's interest, if any, to C, A's only heir apparent.)

11. Rocky → To Adrian for life, then to Adrian's heirs and their heirs.

12. Donald → To Rosie for life, then to Donald's heirs and their heirs.

13. Vito → To Michael for life, then to Vito's heirs and their heirs one day after Michael's funeral.

14. Bubba → To Forrest for life, then to Lt. Dan for life, then to the heirs of Forrest's and their heirs.

15. Tony → To Carmela for life, then to Carmela's heirs and their heirs one day after Carmela's funeral.

Chapter 11

CLASS GIFTS

I. OVERVIEW

Up to this point in the material, almost every conveyance has involved the transfers of a possessory estate and/or future interest to an individual. But there is no requirement that this be the case. A conveyance can be to more than one person or even to a class of individuals.[151]

EXAMPLE 1

O → To A and B and their heirs.

State the title: A and B hold the property *concurrently* in fee simple absolute. There is a separate body of law for *concurrent estates* which addresses the issues inherent in how multiple parties or classes of individuals may simultaneously hold the right to possess the same piece of property. The law of concurrent estates, however, is beyond the scope of this material. This material is concerned only with *class gifts* to the limited extent they overlap with possessory estates and future interests. This overlap occurs primarily *where there is a conveyance of a remainder to a class; and the issue is whether the remainder is vested or contingent.*

II. ANALYSIS

Returning to the three part test for vested remainders:
  (1) the grantee must be *born*,
  (2) the grantee must be *ascertainable*, and
  (3) there must be *no express condition precedent.*[152]
As applied to a single individual, the test is rather straight forward. But when applied to a class, the test is a bit more complicated. This fact becomes apparent when the test is applied to the following conveyance:

---

[151] In large part, a "class" is distinguished from a mere collection of individuals by the common characteristic(s) of the members of the class.

[152] If the remainder fails any part of the test, it is contingent.

EXAMPLE 2

O → To A for life, then to B's children and their heirs.

State the title: A has a life estate, and B's children have a remainder in fee simple absolute. Is the remainder vested or contingent?

Like other conveyances where the recipient is *described generically* as opposed to named specifically, the key is what additional information is given. Assume B has no children yet - would the remainder be vested or contingent? Contingent, because the children are not born or ascertainable. Because the remainder is contingent, O would also hold a reversion in fee simple.

Now assume, however, that B gives birth to a child, X. Apply the test. Well, as to X, he or she is born and ascertainable and there is no express condition precedent - so the remainder is vested. But because B is still alive, B could have more children. *Where there is a remainder to a class, once at least one class member vests, the remainder becomes vested. But if the class is such that more individuals can enter the class, the remainder is classified as vested subject to open.* The "*subject to open*" phrase indicates that more individuals may enter the class. As each new member of the class vests, the shares of each vested member is re-calculated so that each vested member holds an equal share.[153] The "vested remainder subject to open" remains open until the class *closes*.

---

[153] Thus, another way to describe the remainder is to say that it is vested *subject to partial divestment*. As each new member of the class vests, the share of the members who were already vested is reduced, or partially divested. MOYNIHAN, *supra* note 9, at 125-26.

III. CLOSING THE CLASS

A. NATURALLY/PHYSIOLOGICALLY

There are basically two ways for a class to close. First, *a class closes when it becomes impossible for new members to enter the class*. The most common example of this is physiological closure. Returning to the example above ("To A for life, then to B's children and their heirs"), once B dies, it is impossible for B to have any more children (the common law presumed that individuals were fertile up until death, so that physiological closure did not occur until death of the individual with the capacity to create new class members).[154] Assuming that A is still alive, once B dies, however many children B had is the size of the class and the class will close. There is no special terminology to indicate that the class is closed except we drop the phrase "subject to open." The remainder simply is vested.

B. RULE OF CONVENIENCE

The second method for a class to close is by the *rule of convenience*. The rule of convenience is exactly that, a convenient rule the common law courts created to avoid a number of potentially difficult legal and administrative questions. Some background will help understand the rule. Returning to the example above ("To A for life, then to B's children and their heirs"), assume A is still alive, B is still alive, and B has two children: X and Y. State the title: A has a life estate, and B's children, X and Y, have a vested remainder, subject to open, in fee simple.[155] Now assume A dies, but B is still alive. Because B is still alive, more individuals can enter the class. But what happens to the property?

Notice the quandary the courts were in. When A dies, somebody has to have the right to enter and possess the property. X and Y hold the vested

---

[154] Posthumously born children, however, can also qualify as a child of the deceased husband if the child is born within 280 days of the husband's death. The common law (and still general rule) is that for inheritance purposes, a child who qualifies as a posthumously born child is considered as alive from the moment of conception. Notice the common law approach did not take reproductive technology into consideration. Issues raised by such technology are beyond the scope of this introductory coverage of the material.

[155] Notice there is no need for a reversion in O because the remainder in fee simple is vested in at least one individual. Even if B has no more children and X and Y die before A, because X and Y's interests are vested their shares would pass to their heirs or devises.

remainder, but what can they do with the property if there is a chance that they may have to share it if B has more children in the future? Can they transfer their interest if they do not know what their share will be until B dies? If they put the property to profitable use, must they share the profits with future children of B? Rather than dealing with these and other potentially difficult legal and administrative questions, the common law courts created the *rule of convenience*, which provides that *once one member of the class is entitled to take actual possession of the property, the class closes*. Even though physiologically B is capable of having more children, the moment X and Y become entitled to actual possession of the property, the class closes. If one year later,[156] B has a child, Z. Z has no right to claim an interest in the property. X and Y would hold the property jointly in fee simple absolute.

One last wrinkle on the class conveyances. A class conveyance can be coupled with an express condition precedent:

EXAMPLE 3

O → To A for life, then to B's children who survive A and their heirs.

Assume A is alive, B is alive, and B has two children, X and Y.

State the title. A has a life estate. "B's children" means that the remainder is held by a class, and because there is at least one member of the class you might be tempted to state that B's children (X and Y) hold a vested remainder, subject to open, in fee simple. But notice there is an express condition precedent that only those children of B who survive A are entitled to the property. The express condition precedent means the remainder is contingent. If there is a remainder held by a class and there are members of the class born and ascertainable, that does not necessarily mean that the class interest is vested subject to open. You still must check to see if there is an express condition precedent which applies to the class. If there is, the remainder will remain contingent until the express condition is also satisfied.

---

[156] At common law, a child was treated as alive from the moment of conception if it were to the child's advantage. Thus, a child in utero was treated as alive for purposes of construing conveyances.

C. RECAP

Class conveyances present some challenges when determining whether a remainder is vested or contingent. The basic three part test for vested remainders applies, but the wrinkle is that more people may enter the class. Assuming there is no express condition precedent, if no member of the class is born and ascertainable, the class will remain contingent until the first member is born and ascertainable. Once one member of the class is born and ascertainable, the class becomes vested subject to open to reflect the fact that more members may join the class before it closes. The class closes either naturally (the source for new members no longer exists) or under the rule of convenience (the moment one class member is entitled to claim possession of his or her share).

CATEGORY	POSSESSORY ESTATE	FUTURE INTEREST GRANTOR	THIRD PARTY
FEE SIMPLE	FEE SIMPLE ABSOLUTE	NONE	NONE
FEE SIMPLE DEFEASIBLES	FEE SIMPLE DETERMINABLE	POSS REV	--
	FEE SIMPLE SUBJECT TO CONDITION SUBSEQUENT	RT of ENTRY/ POWER TERM	--
	FEE SIMPLE SUBJECT TO AN EXECUTORY LIMITATION	--	EXEC INT
FINITE ESTATES	LIFE ESTATE	REVERSION	REMAINDER
	FEE TAIL	REVERSION	REMAINDER
	TERM OF YEARS	REVERSION	REMAINDER

1. Contingent rem: Must vest prior to, or at, the exp (incl merger/forfeiture/renun) of prec poss estate or it is destroyed
2. Alt cont rem: 1st cont rem must vest prior to merger/forfeiture/renun or both are destroyed
3. Vested rem: remainder must be 1) born, 2) ascertainable, and 3) no express condition precedent (same/prec clause)
4. Vested rem subj to divestmt: vested rem w/ express condition prec in clause subsequent to clause creating remainder
5. Executory interests: shifting (3rd party to 3rd party) vs. springing (grantor to 3rd party: "gap"/future interest only)
6. Rule in Shelley's Case: If rem in heirs of life tenant, give rem to life tenant (check for merger)
7. Doc Worthier Title: If future int (rem or exec int) in heirs of grantor, give future int to grantor (check for merger)
8. Rule in Purefoy's Case: If conveyance can be construed as cont rem or exec int, construe as cont rem
9. Class gifts – vested subject to open: closure either naturally or rule of convenience

CHAPTER 11 PROBLEM SET

State the title for each of the following problems. (Assume that the factual information set forth in sub parts a) through e) are *cumulative*):

1. O → To A for life, then to A's children and their heirs.
   (a) Assume A has no children.

   (b) Assume A has a child, X.

   (c) Assume A has another child, Y.

   (d) Assume A dies.

2. O → To A for life, then to B's children and their heirs.
   (a) Assume B has no children.

   (b) Assume B has a child, X.

   (c) Assume A dies, but B and X are still alive.

   (d) Assume B has a second child, Y.

3. Mike → To Carol for life, then to Carol's children and their heirs.
    (a) Assume Carol is alive and has no children.

    (b) Assume Carol has a child Marsha.

    (c) Assume Marsha dies, survived by a child Gerri.

    (d) Assume Carol has a second child Cindy.

    (e) Assume Carol dies.

4. Tony → To Carmela for life, then to Carmela's children and their heirs who survive Carmela.
    Assume Carmela has two children: Meadow and AJ.

5. Oscar → To Kuala for life, then to Mother Robinson's children and their heirs.

    (a) Assume Kuala is alive and Mother Robinson has no children.

    (b) Assume Mother Robinson has a child Fritz.

(c) Assume Mother Robinson has another child Bertie.

(d) Assume Kuala dies, and thereafter Mother Robinson has another child Ernst.

REVIEW PROBLEM SET 3

State the title to the following problems:

1. Alvy → To Annie and her heirs.

2. Dorothy → To Zeke forever, then to Hickory forever, then to Hunk and his heirs.

3. BB → To Janice and the female heirs of her body, then to Jimi in fee simple absolute, then to BB and his heirs.

4. Arthur → To Lance and his heirs as long as the castle on the property is maintained, then to Guinevere and her heirs.

5. George → To Dick and his heirs, but if Dick goes hunting on the property, then to Rudy and his heirs.

6. Sean → To Chuckie for life, then to Will and his heirs if he graduates from MIT.

   (a) Assume Chuckie and Will are alive, and Will has not graduated.

   (b) Assume Chuckie dies and Will has not graduated from MIT yet.

7. Sean → To Chuckie for life, then to Will and his heirs if Will graduates from MIT, otherwise to Skylar and her heirs.

    (a) Assume Chuckie and Will are alive, and Will has not graduated.

    (b-1) Assume Chuckie dies and Will still has not graduated yet.

    (b-2) Instead, assume Chuckie renounces his interest, and Will has not graduated yet.

    (b-3) Instead, assume Will graduates from MIT, then Will dies, and then Chuckie dies.

8. Mick → To Bert for life, then to Keith and his heirs if Keith snorts Bert's ashes.

9. Todd → To Barbie for life, but if Ken graduates from medical school, then to Ken and his heirs.

10. Robert → To Ernst for life, then to Julio and his heirs as long as Julio maintains the vineyards on the land.

11. Robert → To Ernst for life, then to Julio and his heirs, but if Julio stops growing grapes the land, then Robert may re-enter and reclaim the land.

12. Vizzini →   To Westley for life, then to Buttercup and her heirs, but if Westley stops farming the land, then to Fezzik and his heirs.

13. Rhett →   To Scarlett for life, then to Scarlett's grandchildren and their heirs.

       (a) Assume Scarlett has no grandchildren.

       (b) Assume Scarlett has a grandchild Wilson.

       (c) Assume Scarlett has another grandchild Billie Ray.

       (d) Assume Wilson dies and then Billie Ray dies.

14. Marcus →   To Maximus for life, then to Commodus and his heirs, but if Commodus stops farming the land, then Marcus can re-enter and reclaim the land.

15. Marcus →   To Maximus for life, then to Commodus and his heirs as long as the land is farmed, then to Lucilla and her heirs.

16. Marcus →   To Maximus for life, then to Commodus and his heirs, but if Commodus stops farming the land, then to Lucilla and her heirs.

17. Marcus →   To Maximus for life, then to Commodus and his heirs, but if Maximus stops farming the land, then to Lucilla and her heirs.

18. Richard →   To Emily for life, then to Lorelai and her heirs, but if Lorelai marries Luke, then to Rory and her heirs.

    (a)   Assume Emily, Lorelai, Luke and Rory are alive.

    (b)   Assume Emily dies and Lorelai, Luke and Rory are alive.

19. Arthur →   To Mortimer for life, then to Marian and her heirs if she marries Robin.

20. William →   To Caesar for life, then to Antony and his heirs if Antony attends Caesar's funeral.

21. Alfred →   To Randy for life, then to Newman and his heirs if Newman completes his music requirement and graduates from college.

    (a) State the title as written.

    (b) Assume Randy has died and Newman has not graduated yet.

22. Brad →   To Angelina for life, then to the Angelina's heirs and their heirs.

23. Brad → To Angelina for life, then to Sheryl for life, then to Angelina's heirs and their heirs.

24. Brad → To Angelina for life, then to Angelina's heirs and their heirs if Angelina survives Jennifer.

25. Brad → To Angelina for life, then to Angelina's heirs and their heirs who attend Angelina's funeral.

26. Brad → To Angelina for life, then to Brad's heirs and their heirs.

27. Brad → To Angelina for life, then to Jennifer for life, then to Brad's heirs and their heirs.

28. Brad → To Angelina for life, then to Brad's heirs and their heirs if Angelina survives Jennifer.

29. Thor → To Jacque for life, then to Jacque's heirs and their heirs if they spread Jacque's ashes across the Pacific Ocean.

30. Homer → To Bart for life as long as he does not attend law school.

31. Homer → To Bart for life, but if Bart attends law school, then to Marge and her heirs.

Chapter 12

THE RULE AGAINST PERPETUITIES

I. OVERVIEW

As you probably have noticed, the scheme of possessory estates and future interests gives a property owner the ability to control, to some extent, the property even after conveying the property to another. This control is manifested in the conditions the grantor puts on the possessory estate and/or future interests in the express terms of the conveyance. For example:

EXAMPLE 1

O → To A and her heirs as long as the land is farmed, then to B and her heirs.

A has a fee simple subject to an executory limitation, and B has a shifting executory interest in fee simple.

O continues to exert some control over the property after the conveyance because of the condition O put into the conveyance. A and her heirs have an incentive to continue to farm the land because if they stop farming the land their right to the land will be forfeited; B and her heirs will have the right to claim possession of the property. The problem is that the grantor's wishes as to how the land should be used may not be the highest or best use of the land over time. Even assuming, *arguendo*, that agricultural use was the highest and best use of the land when the conveyance was created, conditions change over time.   Agricultural use may no longer be the highest or best use. If one thinks of the suburban sprawl that occurred following World War II, when farmland was converted to residential use, just think what would have happened if some (or even most) of the land in question had been restricted to agricultural use only. Even without the benefit of formalized law and economics training, the common law courts realized that there had to be a limit on such control by a grantor or the property might not be put to its best use, and society in general would suffer.

To some degree a grantor's ability to control the property by including express conditions in the conveyance is limited by the transferability of the different possessory estates and future interests created. If one party comes along and purchases the possessory estate and the future interest(s), through the merger doctrine the property would be freed from any such conditions. The new owner would be free to use the property as he or she wished. But because contingent remainders, executory interests, and vested remainders subject to open were not transferable, the common law courts had to come up with a different rule to limit their effect. The common law courts were not adverse to some control by a grantor, but the courts reasoned that after a certain amount of time, current owners of the possessory estate should be free to use the property as they wished and/or in the best interests of society. Accordingly, the courts concluded that contingent remainders, executory interests, and vested remainders subject to open had to "vest," if at all, within the "lives in being"[157] plus twenty one years or the future interest in question was void from its attempted creation.

Although the rationale underlying the Rule against Perpetuities is rather comprehensible (to limit the ability of the grantor to exercise control over the property after conveying it), the mechanics of the rule are somewhat more difficult.

II. THE CREATE, KILL, & COUNT APPROACH

The Rule against Perpetuities provides that: "No interest is good unless it must vest, if at all, not later than twenty-one years after some life in being at the creation of the interest." Admittedly this express statement of the Rule is so technical it is difficult to comprehend, but once the Rule is broken down, the Rule is much more comprehensible.

First, although the Rule states that "[n]o *interest* is good ... ," the Rule against Perpetuities does not apply to the vast majority of possessory estates and future interests. The Rule against Perpetuities

---

[157] The "lives in being" constitute *anybody* who was alive at the time of the conveyance – the duration of that person's life. The material will elaborate on the components of the Rule against Perpetuities shortly.

applies only to:

    (1) contingent remainders,

    (2) executory interests, and

    (3) vested remainders subject to open.[158]

Second, the Rule requires these interests "vest, if at all ... ." Although as a technical matter to say that these interests must vest means different things for each interest,[159] as a general rule the interest vests if it has the right to become *possessory*. (This general rule does not apply in all cases because in a small number of cases a contingent remainder may vest without becoming possessory. We will discuss these exceptions to the general rule in greater detail later.)[160]

And third, the future interest must become possessory, if at all, "not later than twenty-one years after some life in being at the creation of the interest." It is this third component of the Rule which creates most of the problems in understanding the Rule. This phrase constitutes the time limit the common law courts settled upon for how long the future interests may tie up the property – for "some life in being at the creation of the interest" plus "twenty-one years." Conceptually, this time limit is analogous to a statute of limitations. The future interest subject to the Rule must vest, if at all, by that point in time (the lives in being at the time the interest was created plus twenty one years – the 'perpetuities period') or the interest is void.

There are, however, two important points to note about the Rule against Perpetuities time limit which distinguish it from the typical statute of limitations.[161] First, unlike the typical statute of limitations where the time period is a set number of years, the time limit under the

---

[158] The Rule against Perpetuities applies to other interests, such as powers of appointments and options to purchase, but those interests are beyond the scope of our introductory materials.

[159] To say that these three different interests must "vest" means different things with respect to the different future interests:

    1) contingent remainders must vest or fail,

    2) executory interests must become possessory, and

    3) vested remainders subject to open must close and completely vest.

[160] You will see that the "must become possessory" shortcut works for everything but conveyances with two successive contingent remainders.

[161] And it is these two points which combine to create most of the problems in understanding the Rule.

Rule against Perpetuities is a formula: the lives in being at the creation of the interest plus 21 years. But how long is that? How do the courts calculate that time limit? (Beginning to see the difficulty with the Rule against Perpetuities?)

The second point about the Rule against Perpetuities time limit which distinguishes it from the typical statute of limitations is how the time limit is applied. Under the typical statute of limitations, the courts wait to see if the claim has been brought within the statutory period in question. The statute of limitations comes into play to bar the claim only if the claim has not been brought by the end of the statutory period but is asserted thereafter. For example, if the statute of limitations for bringing a wrongful termination cause of action is 5 years, the statute of limitations does not kick into effect unless 5 years has passed, and then the plaintiff files his or her cause of action for wrongful termination. The statute of limitations would come into effect and bar the cause of action.

In contrast, under the Rule against Perpetuities, the perpetuities period comes into play and is applied to the future interest *the moment the future interest is created.* Under the traditional common law approach, there was no waiting. Testing the interest immediately upon creation required the courts to identify the relevant measuring life or lives to see if the interest would vest, if at all, within 21 years of the death of the measuring life or lives. Much has been written on (1) how to pick the right individual(s) who were alive at the time of the creation of the interest who should be used as "measuring lives;" and (2) how to test to see if the interest would vest, if at all, within 21 years of their death. This material will offer an alternative analytical approach.

The essence of the Rule against Perpetuities is that the future interest in question *must* vest, if at all, *within the lives in being at the creation of the interest plus 21 years*, or the interest is void from the moment of its attempted creation. Rather than thinking of all the different possible ways that the interest may vest within this time period, approach it from the opposite perspective: *If you can conceive of 1 possible scenario, no matter how implausible, where the interest could vest but only after the lives in being plus 21 years, the interest violates the Rule against Perpetuities.*[162] In attempting to create such a scenario, you should use the '*create, kill, and count*' strategy.

---

[162] Engineers call this type of analysis "proof by counterexample."

Under the '*create, kill, and count*' approach, the first step is to create someone in whom the interest can vest, but only after the perpetuities time period (in theory you can create as many people as you want). By creating this person *after* the conveyance, he or she cannot qualify as a life in being for purposes of the perpetuities time period. Second, kill everyone who was alive at the time of the conveyance (or at least everyone identified in the conveyance/problem). By killing everybody who was alive at the time the property interest was created, we take care of all the possible lives in being so we do not have to worry about identifying the *right* measuring life.[163] Killing everybody who was alive at the time the property interest was created takes care of the "lives in being" part of the rule, but the time period is "the lives in being *plus 21 years*." Then, count twenty-one years. If it is *conceivable (no matter how absurd the scenario sounds)* that one of the parties created can claim possession of the property under the future interest in question, *but only after* the lives in being plus 21 years time period has expired – then we have violated the Rule against Perpetuities and the interest is void from the moment of its attempted creation. *If we cannot create a scenario in which the property interest becomes possessory in a party we created but only after the lives in being plus 21 years, then the property interest does not violate the Rule against Perpetuities and the interest is valid.* Enough of the theoretical description of the approach – time to apply it.

A. CONTINGENT REMAINDERS

State the title to the following conveyance:

EXAMPLE 2

O →   To A for life, then to B and her heirs.

---

[163] If it helps, take a picture of all the people identified by name in the conveyance or in the additional facts to the conveyance. Then *create* as many people as you need in order to create a scenario in which one of the people you created will vest in the property but only after the lives in being plus 21 years. Then *kill* all the people who were in your picture (all the lives in being when the interest was created). Then *count* 21 years and see if you can create a scenario in which one of the people you created can claim possession of the property under the interest in question.

A has a life estate, and B has a vested remainder in fee simple absolute. Does the Rule against Perpetuities apply? No. Remember that you only have to worry about the Rule against Perpetuities if you see one of the three future interests subject to Rule: contingent remainders, executory interests, and/or vested remainders subject to open.

State the title to the following conveyance:

EXAMPLE 3

O → To A for life, then to A's first child to reach age 25 and his or her heirs.

Assume A has two children: B, age 23, and C, age 20.

A has a life estate. A's first child to reach age 25 has a contingent remainder in fee simple, and O has a reversion in fee simple. Is there a future interest which is subject to the Rule against Perpetuities? Yes, the contingent remainder. Does the contingent remainder violate the Rule?

Your gut instinct is probably that the contingent remainder cannot violate the Rule. The time period is lives in being plus 21 years, and B is only two years away from vesting. But not so fast. The Rule against Perpetuities is a harsh rule that is not concerned with probabilities. If there is *any* possible scenario in which the contingent remainder will vest, but not until *after* the running of the Rule's time period, the interest is void. B and C could be killed in a car accident tomorrow, so it is possible that it could be quite awhile before the interest vests. Having now shown you that you cannot jump to assumptions, work through the mechanics of the *"create, kill, and count"* approach.

First, *create* a new life in being (or as the case may be, lives in being). Who should that person be? *You should create someone who will be eligible to claim the interest. If the interest is to vest in someone other than a child, create as far back in the chain of eligible persons as possible.* For example, if the interest was "to A's first grandchild to reach age 21," and A were still alive and had two grandchildren, do not create another grandchild for A, create another child for her. Remember, the goal with the '*create, kill and count'* approach is to create a scenario which *will* violate the rule. If we fail in our quest, then and only then is the interest in the conveyance valid.

Back to the example above:

EXAMPLE 3

O → To A for life, then to A's first child to reach age 25 and his or her heirs.

Assume A has two children, B, age 23, and C, age 20.

State the title. A has a life estate. A's first child to reach age 25 has a contingent remainder in fee simple, and O has a reversion in fee simple.

The contingent remainder at issue is to A's first child to reach age 25. *Create!* Whom do we create? We want to create someone who is eligible to claim the property under the terms of the conveyance so create a new child for A: child X is born to A. We now have a life in being who was not alive at the time of the creation of the interest. What do we do next? *Kill!* Kill whom? All of the people who were alive at the time of the creation of the interest: A, B, C and everybody else in the world (if you want, but you really do not need to – usually all you need to do is kill all the people identified in the problem/conveyance).[164] Then what? That takes care of the lives in being, but we still have to take care of the rest of the time period. *Count!* Count 21 years. How old is child X at the end of the Rule's time period? 21 years old. Is it conceivable that X will live another four years, thereby becoming A's first child to reach age 25 and be entitled to claim the property? Yes. Have we created a scenario in which the interest vests/becomes possessory after the lives in being plus 21 years? Yes. Therefore, the future interest violates the Rule against Perpetuities and is void from its attempted creation. *(Notice that in applying the 'create, kill, and count' approach to the contingent remainder, you suspend the destructibility of contingent remainders rule.)*

---

[164] Again, an easy way to identify all the lives in being is to take a picture of all the people identified in the conveyance and the factual information concerning the time of the conveyance.

If the future interest violates the Rule against Perpetuities, strike the whole clause containing the future interest and restate the title. Here, the original conveyance stated, "To A for life, then to A's first child to reach age 25 and his or her heirs." Striking the whole clause which contains the contingent remainder, the conveyance would read, "To A for life." After applying the Rule against Perpetuities, the state of the title is A has a life estate, and O has a reversion in fee simple.

Applying the rule to a few more problems involving contingent remainders will help you get comfortable with the 'create, kill, and count' approach. State the title for the following conveyance:

EXAMPLE 4

O → To A for life, then to B and her heirs if B reaches age 25.

Assume B is age 23.

A has a life estate. B has a contingent remainder in fee simple, and O has a (default) reversion in fee simple. Because B's remainder is contingent, it is subject to the Rule against Perpetuities. Apply the 'create, kill, and count' approach. Can you create someone who will be eligible to claim the property? No. The condition is tied to B; B is the only person who is eligible to satisfy the condition. *If you cannot create someone who would be eligible to satisfy the condition, then you cannot create a scenario which violates the Rule and the interest must be valid. If the condition is expressly tied to a named person who is alive, as opposed to a generically-described person, the interest will not violate the Rule against Perpetuities.*[165]

---

[165] This is the first of several principles which results from the 'create, kill and count' analysis. While the hope is that these principles help, if you understand the 'create, kill and count' analysis and the mechanics of how to apply it, you do not need to memorize these principles. One of the beauties of the 'create, kill and count' approach is its simplicity. This would be undermined by requiring you to memorize a set of related principles. All you need to know is whether the interest violates the Rule against Perpetuities, not the related principles.

State the title for the following conveyance:

EXAMPLE 5

O → To A for life, then to A's oldest child who survives
A and his or her heirs.

Assume A has two children, B, age 14, and C, age 2.

The contingent remainder in A's oldest child who survives A is subject to
the Rule against Perpetuities. Apply the '*create, kill and count*' approach.
Create – can you create someone who will be eligible to claim the property
under the interest in question? Yes, create a new child X for A. *Kill* – kill
off all the lives in being who were alive at the time the interest was created:
A, B, C and the rest of the world (if you wish). *Count* – count 21 years
and see if the interest might vest *but only after* the Rule's time period.
Will it? No. X will be vested in the property and be eligible to claim
possession, but that occurred the moment A died. There is no way to delay
that vesting until after the lives in being plus 21 years. Because we cannot
create a scenario where the vesting occurs *but only after* the lives in being
plus 21 years, the interest is valid. *If the remainder must vest, if at all,
upon the death of the life tenant (life in being), it is impossible to create a
scenario which it vests/becomes possessory after the lives in being plus 21
years and thus the interest must be valid.*

One more point to note about the Rule against Perpetuities.
Because the test is whether the interest must vest, if at all, within the lives
in being at the time the interest is created, *it is critical that you determine
when an instrument conveying a property interest becomes operative. Inter
vivos* conveyances are typically by deed, and a deed is effective when it is
properly delivered. Testamentary conveyances are by will, and a will is not
effective until the testator dies. The following conveyances will highlight
the importance of this distinction:

EXAMPLE 6

O → To A for life, then to O's first grandchild and his or her heirs.

Assume O has three children, but no grandchildren.

State the title. A has a life estate. O's first grandchild has a contingent remainder in fee simple (contingent because he or she is not born and ascertainable), and O has a reversion in fee simple.

If this conveyance is by *inter vivos* deed, is the contingent remainder valid? Again, the first step is to create a new person, and our goal is to violate the Rule so create as far back in the process as possible. Create a new child for O, child X. Next, kill all the people who were alive at the time of the *inter vivos* conveyance: O, A, and O's 3 children. Then count 21 years. Is it possible that X will have a child thereafter? Yes. Because that child will be O's first grandchild, the remainder will vest upon that child's birth – but we have created a scenario where that birth was delayed until *after* the lives in being plus 21 years. Accordingly, the contingent remainder violates the Rule against Perpetuities and is invalid.

What if the conveyance were by will? Although a will must be properly executed while the testator (the party creating the will) is alive, it has no effect during the testator's life. A will is not effective until the testator dies. At that point, the will becomes effective – the property interests are created. Here, assuming this conveyance was in a will, when O died, A would hold a life estate, with a contingent remainder in O's first grandchild. Is the contingent remainder valid? Put it to the test. First, create someone. Can we create a new child, X, for O? No. O is dead, so we can not create a new child for O. Create a grandchild – but then the interest would vest immediately. The vesting *cannot* be delayed until *after* the lives in being plus 21 years. Because it is impossible to create a scenario where the interest vests, but only after the lives in being plus 21 years, the contingent remainder is valid. (Concluding the interest is valid does not mean it will necessarily vest. O's three children may die without having a child, but the interest will still be valid because it will vest, *if at all*, within the lives in being plus 21 years). Notice how the contingent remainder here is valid if created by will, but invalid if created by deed inter vivos.

The last wrinkle concerning the Rule against Perpetuities and contingent remainders is the stacked contingent remainders conveyance. State the title for the following conveyance:

EXAMPLE 7

O →   To A for life, then to A's oldest child who survives A for life, then to A's oldest grandchild then living and his or her heirs.

Assume A is alive and has two children: B, age 45, and C, age 50.

A has a life estate. A's oldest child who survives A has a contingent remainder in life estate, A's oldest grandchild who survives A's oldest child who survived A has a contingent remainder in fee simple, and O has a reversion in fee simple.

The first point to note is that there are two interests subject to the Rule against Perpetuities: the two contingent remainders. With respect to the first contingent remainder, although we can create a new child for A, the interest must vest, if at all, when we kill all the lives in being. There is no scenario in which we can delay the vesting of the interest until *after* the lives in being plus 21 year. Because we *cannot* create a scenario under the 'create, kill, and count' approach which violates the Rule against Perpetuities, the interest is valid.

With respect to the second contingent remainder, however, we can create a new child for A, child X. Then kill all the lives in being, count 21 years, and envision a scenario in which X has a child Y, who would be A's grandchild. When X dies thereafter, the second contingent remainder would vest in Y, but *only after* the running of the lives in being plus 21 years time period. Here, because we *can* create a scenario under the 'create, kill, and count' approach where the interest vests, but only after the perpetuities time period, the interest is void. *When contingent remainders are stacked one after the other, the second remainder typically will be void unless it vests upon the first contingent remainder becoming possessory.* This principle is borne out in the next two examples.

State the title for the following examples:

EXAMPLE 8

O → To A for life, then to A's widow for life, then to A's children and their heirs.

O → To A for life, then to A's widow for life, then to A's children then living and their heirs.

Assume A is alive and has two children: B, age 45, and C, age 50.

In both conveyances, A has a life estate; A's widow has a contingent remainder in life estate; A's children have a contingent remainder in fee simple; and O has a reversion in fee simple. Again we have two contingent remainders which are subject to the Rule against Perpetuities. With respect to the first contingent remainder in A's widow, although we can create a new person X and have A marry that person so at the time of A's death that person (X) is A's widow, the contingent remainder in A's widow must vest, if at all, upon the expiration of the lives in being (A's life in particular). There is no way to delay its vesting another 21 years (until after the lives in being plus 21 years period). The first contingent remainder is valid.

The second contingent remainder in A's children is trickier. First, note the subtle but critical difference in the wording of the second contingent remainder between the two conveyances. The first conveyance is simply to "A's children ... ," the second is to "A's children *then* living ... ." The first contingent remainder will vest upon A's death (it will not become possessory until after the death of A's widow, but it will vest upon A's death). The vesting cannot be delayed until after the lives in being plus 21 years period, so the contingent remainder in A's children in the first conveyance is valid.

The second contingent remainder in the second conveyance, however, is more difficult. It will not vest until after the death of A's widow because of the express condition that it is only the children of A *then living*. Put it to the test. Create a new person X. Have X and A marry and have a new child Y. Then kill off all the lives in being at the time of the conveyance. The contingent remainder in A's widow immediately vests, but not the contingent remainder in A's children "then living" – living when A's widow dies. Count 21 years. Y's interest is still a contingent remainder. Is it possible that *only after* the additional 21 years X, the widow, will die and Y's interest will become vested and possessory? Yes. The contingent remainder in "A's children then living" is void.[166] *(The first conveyance also shows why it is only a general rule that vested means becomes possessory. Where contingent remainders are stacked, the second contingent remainder can vest even though it is not possessory. The interest only has to vest within the Rule against Perpetuities, it does not necessarily have to become possessory. So while it is easier to think of vested as meaning possessory, you can not do that where there are stacked contingent remainders.)*

---

[166] In Wills & Trusts circles this type of conveyance is commonly known as the "unborn widow" problem.

THE RULE AGAINST PERPETUITIES
CONTINGENT REMAINDER PROBLEM SET

For each of the following problems, (1) state the title of the conveyance as drafted, (2) analyze if any of the interests are subject to the Rule against Perpetuities, and (3) if the interest violates the Rule, restate the title.

1. O → To A for life, then to A's first child, B, if she marries and her heirs.

2. O → To A for life, then to A's first child to marry and his or her heirs. (Assume A has two children, B and C.)

3. O → To A for life, then to A's first grandchild and his or her heirs. (Assume A has two children, B and C.)

4. O → To A for 30 years, then to B and her heirs if B graduates from high school.

5. O → To A for life, then to A's first granddaughter to graduates from law school. (Assume A has two children, and a grandchild who is a first year law student.)

6. O → To A for life, then to whomever is then President of the United States and his or her heirs.

7. O → To A for life, then to A's first child to get a tattoo and his or her heirs. (Assume A has two children, B and C, and neither has a tattoo.)

8. O → To A for 10 years, then to A's first child who agrees to farm the land and his or her heirs. (Assume A has two children, B and C, and neither is interested in staying on the farm and working it.)

9. O → To A and the heirs of her body, then to B and his heirs if B is alive at the time A's interest ends.

10. O → To A for life, then to A's first child to reach age 15. (Assume A has two children, B age 10 and C age 13.)

11. O → To A for 10 years, then to B and her heirs if a woman is elected President of the United States.

12. Mary → To Jane for life, then to Michael and his heirs if he reaches 25. (Assume Michael is 5.)

13. Mary → To Jane for life, then to Jane's first child and his or her heirs. (Assume Jane has no children yet.)

14. Michael → To Lionel for life, then to his first child to reach age 30 and his or her heirs. (Assume Lionel has 2 children: Nicole, age 25, and Myles, age 28.)

15. Pamela → To David for life, then to David's first child to reach age 21 and his or her heirs. (Assume David has 2 children: Taylor, age 19, and Hayley, age 18.)

16. Danny → To Mel for life, then to Mel's first grandchild and his or her heirs. (Assume Mel has 7 children and no grandchildren.)

17. Kirby devises Greenacres to Tony for life, then to Kirby's first grandchild and his or her heirs. (Assume O has no grandchildren yet, but 2 children.)

18. Al → To Brock for life, then to John's first child to graduate from law school and his or her heirs. (Assume John has four children, and one of them is a law student.)

19. Rosemary → To George for life, then to George's widow for life, then to George's children who survive his widow and their heirs. (Assume George has no children yet.)

20. Rosemary → To George for life, then to George's widow for life, then to George's children and their heirs.
    (Assume George has no children yet.)

B.   EXECUTORY INTERESTS.

As complicated as the Rule against Perpetuities is as applied to contingent remainders, it is that easy as applied to executory interests. Remember, there are basically four different scenarios in which there may be an executory interest: (1) following a fee simple defeasible where the future interest is in a third party; (2) following a "future interest only" conveyance; (3) following a vested remainder subject to divestment; and (4) following the "gap" scenario.

> 1. *The Rule against Perpetuities applied to the executory interest following a fee simple defeasible where the future interest is in a third party.*

The most common executory interest is the shifting executory interest following a fee simple subject to an executory limitation:

EXAMPLE 9

O →   To A and his heirs as long as alcohol is not sold on the land, then to B and his heirs.

O →   To A and his heirs, but if alcohol is sold on the land then to B and his heirs.

State the title.   In both conveyances, A has a fee simple subject to an executory limitation, and B has a shifting executory interest in fee simple.

Now that we know executory interests are subject to the Rule against Perpetuities, put B's shifting executory interest to the 'create, kill and count' test.   First, create – who? – X, an heir for A, and Y, an heir for B. Then kill A and B (and assume that the respective interests are inherited by their respective heirs, X and Y).   Now count 21 years.   Is it possible that X, who now holds the fee simple subject to an executory limitation, could sell alcohol on the land, thereby making Y's executory interest possessory? Yes.   Therefore, Ben's executory interest in fee simple is void from the moment of its attempted creation.

Where the interest in question violates the Rule against Perpetuities, strike the whole clause creating the invalid interest and restate the title. B's interest is invalid in both conveyances in Example 9, but the state of the title *after* applying the Rule against Perpetuities is different because of the phrasing in the respective conveyances. In the first conveyance, the original wording was, "To A and his heirs as long as alcohol is not sold on the land, then to B and his heirs." Striking the whole clause which contains the invalid interest results in the conveyance reading as follows: "To A and his heirs as long as alcohol is not sold on the land." State the title following application of the Rule: A has a fee simple determinable, and O has a possibility of reverter in fee simple. In the second conveyance, however, the original wording was, "To A and his heirs, but if alcohol is sold on the land, then to B and his heirs." Striking the whole clause which contains the invalid interest results in the conveyance reading as follows: "To A and his heirs." State the title following application of the Rule: A has a fee simple absolute.

Where the executory interest following a fee simple subject to an executory limitation violates the Rule against Perpetuities, if the conveyance used determinable words of limitation to cut short the fee simple, the possessory estate following application of the Rule is usually a fee simple determinable. Where, however, the executory interest following a fee simple subject to an executory limitation violates the Rule against Perpetuities, if the conveyance used subject to a condition subsequent words of limitation to cut short the fee simple, the possessory estate following application of the Rule is usually a fee simple absolute.

Notice the analysis above of the classic fee simple subject to an executory limitation conveyance would appear to invalidate almost all executory interests following a fee simple subject to an executory limitation. That conclusion is correct. *Where you have a shifting executory interest following a fee simple subject to an executory limitation, if the limiting condition is not tied to a life in being, the executory interest will almost always violate the Rule against Perpetuities.* This point can be driven home by re-drafting the conveyances just slightly:

EXAMPLE 10

O →   To A and his heirs as long as A does not sell alcohol on the land, then to B and his heirs.

O →   To A and his heirs, but if A sells alcohol on the land, then to B and his heirs.

State the title. Again, in both conveyances, A has a fee simple subject to an executory limitation, and B has a shifting executory interest in fee simple.

Notice, these conveyances are essentially the same conveyances as above, except the restricting condition is expressly tied to a life in being, A. Thus the executory interest can only become possessory, if at all, during the lifetime of a life in being. It is impossible for the executory interest to become possessory only after the lives in being plus 21 years. The executory interest is valid.

Where the executory interest follows a fee simple subject to an executory limitation, the executory interest will almost always violate the Rule against Perpetuities unless the restricting condition is expressly tied to a life in being.

One variation on the fee simple defeasible with the future interest in a third party is where the grantor retains possession until a stated condition occurs. The classic variation on that scenario for Rule against Perpetuities purposes is as follows:

EXAMPLE 11

O's will states: To my descendants living at the time my estate is distributed and their heirs.

State the title upon O's death. O's estate has a fee simple subject to an executory limitation, and O's descendants living at the time his estate is distributed have a springing executory interest in fee simple.

Does the executory interest violate the Rule against Perpetuities? Although it would appear impossible for the estate not be distributed in a timely manner, the Rule against Perpetuities is not concerned with practical probabilities, but rather with abstract possibilities. Is it possible, regardless of how unlikely the scenario, that O's estate will not be distributed until after all the lives in being plus 21 years? Put it to the test. Assume that O's executor is A, and that O's descendants then living are B and C. *Create* a new executor, X, and a new descendant, Z. *Kill* all the lives in being at the time the interests were created: A, B and C (and the rest of the world alive at that time if you wish). *Count* 21 years. Is it possible that the new executor, X, may take more than 21 years to complete distribution of O's estate? Yes.[167] Just as with the more traditional executory interest following a fee simple defeasible, *the executory limitation must be tied to a life in being at the time the interest is created.* The future interest in O's descendants living at the time O's estate is distributed is void, and the property would pass to O's heirs at the time of O's death.

2. The Rule against Perpetuities applied to the "future interest only" conveyance.

The classic executory interest is a shifting executory interest following a fee simple defeasible. The executory interest following a "future interest only" conveyance is analogous to the classic executory interest except that in the "future interest only" conveyance the right to possession is being taken from the grantor, not a third party.

For example:

EXAMPLE 12

O → To A and her heirs if she graduates from law school.

State the title. O has a fee simple subject to an executory limitation, and A has a springing executory interest. A's executory interest will cut short O's fee simple if the express condition precedent occurs (here, if A graduates from law school).

---

[167] In Wills & Trusts circles this type of conveyance is commonly known as the "slothful executor" problem.

Just as with the classic executory interest, the key to applying the Rule against Perpetuities to the "future interest only" conveyance is whether the express condition is tied to a life in being or not. Where the express condition is tied to a life in being, it will never violate the Rule against Perpetuities. Where the express condition is not tied to a life in being, it almost always violates the Rule against Perpetuities.

Return to the example above. Does A's springing executory interest violate the Rule against Perpetuities? Put it to the test. First, create someone in whom the interest can vest, but only after the lives in being plus 21 years perpetuities period. You cannot. A is the only person who can satisfy the express condition precedent. A must graduate from law school for the executory interest to vest and become possessory. The interest does not violate the Rule against Perpetuities.

Most "future interest only" conveyances will not violate the Rule against Perpetuities because the express condition typically is tied to a life in being. But it need not be. For example:

EXAMPLE 13

O →   To A and her heirs when a woman is elected
         President of the United States.

State the title. The logical assumption is that at the time the conveyance was created, a woman had not been elected President yet.[168] Accordingly, as written, O has a fee simple subject to an executory limitation, and A has a springing executory interest in fee simple. A's executory interest is subject to the Rule against Perpetuities. Put it to the test. Create a new person in whom the interest can vest, but only after the lives in being plus 21 years perpetuities period – X, an heir of A. Kill A, O and everyone else. Count 21 years. Is it conceivable that a woman will still not have been elected President of the United States? Yes. Is it conceivable that thereafter a woman will be elected President? Yes. Where the express condition is not tied to a life in being, the executory interest typically will violate the Rule against Perpetuities. O holds fee simple absolute.

---

[168] As was the case when this edition was published.

As with classic executory interests, whether an executory interest following a "future interest only" conveyance violates the Rule against Perpetuities usually turns on whether the express condition is tied to a life in being. More often than not, in the "future interest only" conveyance the express condition *will* be tied to a life in being, but you have to read and analyze each conveyance carefully to see whether it violates the Rule against Perpetuities.

3. The Rule against Perpetuities applied to the executory interest following a vested remainder subject to divestment.

In applying the Rule against Perpetuities to executory interests following a vested remainder subject to divestment, the key is whether the divesting condition is one which *must occur, if at all*, during the estate preceding the vested remainder, or whether the divesting condition is one which *may occur* during the estate preceding the vested remainder. The vested remainder subject to divestment almost invariably follows a life estate.[169] If the divesting condition *must occur, if at all*, during the life estate, then the executory interest must become possessory, if at all, either during or upon the expiration of the life estate. Thus where the vested remainder subject to divestment follows a life estate, and the divesting condition *must occur, if at all*, during or upon expiration of the life estate, the executory interest cannot violate the Rule against Perpetuities.

The following example demonstrates that point:

EXAMPLE 14

O → To A for life, then to B and his heirs, but if A sells alcohol on the land, then to C and her heirs.

State the title. A has a life estate. B has a vested remainder in fee simple subject to divestment, and C has a shifting executory interest in fee simple.

---

[169] In theory, the vested remainder subject to divestment could follow a fee tail, in which case there could be a potential Rule against Perpetuities problem, but because the fee tail has practically been abolished and even at common law such a conveyance was extremely rare, those scenarios are beyond the scope of this material. The qualifications in this paragraph, then, pertain to these scenarios which are beyond the scope of this material, and as applied to the norm (the vested remainder subject to divestment following a life estate), there is no Rule against Perpetuities problem.

C's shifting executory interest is subject to the Rule against Perpetuities. Put it to the test. *Create* an heir for B, X, and an heir for C, Y. Kill all the lives in being at the time the executory interest was created: A, B, and C (and whomever else you wish). Here, the problem is that the divesting condition is tied to the life tenant. Thus the executory interest must become possessory, if at all, during, or at the expiration of, the life estate. It is impossible to delay the vesting until after the lives in being plus 21 years. Thus the Rule against Perpetuities is not really a problem for executory interests following a vested remainder subject to divestment where the divesting condition is one which *must occur, if at all*, during the preceding life estate.[170]

On the other hand, if the divesting condition is one which *may* occur during the preceding estate, but may not occur until after the vested remainder has become possessory, for purposes of the Rule against Perpetuities, this scenario is analogous to the fee simple subject to an executory limitation scenario. Unless the divesting condition is tied to a life in being, the executory interest will violate the Rule against Perpetuities and will be void.

4. The Rule against Perpetuities applied to the executory interest following the "gap" scenario.

Although one might think that the Rule against Perpetuities does not have much application to the "gap" scenario, the "gap" scenario is much like the executory interest where the grantor's possessory estate is cut short and for that reason may be deceptively tricky. To the extent the "gap" is tied solely to an express time period less than 21 years, the Rule against Perpetuities will not be a problem. To the extent the "gap" is tied to the occurrence of an event, the Rule is very much applicable.

The Rule typically is not a problem where the "gap" is solely an express time period less than 21 years. For example:

---

[170] If, however, the underlying finite estate is a term of years greater than 21 years, or a fee tail, the Rule against Perpetuities is very much a problem for executory interests which follow a vested remainder subject to divestment.

EXAMPLE 15

O → To A for life, then 1 year after A's death, to B and her heirs.

State the title. A has a life estate, O has a reversion in fee simple subject to an executory limitation, and B has a springing executory interest in fee simple.

B's executory interest is subject to the Rule against Perpetuities. Put it to the test. *Create* a new life in being who will be eligible to claim possession of the property under the interest being tested - X, an heir for B (we also need an heir for O, Y). *Kill* all the lives in being at the time the executory interest was created: O, A and B. *Count* 21 years. Is it possible that the executory interest will become possessory but only *after* the lives in being plus 21 years? No. The executory interest must become possessory one year after the killing of A, a life in being. There is no way to delay the vesting. Thus, where the "gap" is tied to an express time period that is less than 21 years, there is no Rule against Perpetuities problem and the interest is valid.

On the other hand, where the "gap" is tied to an event, if the occurrence can be delayed there will be Rule against Perpetuities problems. For example:

EXAMPLE 16

O → To A for life, then 1 year after the election of a Green Party candidate as President of the United States, to B and her heirs.

State the title. A has a life estate, O has a reversion in fee simple subject to an executory limitation, and B has a springing executory interest in fee simple.

B's executory interest is subject to the Rule against Perpetuities. The scenario here is much like the scenario discussed above where the grantor's possessory estate is being cut short with the future interest being in a third party. If the occurrence is not tied to a life in being, there is going to be a Rule against Perpetuities problem. Put the above example to the test. *Create* the necessary new lives in being: an heir for O and an heir for B. *Kill* all the lives in being at the time the interest was created: O and B. *Count* 21 years. Is it possible that the executory interest will still not be possessory? Yes. Is it possible that thereafter a Green Party candidate could be elected President of the United States? Yes. Therefore, the executory interest violates the Rule against Perpetuities and is void. Strike the interest in question and restate the title. A holds a life estate, and O holds a reversion in fee simple absolute.

THE RULE AGAINST PERPETUITIES EXECUTORY INTERESTS PROBLEM SET

For each of the following problems, (1) state the title of the conveyance as drafted, (2) analyze if any of the interests are subject to the Rule against Perpetuities, and (3) if the interest violates the Rule, restate the title.

1. O → To A and her heirs, but if she stops using the land for charitable purposes, then O has the right to re-enter and re-claim the land.

2. O → To A and her heirs, but if she stops using the land for charitable purposes, then to B and her heirs.

3. O → To A and her heirs as long as the land is farmed, then to B and her heirs.

4. O → To A and her heirs, but if the land is not farmed then to B and her heirs.

5. O → To A and her heirs when her granddaughter graduates from law school. (Assume A has two children, and a grandchild who is a first year law student.)

6. O → To A for life, then 5 years later to whomever is then President of the United States and his or her heirs.

7. O → To A and her heirs if one of her daughters gets a tattoo.

8. O → To A and her heirs as long as she farms the land, then to B and her heirs.

9. O → To A for life, then to A's first child who graduates from law school after A's death and his or her heirs. (Assume A has two children, B and C.)

10. O → To A and her heirs as long as the land is farmed, but if the land is not farmed, then O has the right to re-enter and re-claim the land.

11. Oprah → To Nelson and his heirs as long as the land is used for agricultural purposes; and if it is not used for agricultural purposes, then to Stedman and his heirs.

12. Donor → To whomever is the President of the St. Louis University High at the time of distribution of my estate and his or her heirs.

13. Usher → To Sara for life, then to JoJo and her heirs, but if JoJo ever consumes liquor on the land, to Emma and her heirs.

14. Owner → Donald and his heirs have an option to purchase the land if the option is exercised within the next 25 years.

15. George → To Zuzu and her heirs if she opens a nursery on the property.

C. CLASS GIFTS

As discussed above, conveyances to a class of people create unique challenges when determining whether a remainder is contingent or vested. With respect to class conveyances, there is a third category: vested subject to open. Vested subject to open is like being partially vested. You might think that the same would be true with respect to the Rule against Perpetuities: the conveyance to the class could be valid, invalid, or partially valid/invalid. That is not the case. The general rule is that the whole class, every single possible member of the class, *must* vest within the lives in being or the *whole* class interest (the whole vested remainder subject to open) is invalid. *If you can create one scenario where one class member vests, but after the lives in being plus 21 years from the date of the creation of the conveyance to the class, the interest is void.*

Remainders to a class are typically contingent because not all members of the class are born and thus more members of the class may enter. A class can *also* be contingent because of an express condition precedent. For purposes of the Rule against Perpetuities, the class must close, and if there is an express condition precedent, all members of the class must satisfy the condition precedent, within the lives in being plus 21 years.

Where there is no express condition precedent, there is only one class gift remainder after a life estate, and the identified class does not skip a generation, there is no Rule against Perpetuities problem. For example:

EXAMPLE 17

O → To A for life, then to A's children and their heirs.

State the title. A has a life estate, A's children have a contingent remainder in fee simple, and O has a reversion in fee simple.

The contingent remainder in A's children is subject to the Rule against Perpetuities. But because the class will close upon A's death and there is no express condition precedent, there is no Rule against Perpetuities problem. The remainder will vest, if at all, completely upon A's death. There is no scenario which would delay the vesting in even one class member until *after* the lives in being plus 21 years. The same would be true if the contingent remainder were in another party's children (say B's children). The same would be true if the interest were in A's descendants or A's issue. As long as there is only one class remainder, there is no express condition precedent, and the description of the class is one which does not skip a generation, the class remainder will not violate the Rule against Perpetuities because it must vest, if at all, upon the expiration of the life estate (it cannot be delayed until after the lives in being plus 21 years).

If however, there is only one class gift remainder after a life estate, there is no express condition precedent, but the description of the class skips a generation, the class interest typically will violate the Rule against Perpetuities. Return to the example above and modify it slightly:

EXAMPLE 18

O → To A for life, then to A's grandchildren and their heirs.

State the title. A has a life estate, A's grandchildren have a contingent remainder in fee simple, and O has a reversion in fee simple.

The remainder in A's grandchildren, be it contingent or vested subject to open, is subject to the Rule against Perpetuities. Put it to the test. *Create* someone who will be eligible to claim possession of the property under the interest but after the lives in being plus 21 years, so create as far back in the chain as possible: create a new child for A, child X. *Kill* all the lives in being at the time the interest was created: O, A, all of A's children alive at the time of the conveyance, if any, and all of A's grandchildren alive at the time of the conveyance, if any. *Count* 21 years. Is it possible that thereafter X will have a child, Y, a grandchild of A, who would be able to claim possession of the property pursuant to the remainder?[171] Yes. Thus the remainder in A's grandchildren, be it contingent or vested subject to open, is invalid. *Where there is only one class remainder and no express condition precedent, but the description of the class skips a generation, the remainder typically will violate the Rule against Perpetuities.*

---

[171] Remember, for analytical purposes, the Rule against Perpetuities ignores the destructibility of contingent remainders doctrine.

The trickier problems develop when either (1) there are stacked contingent or vested subject to open remainders, and/or (2) there is an express condition precedent on the class. Start with the former:

EXAMPLE 19

O → To A for life, then to B's children for life, then to B's grandchildren and their heirs.

Assume A and B are alive, that B has 4 children (K, L, M, and N) and 2 grandchildren (R and S).

State the title. A has a life estate, B's children have a vested remainder subject to open in life estate, and B's grandchildren have a vested remainder subject to open in fee simple. There are two remainders which are subject to the Rule against Perpetuities. Notice even if one or both of them were contingent remainders, they would still be subject to the Rule against Perpetuities. The analysis would be the same. But the example involves a vested subject to open because it was assumed that you would probably be more inclined to find vested remainders subject to open valid than contingent remainders. But even with the vested subject to open, you have to put it to the test.

First, test the vested remainder subject to open in B's children. *Create* a new being who would be eligible to claim the interest in question: another child for B, X. *Kill* all the lives in being at the time the first remainder was created: O, A, B, K, L, M, N, R and S. *Count* 21 years. Is it possible that X's remainder will vest but *only* after the lives in being plus 21 years? No. X's interest will vest, if at all, only upon the killing of the lives in being, not after the additional 21 years. There is no Rule against Perpetuities problem with the first remainder (which is consistent with the observation above that when there is only one remainder with no express condition precedent, there is no Rule against Perpetuities problem).

When there is no express condition precedent, but stacked contingent or vested subject to open remainders, the Rule against Perpetuities problem is with the second contingent or vested subject to open remainder. Returning to the example above, test the vested remainder subject to open in B's grandchildren. *Create* as far back in the process as possible, so create a new child for B, child X, and a new grandchild for B, grandchild Y. *Kill* all the lives in being at the time the first remainder was created: O, A, B, K, L, M, N, R and S. *Count* 21 years. Is it possible that thereafter X will die, thereby closing the class of B's grandchildren and making the interest possessory in Y? Certainly. Thus, because we created a scenario in which the vested remainder subject to open became possessory in a class member after the lives in being plus 21 years, the class gift is void. *Whenever there is no express condition precedent but there are contingent or vested subject to open conveyances which are stacked, the second contingent or vested subject to open invariably will be void.*

The other class gift scenario that has potential Rule against Perpetuities problems is a remainder to a class which contains an express condition precedent which can take more than 21 years to satisfy. For example:

EXAMPLE 20

O →   To A for life, then to B's children who reach age 30 and their heirs.

Assume A and B are alive, and B has 4 children (F, age 39, G, age 36, H, age 33, and J, age 31).

State the title. A has a life estate, and B's children who reach the age of 30 have a vested remainder subject to open in fee simple.

Why is the remainder vested subject to open if all of B's children are over the age of 30? Because B can have more children. What if B were an 85 year old woman? Putting aside the advances in reproductive technology and techniques, the common law presumed each individual was fertile until death.[172] Put the interest to the test. *Create* a new being who could claim the property under the interest being challenged - a new child for B, X. *Kill* all the lives in being at the time the interest was created: O, A, B, F, G, H, and J. Notice killing B closes the class but does not fully vest the class because X has not satisfied the express condition precedent. *Count* 21

---

[172] In Wills & Trusts circles, this possibility is commonly known as the "fertile octogenarian." The fertile octogenarian often creates Rule against Perpetuities problems.

years. Is it possible that X could live another 9 years, thereby satisfying the express condition precedent and being able to claim possession of the property? Yes. Thus the vested remainder subject to open in B's children who reach the age of 30 is void. A would hold a life estate, and O would hold a reversion in fee simple absolute.

If the express condition precedent for the class is one which must be satisfied, if at all, within 21 years, then there is no Rule against Perpetuities problem. Modify the above example just slightly:

EXAMPLE 21

O →   To A for life, then to B's children who reach age 20 and their heirs.

      Assume A and B are alive, and B has 4 children (F, age 39, G, age 36, H, age 33, and J, age 31).

State the title. A has a life estate, and B's children who reach the age of 20 have a vested remainder subject to open in fee simple.

Again, the vested remainder subject to open in the children of B who reach age 20 is subject to the Rule against Perpetuities. Put the interest to the test. *Create* a new being who could claim the property under the interest being challenged - a new child for B, X. *Kill* all the lives in being at the time the interest was created: O, A, B, F, G, H, and J. Notice B's death closes the class but does not fully vest the class because X has not satisfied the express condition precedent. *Count* 21 years. Is it possible that X could satisfying the express condition precedent and be able to claim possession of the property but not until *after* the running of the 21 years? No. X will have to turn 20 before the 21 years has fully run. Because the express condition is one which must be satisfied, if at all, within 21 years, it cannot violate the Rule against Perpetuities.

THE RULE AGAINST PERPETUITIES
CLASS GIFTS PROBLEM SET

For each of the following problems, (1) state the title of the conveyance as drafted, (2) analyze if any of the interests are subject to the Rule against Perpetuities, and (3) if the interest violates the Rule, restate the title. (Treat the sub parts under each conveyance as cumulative factual developments.)

1. O → To A for life, then to A's children and their heirs.
   (Assume A has two children, B and C.)

2. O → To A for life, then to A's grandchildren and their heirs.
   (Assume A has no children but grandchildren, B and C.)

3. O → To A for life, then to A's children who reach age 30 and his or her heirs. (Assume A has two children, B, age 35, and C, age 25.)

4. O → To A for life, then to A's grandchildren who reach age 20 and his or her heirs. (Assume A has no children and two grandchildren, B, age 10, and C, age 3.)

5. O → To A for 10 years, then to A's children who reach age 20 and his or her heirs. (Assume A has two children, B, age 25, and C, age 15.)

D. MODERN TREND

Like the other common law rules which promoted the marketability of the property, the modern trend views the Rule against Perpetuities with disfavor – so much so that a good number of jurisdictions have abolished it. Others have adopted the "wait-and-see" approach, which is exactly as it sounds. Instead of testing future interests the moment they are created to see if there is a hypothetical scenario in which the interest violates the Rule against Perpetuities, the "wait-and-see" approach takes the traditional statute of limitations approach and waits to see what happens. Both of these developments are beyond the scope of this coverage. Listen carefully to your professor to see if he or she expects you to be familiar with both the common law and the modern trend approach to the Rule against Perpetuities.

Appendix A

ANSWERS TO PROBLEM SETS

ANSWERS TO CHAPTER 2 PROBLEM SET

1. (a) **Common law**: A fee simple absolute is conveyed - proper words of limitation for common law conveyance.

   (b) **Modern trend**: A fee simple absolute is conveyed. The modern trend is more lenient, so any language that would convey a fee simple absolute under the common law approach should be equally effective under the modern trend.

2. (a) **Common law**: No fee simple absolute. The words of limitation necessary to create a fee simple absolute are missing. The common law approach is very strict, insisting on proper words of limitation as opposed to presuming intent.

   (b) **Modern trend**: A fee simple absolute is conveyed. The modern trend focuses on the grantor's intent. The starting assumption is that a grantor intends to convey all that he or she owns. Here, assuming O owned fee simple absolute, she is presumed to intend to convey fee simple absolute, even though she did not use the traditional words of limitation.

3. (a) **Common law**: No fee simple absolute. Improper words of limitation. The common law approach is very strict, insisting on proper words of limitation as opposed to focusing on intent.

   (b) **Modern trend**: A fee simple absolute is conveyed. The modern trend focuses on the grantor's intent. Here, the grantor clearly intends to convey a fee simple absolute even though he or she did not use the traditional words of limitation.

4. (a) **Common law**: No fee simple absolute. Improper words of limitation. Although the conveyance uses the word "heirs" the use is in the word of purchase – they describe who is taking the interest.

(b) **Modern trend**: Unclear; may or may not convey a fee simple absolute. You have not covered enough material to see all the ambiguities inherent in the language of this conveyance. The biggest obstacle to finding that this conveys a fee simple absolute to Abigail is that the words of purchase technically give the property to the *heirs* of Abigail, not Abigail. But the court may take extrinsic evidence to try to resolve the ambiguity. If the only evidence, however, is the language of the conveyance, it is unclear whether the grantor meant for Abigail to have a fee simple or the heirs of Abigail (and the facts do not indicate whether Abigail is alive or dead – another issue).

5. (a) **Common law**: No fee simple absolute. Improper words of limitation. (You will learn later that this language would convey the property to Beth for the duration of his or her life – a life estate.)

   (b) **Modern trend**: A fee simple absolute is conveyed. Absent extrinsic evidence to the contrary, the presumption would be that the grantor intended to convey all that he or she had to the grantee. Because there are no words limiting what the grantee is to take, assuming Oscar held a fee simple absolute, Beth would take a fee simple absolute.

6. (a) **Common law**: No fee simple absolute. Improper words of limitation. The common law approach is very strict, insisting on proper words of limitation as opposed to focusing on intent.

   (b) **Modern trend**: Fee simple absolute. Absent extrinsic evidence to the contrary, the presumption would be that the grantor intended to convey all that he or she had to the grantee. Because there are no words limiting what the grantee is to take, assuming Olivia held a fee simple absolute, Allison would take a fee simple absolute.

7. (a) **Common law**: No fee simple absolute. Improper words of limitation. The common law approach is very strict, insisting on proper words of limitation as opposed to focusing on intent.

   (b) **Modern trend**: A fee simple absolute is conveyed. The modern trend focuses on the grantor's intent. Here, Olivia clearly intends to convey a fee simple absolute even though she did not use the traditional words of limitation.

ANSWERS TO CHAPTER 3 PROBLEM SET

1.   A has a fee simple determinable, and
     O has a possibility of reverter in fee simple absolute.

     O →| A – FSD | O – POSS REV in FSA

2.   A has a fee simple subject to a condition subsequent, and
     O has a right of entry/power of termination in fee simple absolute.

     O →| A – FSSCS | O – RT ENTRY in FSA

3.   A has a fee simple subject to an executory limitation, and
     B has a shifting executory interest in fee simple.

     O → A – FSSEL   B – Sh EX INT in FSA

4.   A has a fee simple subject to a condition subsequent, and
     O has a right of entry/power of termination in fee simple absolute.

     O →| A – FSSCS | O – RT ENTRY in FSA

5.   A has a fee simple determinable, and
     O has a possibility of reverter in fee simple absolute.

     O →| A – FSD | O – POSS REV in FSA

6.   A has a fee simple subject to an executory limitation, and
     C has a shifting executory interest in fee simple.

     O → A – FSSEL   C – Sh EX INT in FSA

7.   A has a fee simple subject to a condition subsequent, and
O has a right of entry/power of termination in fee simple absolute.

8.   A has a fee simple determinable, and
O has a possibility of reverter in fee simple absolute.

9.   A has a fee simple subject to a condition subsequent, and
O has a right of entry/power of termination in fee simple absolute.

10.   A has a fee simple subject to an executory limitation, and
B has a shifting executory interest in fee simple.

11.   A has a fee simple subject to a condition subsequent, and
O has a right of entry/power of termination in fee simple absolute.

(Notice the ambiguity in this conveyance – it has both determinable words of limitation, "as long as … ," as well as condition subsequent words of limitation, "but if … ." Because the fee simple determinable includes an automatic termination of interest, and because the courts dislike forfeiture of property, an ambiguous fee simple defeasible is construed as a fee simple subject to condition subsequent.)

12.   A has a fee simple subject to a condition subsequent, and
O has a right of entry/power of termination in fee simple absolute.

13.   A has a fee simple determinable, and
O has a possibility of reverter in fee simple absolute.

14.   A has a fee simple subject to an executory limitation, and
B has a shifting executory interest in fee simple absolute.

15.   A has a fee simple determinable, and
O has a possibility of reverter in fee simple absolute.

16.   A has a fee simple subject to a condition subsequent, and
O has a right of entry/power of termination in fee simple absolute.

17.   A has a fee simple subject to a condition subsequent, and
O has a right of entry/power of termination in fee simple absolute.

18.   A has a fee simple subject to an executory limitation, and
        B has a shifting executory interest in fee simple.

19.   A has a fee simple subject to a condition subsequent, and
        O has a right of entry/power of termination in fee simple absolute.

20.   A has a fee simple subject to a condition subsequent, and
        O has a right of entry/power of termination in fee simple absolute.

21.   A has a fee simple determinable, and
        O has a possibility of reverter in fee simple absolute.

22.   A has a fee simple subject to an executory limitation, and
        B has a shifting executory interest in fee simple.

23.   A has a fee simple subject to a condition subsequent, and
        O has a right of entry/power of termination in fee simple absolute.

24.   A has a fee simple determinable, and
        O has a possibility of reverter in fee simple absolute.

25.   A has a fee simple subject to an executory limitation, and
        B has a shifting executory interest in fee simple.

26.   Hank has a fee simple subject to an executory limitation, and
        Barry has a shifting executory interest in fee simple.

27.   Katie has a fee simple determinable, and
        Tom has a possibility of reverter in fee simple.

28.   Ferris has a fee simple subject to a condition subsequent, and
        Rooney has a right of entry/power of termination in fee simple.

29.   Dude has a fee simple subject to an executory limitation, and
        Lebowski has a shifting executory interest in fee simple.

30.   Merlin has a fee simple subject to an executory limitation, and
        Harry has a springing executory interest in fee simple.

ANSWERS TO CHAPTER 4 PROBLEM SET

1.   A has a life estate, and B has a remainder in fee simple.

2.   A has a fee tail,
       B has a remainder in life estate, and
       O has a reversion in fee simple

3.   **Common law**:A has a life estate,
                     B has a remainder in life estate, and
                     C has a remainder in fee simple.

       Modern trend: Unclear. On the one hand, the grantor is presumed to convey all that he or she held. A can argue that A received a fee simple absolute and all the other parties took nothing then. On the other hand, the use of the "and her heirs" words of limitation in the clause giving C's interest to C arguably shows that the grantor knew how to convey a fee simple absolute when he or she wanted to. Under this construction, the state of the title is the same as the common law. This latter construction is the better construction.

4.   A has a life estate,
       B has a remainder in fee simple subject to a condition subsequent, and
       O has a right of entry/power of termination in fee simple.

5.   A has a fee tail,
       B has a remainder in fee simple subject to an executory limitation, and
       C has a shifting executory interest in fee simple.

6.   A has a fee tail, and O has a reversion in fee simple.

7.   A has a life estate,
       B has a remainder in fee simple determinable, and
       O has a possibility of reverter in fee simple.

8.   A has a term of years,
       B has a remainder in fee simple subject to an executory limitation, and
       C has a shifting executory interest in fee simple.

9.   A has a life estate,
      B has a remainder in fee tail,
      C has a remainder in term of years, and
      O has a reversion in fee simple absolute.

10.   A has a fee tail,
      B has a remainder in fee simple subject to a condition subsequent, and
      O has a right of entry/power of termination in fee simple.

11.   A has a term of years,
      B has a remainder in life estate,
      C has a remainder in fee tail, and
      D has a remainder in fee simple.

12.   A has a fee tail,
      B has a remainder in life estate,
      C has a remainder in fee simple subject to a condition subsequent, and
      O has a right of entry/power of termination in fee simple.

13.   **Common law**: A has a term of years,
                        B has a remainder in life estate,
                        C has a remainder in life estate, and
                        D has a remainder in fee simple.

      Modern trend: Unclear. On the one hand, the grantor is presumed to convey all that he or she held. B can argue that because B's interest is not expressly limited, B received a fee simple absolute and all the subsequent parties took nothing then. On the other hand, the use of the "and her heirs" words of limitation in the clause giving D's interest to D arguably shows that the grantor knew how to convey a fee simple absolute when he or she wanted to. Under this construction, the state of the title is the same as the common law. This latter construction is the better construction.

14.   A has a life estate,
      B has a remainder in fee simple subject to an executory limitation, and
      C has a shifting executory interest in fee simple.

15.   **Common law**: A has a life estate,
                            B has a remainder in life estate,
                            C has a remainder in life estate, and
                            O has a reversion in fee simple.

       Modern trend: A has a life estate,
                            B has a remainder in life estate, and
                            C has a remainder in fee simple absolute.

16.   Bert has a life estate, and Ernie has a remainder in fee simple absolute.

17.   Mary has a life estate, and
       George has a reversion in fee simple absolute.

18.   Gonzo has a fee tail, and Ralph has a remainder in fee simple absolute.

19.   Rizzo has a fee tail, and Olivia has a reversion in fee simple absolute.

20.   Bird has a fee simple determinable, and
       Olivia has a possibility of reverter in fee simple absolute.

21.   **Common law**: Groucho has a life estate,
                            Harpo has a remainder in life estate, and
                            Zeppo has a remainder in fee simple absolute.

       Modern trend: Unclear. On the one hand, the grantor is presumed to convey all that he or she held. Groucho can argue that because his interest is not expressly limited, he received a fee simple absolute and all the subsequent parties took nothing. On the other hand, the use of the "and his heirs" words of limitation in the clause giving Zeppo his interest shows that Olivia knew how to convey a fee simple absolute when she wanted to. Under this construction, the state of the title is the same as the common law. This latter construction is the better construction.

22.   Hannibal has a term of years, and
       Olivia has a reversion in fee simple absolute.

23.   Oscar has a fee simple absolute, and Felix has nothing (one cannot give away the same property twice).

24. **Common law**: Jeff has a life estate, and
    Mutt has a reversion in fee simple absolute.

    Modern trend: Jeff has a fee simple absolute.

25. **Common law**: Harriette has a life estate, and
    Ozzie has a reversion in fee simple absolute.

    Modern trend: Harriette has a fee simple absolute.

26. **Common law**: Juliette has a life estate, and
    Romeo has a reversion in fee simple absolute.

    Modern trend: Juliette has a fee simple absolute.

27. Dick has a fee simple subject to an executory limitation, and
    Howard has a shifting executory interest in fee simple.

28. Rosie has a life estate, and
    Barbara has a remainder in fee simple absolute.

    Thereafter, Rosie transfers her interest to Ellen.

    Ellen has a life estate pur autre vie (measured by Rosie's life), and
    Barbara has a remainder in fee simple absolute.

29. Bill has a fee simple subject to an executory limitation, and
    Hillary has a shifting executory interest in fee simple.

30. Simon has a fee simple determinable, and
    Oliver has a possibility of reverter in fee simple.

ANSWERS TO CHAPTER 6 PROBLEM SET

1. A has a life estate,
    B has a contingent remainder in fee simple, and
    O has a reversion in fee simple.

2. **Common law**: A has a life estate,
         B has a vested remainder in fee tail,
         C has a vested remainder in a term of years, and
         O has a reversion in fee simple.

    Modern trend: Unclear. On the one hand, the grantor is presumed to convey all that he or she held. A can argue that because A's interest is not expressly limited, A received a fee simple absolute and all the subsequent parties took nothing. On the other hand, the other parties will argue that the extra clauses evidence that O did not intend to give A a fee simple absolute or those clauses would be null and void. They would argue that the court should construe the conveyance to give effect to all the clauses. Under this construction, the state of the title is the same as the common law. The court could rule either way.

3. A has a fee tail,
    B has a contingent remainder in fee simple,
    C has an alternative contingent remainder in fee simple, and
    O has a reversion in fee simple.

4. **Common law**: A has a life estate,
         B has a vested remainder in life estate,
         C has a contingent remainder in fee simple, and
         O has a reversion in fee simple.

    Modern trend: Unclear. On the one hand, the grantor is presumed to convey all that he or she held. B can argue that because B's interest is not expressly limited, B received a fee simple absolute and all the subsequent parties took nothing. On the other hand, the use of the "and his heirs" words of limitation in the clause giving C her interest shows that O knew how to convey a fee simple absolute when she wanted to. Under this construction, the state of the title is the same as the common law. This latter construction is the better construction.

5.   A has a term of years,
     B has a vested remainder in fee tail,
     C has a vested remainder in fee simple determinable, and
     O has a possibility of reverter in fee simple.

6.   A has a life estate, and
     B has a contingent remainder in fee simple, and
     O has a reversion in fee simple.

7.   Common law: A has a life estate
                   B has a vested remainder in life estate,
                   C has a contingent remainder in life estate, and
                   O has a reversion in fee simple.

     Modern trend: Unclear. On the one hand, the grantor is presumed
     to convey all that he or she held. A can argue that because A's interest
     is not expressly limited, A received a fee simple absolute and all the
     subsequent parties took nothing. On the other hand, the other parties
     will argue that the extra clauses evidence that O did not intend to give
     A a fee simple absolute or those clauses would be null and void. They
     would argue that the court should construe the conveyance to give
     effect to all the clauses. Under this construction, the state of the title is
     the same as the common law. The court could rule either way.

8.   A has a life estate,
     B has a contingent remainder in fee simple,
     C has an alternative contingent remainder in fee simple, and
     O has a reversion in fee simple.

9.   Bilbo has a life estate,
     Frodo has a vested remainder in fee simple, and
     Gollum has nothing.

10. Smeagol has a life estate,
     Bilbo has a vested remainder in fee tail,
     Frodo has a vested remainder in fee simple absolute, and
     Deagol has nothing.

11.   John has a fee tail,
        George has a vested remainder in life estate,
        Ringo has a vested remainder in fee simple determinable, and
        Paul has a possibility of reverter in fee simple absolute.

12.   Raphael has a life estate,
        Donatello has a vested remainder in life estate,
        Michelangelo has a vested remainder in life estate, and
        Bernini has a reversion in fee simple absolute.

13.   Ted has a term of years,
        Carol has a vested remainder in fee tail,
        Alice has a vested remainder in life estate, and
        Bob has a reversion in fee simple absolute.

14.   Kate has a life estate, and
        Goldie has a reversion in fee simple absolute.

15.   Chandler has a fee tail,
        Monica has a vested remainder in fee tail,
        Joey has a vested remainder in fee simple subject to a condition
            subsequent,
        Ross has a right of entry/power of termination in fee simple absolute.

ANSWERS TO REVIEW PROBLEM SET 1

1.   **Common law**: A has a life estate,
                           B has a vested remainder in life estate, and
                           O has a reversion in fee simple.

       Modern trend: A has a life estate, and
                           B has a vested remainder in fee simple.

2.   A has a fee tail,
       B has a contingent remainder in life estate, and
       O has a reversion in fee simple.

3.   **Common law**: A has a life estate,
                           B has a vested remainder in fee tail,
                         C has a vested remainder in fee simple determinable, and
                         O has a possibility of reverter in fee simple.

       Modern trend: Unclear. On the one hand, the grantor is presumed to convey all that he or she held. A can argue that because A's interest is not expressly limited, A received a fee simple absolute and all the subsequent parties took nothing. On the other hand, the use of the "and his heirs" words of limitation in the clause giving C his interest shows that O knew how to convey a fee simple absolute when she wanted to. Under this construction, the state of the title is the same as the common law. This latter construction is the better construction.

4.   A has a life estate,
       B has a vested remainder in fee simple subject to a condition subsequent, and
       O has right of entry/power of termination in fee simple.

5.   A has a term of years,
       B has a contingent remainder in fee simple,
       C has an alternative contingent remainder in fee simple, and
       O has a reversion in fee simple.

6. **Common law**: A has a life estate,
    B has a vested remainder in fee simple determinable, and
    O has a possibility of reverter in fee simple.

    Modern trend: Unclear. On the one hand, the grantor is presumed to convey all that he or she held. A can argue that because A's interest is not expressly limited, A received a fee simple absolute and all the subsequent parties took nothing. On the other hand, the use of the "and his heirs" words of limitation in the clause giving B his interest shows that O knew how to convey a fee simple absolute when she wanted to. Under this construction, the state of the title is the same as the common law. This latter construction is the better construction.

7. **Common law**: A has a life estate,
    B has a contingent remainder in life estate, and
    O has a reversion in fee simple.

    Modern trend: A has a life estate, and
    B has a contingent remainder in fee simple, and
    O has a reversion in fee simple.

8. A has a fee simple subject to an executory limitation, and
    B has a shifting executory interest in fee simple.

9. A has a life estate,
    B has a contingent remainder in fee simple,
    C has an alternative contingent remainder in fee simple, and
    O has a reversion in fee simple.

10. A has a fee simple subject to a condition subsequent, and
    O has a right of entry/power of termination in fee simple.

11. **Common law**: A has a life estate,
    B has a vested remainder in life estate,
    C has a contingent remainder in fee simple, and
    O has a reversion in fee simple.

Modern trend: Unclear. On the one hand, the grantor is presumed to convey all that he or she held. A can argue that because A's interest is not expressly limited, A received a fee simple absolute and all the subsequent parties took nothing. On the other hand, the use of the "and his heirs" words of limitation in the clause giving C her interest shows that O knew how to convey a fee simple absolute when she wanted to. Under this construction, the state of the title is the same as the common law. This latter construction is the better construction.

12.   A has a life estate,
       B has a vested remainder in life estate,
       C has a vested remainder in fee simple subject to a condition
            subsequent, and
       O has a right of entry/power of termination in fee simple.

13.   **Common law**: A has a life estate,
                        B has a vested remainder in term of years,
                        C has a vested remainder in life estate,
                        D has a contingent remainder in fee simple, and
                        O has a reversion in fee simple.

       Modern trend: Unclear. On the one hand, the grantor is presumed to convey all that he or she held. A can argue that because A's interest is not expressly limited, A received a fee simple absolute and all the subsequent parties took nothing. On the other hand, the use of the "and his heirs" words of limitation in the clause giving D her interest shows that O knew how to convey a fee simple absolute when she wanted to. Under this construction, the state of the title is the same as the common law. This latter construction is the better construction.

14.   A has a life estate,
       B has a contingent remainder in fee simple,
       C has an alternative contingent remainder in fee simple, and
       O has a reversion in fee simple.

15.   **Common law**: A has a life estate,
                        B has a vested remainder in fee tail,
                        C has a vested remainder in life estate, and
                        O has a reversion in fee simple.

Modern trend: A has a life estate, and
B has a vested remainder in fee tail, and
C has a vested remainder in fee simple.

16. A has a term of years,
B has a vested remainder in fee simple subject to an executory
limitation, and
C has a shifting executory interest in fee simple.

17. A has a fee simple determinable, and
O has a possibility of reverter in fee simple.

18. A has a fee simple subject to a condition subsequent, and
O has a right of entry/power of termination in fee simple.

19. A has a life estate,
B has a vested remainder in fee simple subject to an executory
limitation, and
C has a shifting executory interest in fee simple.

20 A has a life estate,
B has a contingent remainder in fee simple, and
O has a reversion in fee simple.

21 Common law: Adrian has a life estate, and
Rocky has a reversion in fee simple absolute.

Modern trend: Adrian has a fee simple absolute, and
Rocky has nothing.

22. Adrian has a fee simple absolute (and Rocky has nothing).

23. Adrian has a life estate, and
Rocky has a reversion in fee simple absolute.

24. Nelson has a fee simple determinable, and
Oprah has a possibility of reverter in fee simple absolute.

25.   Shoeless has a fee simple subject to a condition subsequent, and
Ray has a right of entry/power of termination in fee simple absolute.

26.   Marilyn has a fee tail, and
Joe has a reversion in fee simple absolute.

27.   Nelson has a fee simple subject to an executory limitation, and
Stedman has a shifting executory interest in fee simple absolute.

28.   Paris has a fee simple subject to an executory limitation, and
Nicole has a shifting executory interest in fee simple absolute.

29.   Paris has a fee tail, and
Nicole has a vested remainder in fee simple.

30.   Barbara has a fee tail,
Rosie has a contingent remainder in fee simple absolute, and
Oprah has a reversion in fee simple absolute.

31.   **Common law**: The only thing certain is that Tom does not have a fee simple absolute. Depending on how strictly the courts construed the poorly drafted instrument, Tom could have either a life estate all alone, with Oprah having a reversion in fee simple absolute; or Tom and his children could have joint life estates with Oprah having a reversion in fee simple absolute.

(b) **Modern trend**: Unclear. Tom and his children could hold title concurrently (joint tenants or tenants in common – common law vs. modern trend) in fee simple; or Tom could hold a fee simple absolute (if the court construed the grantor as intended to give it all to Tom and reads the words 'and his children' as if they were 'and his heirs.')

32.   Fidel has a life estate, and
Hugo has a vested remainder in fee simple.

33.   Randy has a life estate,
Ryan has a contingent remainder in fee simple,
Paula has an alternative contingent remainder in fee simple, and
Simon has a reversion in fee simple.

34.   Randy has a life estate,
        Simon has a contingent remainder in fee simple, and
        Paula has a reversion in fee simple absolute.

35.   Susan has a life estate,
        The "then" Dean has a contingent remainder in fee simple, and
        Kingsfield has a reversion in fee simple.

36.   Ali has a life estate,
        Leon has a vested remainder in life estate,
        Oscar's heirs have a contingent remainder[173] in fee simple, and
        Joe has a reversion in fee simple.

37.   Ralph has a life estate,
        Horace has a vested remainder in fee simple determinable, and
        Thoreau has a possibility of reverter in fee simple.

38.   Ralph has a life estate,
        Horace has a contingent remainder in fee simple, and
        Thoreau has a reversion in fee simple.

39.   William has a life estate,
        Harry has a contingent remainder in fee simple, and
        Elizabeth has a reversion in fee simple.

40.   Hank has a life estate,
        Barry has a contingent remainder in fee simple, and
        Babe has a reversion in fee simple.

        (Remember to construe each conveyance as written based upon the
        logical assumptions about the facts at the time the conveyance is
        created in light of the phrasing in the conveyance.)

---

[173] A person does not have heirs until he or she dies, only apparent heirs. To qualify as an heir you have to survive the decedent. Thus C's heirs are not ascertainable while C is still alive.

ANSWERS TO CHAPTER 7 PROBLEM SET

1. A has a life estate,
    B has a vested remainder in fee simple subject to divestment, and
    C has a shifting executory interest in fee simple.

2. A has a fee tail,
    B has a vested remainder in fee simple subject to a condition
          subsequent, and
    O has a right of entry/power of termination in fee simple.

3. (a) Common law:

    A has a life estate,
    B has a vested remainder in fee simple subject to an executory
          limitation, and
    C has a shifting executory interest in fee simple.

    (b) Modern trend:

    Unclear. A will argue that she holds a fee simple absolute because
    there are no words of limitation qualifying her interest and indicating
    that the grantor intended to convey something other than the default to
    her – a fee simple absolute. The other grantees will argue that the use
    of the words "and her heirs" in the gift to C shows that the grantor
    knew how to create a fee simple absolute when he or she wanted, and
    they will argue that the conveyance should be construed to give effect
    to all clauses. Under this construction, the title would be the same as
    under the common law. The latter construction is the better, and more
    likely, construction even under the modern trend.

4. O has a fee simple subject to an executory limitation, and
    A has a springing executory interest in fee simple.

5. A has a term of years,
    B has a vested remainder in fee simple subject to an executory
          limitation, and
    C has a shifting executory interest in fee simple.

6.   (a) Common law:

A has a life estate,
B has a vested remainder in fee simple, subject to divestment, and
C has a shifting executory interest in fee simple.

(b) Modern trend – same as number 3(b) above.

7.   A has a life estate,
B has a vested remainder in fee simple determinable, and
O has a possibilitiy of reverter in fee simple.

8.   A has a fee simple subject to an executory limitation, and
B has a shifting executory interest in fee simple.

9.   A has a life estate,
B has a vested remainder in fee simple subject to divestment, and
C has a shifting executory interest in fee simple.

10.   A has a fee simple subject to an executory limitation, and
B has a shifting executory interest in fee simple.

11.   Scottie has a life estate,
Kirk has a contingent remainder in fee simple, and
Spock has a reversion in fee simple.

12.   Walter has a fee simple subject to an executory limitation, and
Dude has a springing executory interest in fee simple.

13.   Mary has a life estate,
Zuzu has a vested remainder in fee simple determinable, and
George has a possibility of reverter in fee simple.

14.   Sulu has a life estate,
Uhura has a vested remainder in fee simple subject to divestment, and
McCoy has a shifting executory interest in fee simple.

15.   Scottie has a life estate,
Shaq has a contingent remainder in fee simple, and
Michael has a reversion in fee simple.

16. Lance has a life estate,
     Floyd has a vested remainder in fee simple determinable, and
     Pierre has a possibility of reverter in fee simple.

17. Shaq has a life estate,
     Kobe has a vested remainder in fee simple subject to divestment, and
     Nash has a shifting executory interest in fee simple.

18. Jack has a life estate,
     Jill has a vested remainder in fee simple determinable, and
     Mother has a possibility of reverter in fee simple absolute.

19. Jack has a life estate,
     Jill has a vested remainder in fee simple subject to a condition
         subsequent, and
     Mother has a right of entry/power to terminate in fee simple absolute.

20. Jack has a life estate,
     Jill has a vested remainder in fee simple subject to an executory
         limitation, and
     Bo has a shifting executory interest in fee simple absolute.

21. Jack has a life estate,
     Jill has a vested remainder in fee simple subject to an executory
         limitation, and
     Bo has a shifting executory interest in fee simple absolute.

22. (a) Common law:

     Hewey has a life estate, and
     Dewey has a vested remainder in fee simple.
     Louie has nothing. (Once Walt conveyed an unqualified fee simple to
         Dewey, Walt had nothing left to give to Louis.)

     (b) Modern trend:

     Hewey has a life estate,
     Dewey has a vested remainder in fee simple, and
     Louie has nothing.

(Louie can argue that Walt arguably intended to give Louie some interest because he expressly refers to him in the conveyance. Nevertheless, it is unlikely that a court would give Louie an interest. There is no express condition indicating when Dewey's fee simple is to be cut other than the inconsistent gift to Dewey; and Walt showed he knew how to create a life estate when he wanted to by the express clause "for life" in the gift to Hewey. If, by chance, the court adopted Louie's argument, Dewey would hold a vested remainder in life estate, and Louie would hold a vested remainder in fee simple – or possibly only in life estate. If Dewey holds only a life estate, so too arguably should Louie since the language in the respective clauses is the same. In which case Walt would hold a reversion in fee simple.)

23. (a) Jill has a life estate,
     Bo has a vested remainder in fee simple subject to an executory
             limitation, and
     Alice has a shifting executory interest in fee simple absolute.

    (b) Bo has a fee simple subject to an executory limitation, and
     Alice has a shifting executory interest in fee simple absolute.

24.   Woody has a life estate,
     Buzz has a contingent remainder in fee simple absolute, and
     Andy has a reversion in fee simple absolute.

25.   Buzz has a fee simple subject to an executory limitation, and
     Woody has a springing executory interest in fee simple absolute.

ANSWERS TO REVIEW PROBLEM SET 2

1.   A has a fee simple absolute.

2.   A has a fee simple subject to a condition subsequent, and
O has a right of entry/power of termination in fee simple.

3.   A has a fee simple determinable, and
O has a possibility of reverter in fee simple.

4.   A has a fee simple subject to an executory limitation, and
B has a shifting executory interest in fee simple absolute.

5.   O has a fee simple subject to an executory limitation, and
A has a springing executory interest in fee simple.

6.   A has a life estate, and
O has a reversion in fee simple.

7.   B has a life estate *pur autre vie* (measured by A's life), and
O has a reversion in fee simple.

8.   A has a fee tail, and
O has a reversion in fee simple absolute.

9.   (a) Common law:

A has a life estate,
B has a contingent remainder in *life estate*, and
O has a reversion in fee simple.

(b) Modern trend:

A has a life estate,
B has a contingent remainder in fee simple, and
O has a reversion in fee simple.

10.   A has a life estate,
B has a vested remainder in fee simple determinable, and
O has a possibility of reverter in fee simple.

11.   A has a life estate,
         B has a contingent remainder in fee simple, and
         O has a reversion in fee simple.

12.   A has a life estate,
         B has a contingent remainder in fee simple, and
         O has a reversion in fee simple.

13.   A has a life estate,
         A's first child has a contingent remainder in fee simple, and
         O has a reversion in fee simple.

14.   A has a life estate,
         The next President has a contingent remainder in fee simple, and
         O has a reversion in fee simple.

15.   A has a life estate,
         The 'then' President has a contingent remainder in fee simple, and
         O has a reversion in fee simple.

16.   A has a life estate,
         B has a contingent remainder in fee simple, and
         O has a reversion in fee simple.

17.   A has a life estate,
         B has a contingent remainder in fee simple,
         C has an alternative contingent remainder in fee simple, and
         O has a reversion in fee simple.

18.   A has a life estate,
         B has a contingent remainder in fee simple,
         C has an alternative contingent remainder in fee simple, and
         O has a reversion in fee simple.

19.   As written:

         A has a life estate,
         B has a contingent remainder in fee simple,
         C has an alternative contingent remainder in fee simple, and
         O has a reversion in fee simple.

(a) After A transfers her interest to O

O holds fee simple absolute (per the merger doctrine).

20.   A has a life estate,
        O has a reversion in fee simple subject to an executory limitation, and
        B has a springing executory interest in fee simple.

21.   A has a life estate,
        B has a vested remainder in fee simple subject to an executory
                limitation, and
        C has a shifting executory interest in fee simple.

22.   A has a life estate,
        B has a vested remainder in fee simple subject to divestment, and
        C has a shifting executory interest in fee simple.

        (This is a bit tricky due to the mixed words of limitation – but since
        the condition is one which will occur, if at all, during the preceding
        finite estate, the better characterization is that B holds a vested
        remainder subject to divestment, not subject to an executory
        limitation.)

23.   A has a life estate,
        B has a vested remainder in fee simple subject to divestment, and
        C has a shifting executory interest in fee simple.

24.   B has a fee simple subject to an executory limitation, and
        C holds a shifting executory limitation in fee simple.

25.   Jack has a life estate,
        Bo has a vested remainder in fee simple determinable, and
        Mother has a possibility of reverter in fee simple absolute.

26.   Jack has a life estate,
        Bo has a vested remainder in fee simple subject to a condition
                subsequent, and
        Mother has a right on entry/power to terminate in fee simple absolute.

27.   Mongo has a life estate,
      Bart has a vested remainder in fee simple subject to an executory
          limitation, and
      Waco has a shifting executory interest in fee simple absolute.

28.   Little Joe has a life estate,
      Hoss has a vested remainder in fee simple subject to an executory
          limitation, and
      Adam has a shifting executory interest in fee simple absolute.

29.   Little Joe has a life estate,
      Hoss has a vested remainder in fee simple subject to divestment,[174]
          and
      Adam has a shifting executory interest in fee simple absolute.

30.   Charles has a life estate,
      William has a vested remainder in fee simple subject to divestment,[175]
          and
      Harry has a shifting executory interest in fee simple absolute.

      (b) Assume Charles dies and William, Harry and Kate are still alive.

      William has a fee simple subject to an executory limitation, and
      Harry has a shifting executory interest in fee simple absolute.

31.   Archie has a life estate,
      Jughead has a contingent remainder in fee simple, and
      Veronica has a reversion in fee simple.

32.   Elmer has a life estate,
      Bugs has a vested remainder in fee simple subject to divestment, [176]
          and
      Yosemite has a shifting executory interest in fee simple absolute.

---

[174] Whether the divesting condition would also cut short the life estate is beyond the scope of this introductory coverage.

[175] Whether the divesting condition would also cut short the life estate is beyond the scope of this introductory coverage.

[176] Whether the divesting condition would also cut short the life estate is beyond the scope of this introductory coverage.

33.   Doc has a life estate,
         Sleepy has a contingent remainder in fee simple,
         Dopey has an alternative contingent remainder in fee simple, and
         White has a reversion in fee simple.

34.   Wendy has a life estate,
         Peter has a vested remainder in fee simple determinable, and
         Hook has a possibility of reverter in fee simple.

35.   Ginger has a life estate,
         MaryAnne has a vested remainder in fee simple subject to
               divestment,[177] and
         Gilligan has a shifting executory interest in fee simple absolute.

---

[177] Whether the divesting condition would also cut short the life estate is beyond the scope of this introductory coverage.

ANSWERS TO CHAPTER 8 PROBLEM SET

1. A has a fee tail,
    A's first child has a contingent remainder in fee simple, and
    O has a reversion in fee simple absolute.

2. A has a life estate,
    B has a contingent remainder in fee simple, and
    O has a reversion in fee simple.

3. A has a life estate,
    B has a contingent remainder in fee simple,
    C has an alternative contingent remainder in fee simple, and
    O has a reversion in fee simple.

4. A has a life estate,
    B has a vested remainder in fee simple, subject to divestment, and
    C has a shifting executory interest in fee simple.

5. A has a fee tail,
    B has a vested remainder in fee simple subject to an executory
        limitation, and
    C has a shifting executory interest in fee simple.

6. O has a fee simple subject to an executory limitation, and
    A has a springing executory interest in fee simple.

7. A has a life estate,
    O has a reversion in fee simple subject to an executory limitation, and
    B has a springing executory interest in fee simple.

8. A has a life estate,
    B has a vested remainder in fee simple determinable, and
    O has a possibility of reverter in fee simple.

9. A has a life estate,
    B has a vested remainder in fee simple subject to an executory
        limitation, and
    C has a shifting executory interest in fee simple.

10. A has a life estate,
   B has a vested remainder in fee simple subject to divestment, and
   C has a shifting executory interest in fee simple.

11. Harry has a life estate,
   Bill has a reversion in fee simple subject to an executory limitation, and
   Jack has a springing executory interest in fee simple absolute.

12. (a) Felix has a life estate,
   Oscar has a contingent remainder in fee simple, and
   Neil holds a reversion in fee simple.

   (b) Neil has fee simple absolute. (Oscar's contingent remainder did not vest by the end of the preceding life estate, so it is destroyed by operation of law).

13. Westley has a fee simple subject to an executory limitation, and
   Buttercup has a shifting executory interest in fee simple absolute.

14. Joni has a fee simple subject to an executory limitation, and
   Jimi has a shifting executory interest in fee simple absolute.

15. Obi has a fee simple subject to an executory limitation, and
   Luke has a springing executory interest in fee simple absolute.

16. Neo has a life estate,
   Oracle has a reversion in fee simple subject to an executory limitation, and Trinity has a springing executory interest in fee simple absolute.

17. Dorothy has a life estate,
   Tinman has a vested remainder in fee simple subject to an executory limitation, and
   Scarecrow has a shifting executory interest in fee simple.

18.   Dorothy has a life estate,
       Tinman has a vested remainder in fee simple subject to divestment, [178]
           and
       Scarecrow has a shifting executory interest in fee simple absolute.

19.   Gerri has a life estate,
       Carolyn has a vested remainder in fee simple subject to divestment,
               and
       Paul has a shifting executory interest in fee simple.

20.   Dr. Brown has a life estate,
       Marty has a contingent remainder in fee simple absolute,
       Bill has an alternative contingent remainder in fee simple, and
       George has a reversion in fee simple.

---

[178] Whether the divesting condition would also cut short the life estate is beyond the scope of this introductory coverage.

ANSWERS TO CHAPTER 9 PROBLEM SET

1. This problem highlights the subtle difference between the common law and the modern trend with respect to the default estate when improper drafting words of limitation are not used.

    Under the common law, the default estate is a life estate. Because there are no words of limitation expressly indicating the duration of A's estate, A has a *life estate* determinable, and O has a *reversion* in fee simple.

    Under the modern trend, the default estate is the fee simple. Because there are no words of limitation expressly *limiting* the estate O conveyed, O is presumed to have conveyed a fee simple – here a fee simple defeasible. Under the modern trend, A holds a *fee simple* determinable, and O holds a *possibility of reverter* in fee simple.

    You need to read the wording of each conveyance very carefully.

2, A has a life estate subject to a condition subsequent, and
    O has a reversion in fee simple.

3. A has a life estate determinable, and
    O has a reversion in fee simple.

4. A has a life estate,
    B has a vested remainder in life estate subject to an executory
        limitation,
    C has a shifting executory interest in fee simple, and
    O has a reversion in fee simple.

5. A has a life estate determinable, and
    B has a vested remainder in fee simple.

6. A has a life estate subject to an executory limitation,
    B has a shifting executory interest in fee simple, and
    O has a reversion in fee simple.

7.   (a) Common law:

A has a life estate,
B has a vested remainder in life estate determinable, and
B has a vested remainder in fee simple.

(b) Modern trend:

A has a life estate,
B has a vested remainder in fee simple determinable, and
O has a possibility of reverter in fee simple.

8.   A has a life state,
B has a vested remainder in life estate subject to an executory
       limitation,
C has a shifting executory interest in fee simple, and
O has a reversion in fee simple.

9.   A has a life estate,
B has a vested remainder in life estate subject to a condition
       subsequent, and
O has a reversion in fee simple.

10.   A has a life estate,
B has a vested remainder in life estate determinable, and
O has a reversion in fee simple.

11.   A has a life estate,
B has a vest remainder in life estate subject to an executory
       limitation,
C has a shifting executory interest in fee simple, and
O has a reversion in fee simple.

12.   Common law:

A has a life estate,
B has a vested remainder in *life estate* determinable, and
O has a *reversion* in fee simple.

Modern trend:

A has life estate,
B has a vested remainder in *fee simple* determinable, and
O has a *possibility of reverter* in fee simple.

13.   Common law:

A has a life estate,
B has a vested remainder in *life estate* subject to an executory
        limitation,
C has a shifting executory interest in fee simple, and
O has a *reversion* in fee simple.

Modern trend:

A has life estate,
B has a vested remainder in *fee simple* subject to an executory
        limitation, and
C has a shifting executory interest in fee simple.

14.   Carolyn has a life estate determinable, and
        Paul has a vested remainder in fee simple absolute.

15.   (a) Common law:

Rick has a life estate determinable, and
Victor has a vested remainder in fee simple absolute.

(b) Modern trend:

Rick has a fee simple determinable, and
Victor has a possibility of reverter in fee simple.

16.   Priscilla has a life estate subject to an executory limitation,
        Lisa Marie has a shifting executory interest in fee simple, and
        The King has a reversion in fee simple.

17.   Clark has a *fee simple* subject to an executory limitation, and
        Martha has a shifting executory interest in fee simple.

(Read carefully – the express words of limitation "and his heirs" indicates that Clark is taking a fee simple defeasible, not a life estate defeasible – threw that in just to make sure you were paying attention.)

18.   Common law:

Clark has a *life estate* determinable, and
Martha has a vested remainder in fee simple.

Modern trend:

Clark has *fee simple* subject to an executory limitation, and
Martha has a shifting executory interest in fee simple.

19.   Bart has a life estate determinable, and
Homer has a reversion in fee simple absolute.

20.   (a) Common law:

Clark has a life estate subject to a condition subsequent, and
Jonathon has a reversion in fee simple absolute.

(b) Modern trend:

Clark has a fee simple subject to an executory limitation, and
Martha has a shifting executory interest in fee simple.

ANSWERS TO CHAPTER 10 PROBLEM SET

1.   A has a life estate,
A's heirs have a contingent remainder in fee simple, and
O has a reversion in fee simple.

The Rule in Shelley's Case applies, as does merger:

A has fee simple absolute.

2.   A has a life estate,
O has a reversion in fee simple subject to an executory limitation, and
A's heirs who attend A's funeral have a springing executory interest in fee simple.

3.   A has a life estate,
A's children have a contingent remainder in fee simple, and
O has a reversion in fee simple

4.   A has a life estate,
O's heirs have a contingent remainder in fee simple, and
O has a reversion in fee simple.

The Doctrine of Worthier Title applies, as does merger:

A has a life estate, and O has a reversion in fee simple.

5.   A has a life estate,
O has a reversion in fee simple subject to an executory limitation, and
O's heirs have a springing executory interest in fee simple.

The Doctrine of Worthier Title applies, as does merger:

A has a life estate, and O has a reversion in fee simple

6.   A has a life estate,
O's children have a contingent remainder in fee simple, and
O has a reversion in fee simple.

7.   A has a life estate,
        B has a contingent remainder in fee simple, and
        O has a reversion in fee simple.
        (Rule in Purefoy's Case applies to the extent you thought the
                conveyance ambiguous.)

8.   A has a life estate,
        O has a reversion in fee simple absolute, and
        B has a springing executory interest in fee simple.

9.   A has a life estate,
        O has a reversion in fee simple subject to an executory limitation,
                and
        A's heirs have a springing executory interest in fee simple.

10.   A has a life estate,
        B has a contingent remainder in fee simple, and
        O has a reversion in fee simple.

        Following the transfer:

        A has a life estate,
        B has a contingent remainder in fee simple, and
        C has a reversion in fee simple.
        (The Rule in Shelley's Case does not apply.)

11.   Adrian has a life estate,
        Adrian's heirs have a contingent remainder in fee simple, and
        Rocky has a reversion in fee simple.

        The Rule in Shelley's Case applies, as does merger:

        Adrian has a fee simple absolute.

12.   Rosie has a life estate,
        Donald's heirs have a contingent remainder in fee simple, and
        Donald has a reversion in fee simple.

        The Doctrine of Worthier Title applies, as does merger:

Rosie has a life estate, and
Donald has a reversion in fee simple absolute.

13.   Michael has a life estate,
        Vito has a reversion in fee simple subject to an executory limitation,
            and
        Vito's heirs have a springing executory interest in fee simple.

        The Doctrine of Worthier Title applies, as does merger:

        Michael has a life estate, and
        Vito has a reversion in fee simple absolute.

14.   Forrest has a life estate,
        Lt. Dan has a vested remainder in life estate,
        Forrest's heirs have a contingent remainder in fee simple, and
        Bubba has a reversion in fee simple absolute.

        The Rule in Shelley's Case applies, but not merger:

        Forrest has a life estate,
        Lt. Dan has a vested remainder in life estate,
        Forrest has a vested remainder in fee simple.

15.   Carmela has a life estate,
        Tony has a reversion in fee simple subject to an executory limitation,
            and
        Carmela's heirs have a springing executory interest in fee simple
            absolute.

ANSWERS TO CHAPTER 11 PROBLEM SET

1.   (a) *Assume A has no children.*

A has a life estate,
A's children have a contingent remainder in fee simple, and
O has a reversion in fee simple.

(b) *Assume A has a child, X.*

A has a life estate, and
A's child, X, has a vested remainder, subject to open, in fee simple.

(c) *Assume A has another child, Y.*

A has a life estate, and
A's children, X and Y, have a vested remainder, subject to open, in fee
      simple.

(d) *Assume A dies.*

X and Y hold the property in fee simple absolute.

2.   (a) *Assume B has no children.*

A has a life estate,
B's children have a contingent remainder in fee simple, and
O has a reversion in fee simple.

(b) *Assume B has a child, X.*

A has a life estate, and
B's child, X, has a vested remainder, subject to open, in fee simple.

(c) *Assume A dies and B is still alive..*

X holds the property in fee simple absolute.

(d) *Assume B has a second child, Y.*

X holds the property in fee simple absolute (per the Rule of Convenience, the class closed when A died).

3.   (a) *Assume Carol is alive and has no children.*

Carol has a life estate,
Carol's children have a contingent remainder in fee simple, and
Mike has a reversion in fee simple absolute.

(b) *Assume Carol has a child Marsha.*

Carol has a life estate, and
Carol's child Marsha has a vested remainder, subject to open, in fee
         simple.

(c) *Assume Marsha dies, survived by a child Gerri.*

Carol has a life estate, and
Carol's child, Marsha/Gerri, has a vested remainder, subject to open,
         in fee simple (Marsha's share, because it was vested, descended to
         her heir Gerri).

(d) *Assume Carol has a second child Cindy.*

Carol has a life estate, and
Carol's children, Marsha/Gerri and Cindy, have a vested remainder,
         subject to open, in fee simple (Marsha's share, because it was
         vested, descended to her heir Gerri).

(e) *Assume Carol dies.*

Gerri and Cindy hold the property in fee simple absolute.

4.   Carmela has a life estate,
      Carmela's children who survive her have a contingent remainder in fee
            simple absolute, and
      Tony has a reversion in fee simple absolute.

      (The interest in Carmela's children is still contingent, even though
      they are born and ascertainable, because of the express condition
      precedent that they survive her.)

5.   (a) *Assume Kuala is alive and Mother Robinson has no children.*

      Kuala has a life estate,
      Mother Robinson's children have a contingent remainder in fee
            simple, and
      Oscar has a reversion in fee simple absolute.

      (b) *Assume Mother Robinson has a child Fritz.*

      Kuala has a life estate, and
      Mother Robinson's child, Fritz, has a vested remainder, subject to
            open, in fee simple.

      (c) *Assume Mother Robinson has another child Bertie.*

      Kuala has a life estate, and
      Mother Robinson's children, Fritz and Bertie, have a vested
            remainder, subject to open, in fee simple.

      (d) *Assume Kuala dies, and thereafter Mother Robinson has another
            child Ernst.*

      Fritz and Bertie hold the property in fee simple.

ANSWERS TO REVIEW PROBLEM SET 3

1.   Annie holds a fee simple absolute.

2.   (a) *Common law*:

Zeke has a life estate,
Hickory has a vested remainder in life estate, and
Hunk has a vested remainder in fee simple absolute.

(b) *Modern trend*:

Ambiguous – unclear how a court would resolve it. One approach would be to grant Zeke a fee simple absolute and void all the other possible interest; the other would be to grant Zeke a life estate, Hickory a vested remainder in life estate, and Hunk a vested remainder in fee simple absolute.

3.   (a) *Common law*:

Janice has a fee tail female,
Jimi has a vested remainder in life estate, and
BB has a reversion in fee simple absolute.

(b) *Modern trend (but not so modern as to have abolished the fee tail)*:

Ambiguous – unclear how a court would resolve it. One approach would be to grant Janice a fee tail female, Jimi a vested remainder in fee simple absolute, and void the other possible interest in BB; the other would be to grant Janice a fee tail female, Jimi a vested remainder in life estate, and BB a reversion in fee simple absolute.

4.   Lance has a fee simple subject to an executory limitation, and
Guinevere has a shifting executory interest in fee simple.

5.   Dick has a fee simple subject to an executory limitation, and
Rudy has a shifting executory interest in fee simple.

6.   (a) *Assume Chuckie and Will are alive.*

Chuckie has a life estate,
Will has a contingent remainder in fee simple absolute, and
Sean has a reversion in fee simple absolute.

(b) *Assume Chuckie dies and Will has still not graduated.*

Common law:
Sean has a fee simple absolute.

Modern trend (if the jurisdiction has abolished the destructibility of
          contingent remainders):
Sean has a fee simple subject to an executory limitation, and
Will has a springing executory interest in fee simple.

7.   (a) *Assume Chuckie and Will are alive.*

Chuckie has a life estate,
Will has a contingent remainder in fee simple,
Skylar has an alternative contingent remainder in fee simple, and
Sean has a reversion in fee simple.

(b-1)   *Assume Chuckie dies and Will has not graduated yet.*

Skylar holds the property in fee simple absolute.

(b-2)   *Assume Chuckie renounces his interest and B has not
          graduated from medical school yet.*

Sean holds the property in fee simple absolute.

(b-3)   *Assume Will graduates, then Will dies, and then Chuckie dies.*

Will held a vested remainder in fee simple absolute. Will's interest is
          inheritable, so it will pass to Will's heirs.

8.   Bert has a life estate,
       Mick has a reversion in fee simple subject to an executory limitation, and
       Keith has a springing executory interest in fee simple absolute.

9.   Barbie has a life estate subject to an executory limitation,
       Ken has a shifting executory interest in fee simple, and
       Todd has a reversion in fee simple.

10.   Ernst has a life estate,
       Julio has a vested remainder in fee simple determinable, and
       Robert has a possibility of reverter in fee simple.

11.   Ernst has a life estate,
       Julio has a vested remainder in fee simple subject to a condition
             subsequent, and
       Robert has a right of entry/power of termination in fee simple.

12.   Westley has a life estate,
       Buttercup has a vested remainder, subject to divestment, in fee simple, and
       Fezzik has a shifting executory interest in fee simple absolute.

13.   (a) *Assume Scarlett has no grandchildren.*

       Scarlett has a life estate,
       Scarlett's grandchildren have a contingent remainder in fee simple, and
       Rhett has a reversion in fee simple.

       (b) *Assume Scarlett has a grandchild Wilson.*

       Scarlett has a life estate,
       Scarlett's grandchild, Wilson, has a vested remainder in fee simple subject to open.

       (c) *Assume Scarlett has another grandchild Billie Ray.*

       Scarlett has a life estate,

Scarlett's grandchildren, Wilson and Billie Ray, have a vested remainder in fee simple subject to open.

(d) *Assume Wilson dies and then Billie Ray dies.*

Scarlett has a life estate,
Scarlett's grandchildren, Wilson and Billie Ray, have a vested remainder in fee simple subject to open – their shares will pass to their respective heirs.

14.   Maximus has a life estate,
      Commodus has vested remainder in fee simple subject to a condition subsequent, and
      Marcus has a right of entry/power of termination in fee simple absolute.

15.   Maximus has a life estate,
      Commodus has a vested remainder in fee simple subject to an executory limitation, and
      Lucilla has a shifting executory interest in fee simple absolute.

16.   Maximus has a life estate,
      Commodus has a vested remainder in fee simple subject to an executory limitation, and
      Lucilla has a shifting executory interest in fee simple absolute.

17.   Maximus has a life estate,
      Commodus has a vested remainder in fee simple subject to divestment, and
      Lucilla has a shifting executory interest in fee simple absolute.

18.   (a) *Assume Emily, Lorelai, Rory and Luke are alive.*

      Emily has a life estate,
      Lorelai has a vested remainder subject to divestment in fee simple, and
      Rory has a shifting executory interest in fee simple absolute.

      (b) *Assume Emily dies and Lorelai, Rory and Luke are alive.*

      Lorelai has a fee simple subject to an executory limitation, and

Rory has a shifting executory interest in fee simple.

19. Mortimer has a life estate,
Marian has a contingent remainder in fee simple, and
Arthur has a reversion in fee simple.

20. Ceasar has a life estate,
William has a reversion in fee simple subject to an executory
limitation, and
Antony has a springing executory interest in fee simple absolute.

21. Randy has a life estate,
Newman has a contingent remainder in fee simple, and
Alfred has a reversion in fee simple.

(b) Assume Randy has died, and Newman has not graduated yet.

Alfred has a fee simple absolute. (Assuming the jurisdiction still
applies the destructibility of contingent remainders –
otherwise, Alfred has a fee simple subject to an executory
limitation, and Newman holds a springing executory interest in
fee simple.)

22. Angelina has a life estate,
Angelina's heirs have a contingent remainder in fee simple, and
Brad has a reversion in fee simple absolute.

Angelina has fee simple (per the Rule in Shelley's Case and merger).

23. Angelina has a life estate,
Sheryl has a vested remainder in life estate,
Angelina's heirs have a contingent remainder in fee simple, and
Brad has a reversion in fee simple.

Angelina has a life estate,
Sheryl has a vested remainder in life estate, and
Angelina has a vested remainder in fee simple.
(The Rule in Shelley's Case applies, but not merger.)

24.   Angelina has a life estate,
      Angelina's heirs have a contingent remainder in fee simple, and
      Brad has a reversion in fee simple.

      Angelina has a life estate,
      Angelina has a contingent remainder in fee simple, and
      Brad has a reversion in fee simple absolute.

25.   Angelina has a life estate,
      Brad has a reversion in fee simple subject to an executory limitation,
            and
      Angelina's heirs have a springing executory interest in fee simple
            absolute.

26.   Angelina has a life estate, and
      Brad's heirs have a contingent remainder in fee simple, and
      Brad has a reversion in fee simple.

      Angelina has a life estate, and
      Brad has a reversion in fee simple absolute (per the Doctrine of
            Worthier Title)

27.   Angelina has a life estate,
      Jennifer has a vested remainder in life estate,
      Brad's heirs have a contingent remainder in fee simple, and
      Brad has a reversion.

      Angelina has a life estate,
      Jennifer has a vested remainder in life estate, and
      Brad has a reversion in fee simple absolute (per the Doctrine of
            Worthier Title)

28.   Angelina has a life estate,
      Brad's heirs have a contingent remainder in fee simple, and
      Brad has a reversion in fee simple.

      Angelina has a life estate, and
      Brad has a reversion in fee simple absolute (per the Doctrine of
            Worthier Title)

29.   Jacque has a life estate,
       Thor has a reversion in fee simple subject to an executory limitation, and
       Jacque's heirs have a springing executory interest in fee simple absolute.

30.   Bart has a life estate determinable, and
       Homer has a reversion in fee simple absolute.

31.   Bart has a life estate subject to an executory limitation,
       Marge has a shifting executory interest in fee simple, and
       Homer has a reversion in fee simple absolute.

CHAPTER 12 PROBLEM SET – CONTINGENT REMAINDERS

1. A has a life estate,
    A's first child B has a contingent remainder in fee simple if she
        marries, and
    O has a reversion in fee simple.

    Put B's contingent remainder to the test: *create* – X, a new child
    for A (and a new life in being); *kill* – O, A and B; *count* 21 yrs.
    Can you create a scenario in which the interest will vest, but only
    after the lives in being plus 21 years have passed?

    No. Because the remainder will vest only if B marries, there is no
    way to satisfy the condition but after the lives in being plus 21
    years. Because we could not create a scenario in which the
    contingent remainder vests, but only after the lives in being plus 21
    years, the contingent remainder is valid.

2. A has a life estate,
    A's first child to marry has a contingent remainder in fee simple,
        and
    O has a reversion in fee simple.

    Put the contingent remainder to the test: *create* – X, a new child
    for A (and a new life in being); *kill* – O, A and B; *count* 21 yrs.
    Can you create a scenario in which the interest will vest, but only
    after the lives in being plus 21 years have passed?

    Yes. Is it possible that X will marry sometime after the lives in
    being have died and 21 years has passed? Sure. Because a
    scenario exists where the remainder vests but only after the lives in
    being plus 21 years, the contingent remainder is invalid.

    Strike the interest and restate the title:

    A has a life estate, and O has a reversion in fee simple.

3. A has a life estate,
    A's first grandchild has a contingent remainder in fee simple, and
    O has a reversion in fee simple.

Put the contingent remainder to the test: *create* – X, a new child for A (and a new life in being); *kill* – O, A and B; *count* 21 yrs. Can you create a scenario in which the interest will vest, but only after the lives in being plus 21 years has passed?

Yes. Is it possible that X will give birth to a child – A's first grandchild – but only sometime after the lives in being have died and 21 years have passed? Sure. Because a scenario exists where the remainder vests but only after the lives in being plus 21 years, the contingent remainder is invalid.

Strike the interest and restate the title:

A has a life estate, and O has a reversion in fee simple.

4.   A has a term of years,
        B has a contingent remainder in fee simple, and
        O has a reversion in fee simple.

Put the contingent remainder to the test. Can you create a scenario in which the interest vests, but not until after the lives in being plus 21 years? No. The condition is tied to a life in being – B. Either B will graduate from high school or not during B's lifetime. It cannot vest in anyone else, and the vesting cannot be delayed until after the lives in being plus 21 years. The contingent remainder is valid.

5.   A has a life estate,
        A's first granddaughter to graduate from law school has a
                contingent remainder in fee simple, and
        O has a reversion in fee simple.

Put the contingent remainder to the test. Can you create a scenario in which the interest vests, but not until after the lives in being plus 21 years? Yes. Create a new grandchild for A, grandchild X. Kill all the lives in being at the time the interest was created (O, A, the two kids and the grandchild), and count 21 years. Is it possible that X might graduate from law school thereafter? Sure. Because a scenario exists where the remainder vests but only after the lives in being plus 21 years, the contingent remainder is invalid.

Strike the interest and restate the title:

A has a life estate, and O has a reversion in fee simple.

6.   A has a life estate,
The President has a contingent remainder in fee simple, and
O has a reversion.

Put the contingent remainder to the test. Can you create a scenario
in which the interest vests, but not until after the lives in being plus
21 years? No. The condition is tied to a life in being – the next
President of the United States. Whoever that is, the interest will
vest immediately upon the death of all the relevant lives in being.
As soon as you kill A, the contingent remainder vests. You cannot
delay the vesting until after the lives in being plus 21 years time
period. The contingent remainder is valid.

7.   A has a life estate,
A's first child to get a tattoo has a contingent remainder in fee
        simple, and
O has a reversion in fee simple.

Put the contingent remainder to the test. Can you create a scenario
in which the interest vests, but not until after the lives in being plus
21 years? Yes. Create a new child for A, child X. Kill all the
lives in being at the time the interest was created (O, A, the two
kids B and C), and count 21 years. Is it possible that thereafter X
might get a tattoo? Sure. Because a scenario exists where the
remainder vests but only after the lives in being plus 21 years, the
contingent remainder is invalid.

Strike the interest and restate the title:

A has a life estate, and O has a reversion in fee simple.

8.   A has a life estate,
A's first child who agrees to farm the land has a contingent
        remainder in fee simple, and
O has a reversion in fee simple.

Put the contingent remainder to the test. Can you create a scenario in which the interest vests, but not until after the lives in being plus 21 years? Yes. Create a new child for A, child X. Kill all the lives in being at the time the interest was created (O, A, the two kids B and C), and count 21 years. Is it possible that thereafter X might agree to farm the land? Sure. Because a scenario exists where the remainder vests but only after the lives in being plus 21 years, the contingent remainder is invalid.

Strike the interest and restate the title:

A has a life estate, and O has a reversion in fee simple.

9.   A has a term of years,
          B has a contingent remainder in fee simple, and
          O has a reversion in fee simple.

Put the contingent remainder to the test. Can you create a scenario in which the interest vests, but not until after the lives in being plus 21 years? No. The condition is tied to a life in being – B. Either B will be alive when A's interest ends or not. It cannot vest in anyone else, and the vesting cannot be delayed until after the lives in being plus 21 years. The contingent remainder is valid.

10.   A has a life estate,
          A's first child to reach age 15 has a contingent remainder in fee
              simple, and
          O has a reversion in fee simple.

Put the contingent remainder to the test. Can you create a scenario in which the interest vests, but not until after the lives in being plus 21 years? No. Although you can create a new child for A, child X, and kill all the lives in being at the time the interest was created, you cannot delay the vesting until after you count 21 years. The interest would vest in child X, the new child, at the latest when you reach year 15. X will become A's first child to reach age 15, but before the lives in being plus 21 years period has run. The vesting cannot be delayed until after the lives in being plus 21 years. The contingent remainder is valid.

11.   A has a term of years,
       B has a contingent remainder in fee simple, and
       O has a reversion in fee simple.

       Put the contingent remainder to the test. Can you create a scenario
       in which the interest vests, but not until after the lives in being plus
       21 years? Yes. Create an heir for B, child X. Kill all the lives in
       being at the time the interest was created (O, A, and B), and count
       21 years. Is it possible that thereafter a woman might be elected
       President? Sure. Because a scenario exists where the remainder
       vests but only after the lives in being plus 21 years, the contingent
       remainder is invalid. (Is it possible, even probable, that a woman
       will be elected President before the lives in being plus 21 years has
       passed? Sure – but that is not the test. As long as there is one
       possible scenario where the interest does not vest until *after* the
       lives in being plus 21 years, the interest if invalid.)

       Strike the interest and restate the title:

       A has a life estate, and O has a reversion in fee simple.

12.   Jane has a life estate,
       Michael has a contingent remainder in fee simple, and
       Mary has a reversion in fee simple.

       Put Michael's contingent remainder to the test: *create* – X, an heir
       for Michael (and a new life in being); *kill* – Mary, Jane, and
       Michael; *count* 21 yrs. Can you create a scenario in which the
       interest will vest, but only after the lives in being plus 21 years has
       passed?

       No. The remainder will vest only if *Michael* reaches age 25. The
       condition is tied to a live in being. There is no way to satisfy the
       condition but after the lives in being plus 21 years. Because we
       could not create a scenario in which the contingent remainder
       vests, but only after the lives in being plus 21 years, the contingent
       remainder is valid.

13.   Jane has a life estate,
        Jane's first child has a contingent remainder in fee simple, and
        Mary has a reversion in fee simple.

        Put the contingent remainder in Jane's first child to the test: *create*
        – X, a child for Jane (and a new life in being); *kill* – Mary and
        Jane; *count* – 21 years. Can you create a scenario in which the
        interest will vest, but only after the lives in being plus 21 years has
        passed?

        No. The contingent remainder in Jane's first child will vest
        immediately upon the creation of the first child, X, and there is no
        way to delay the vesting until after the lives in being plus 21 years.
        The condition is tied to a life in being, so there is no way to delay
        the vesting until after the lives in being plus 21 years. Therefore,
        the contingent remainder is valid.

14.   Lionel has a life estate,
        Lionel's first child to reach age 30 has a contingent remainder in
             fee simple, and
        Michael has a reversion in fee simple.

        Put the contingent remainder in Lionel's first child to reach age 30
        to the test: *create* – X, a new child for Lionel (and a new life in
        being); *kill* – Michael, Lionel, Nicole and Myles; *count* – 21 years.
        Can you create a scenario in which the interest will vest, but only
        after the lives in being plus 21 years has passed?

        Yes. Is it possible that X will live for another 9 years and reach
        age 30, at which time the contingent remainder will vest. Because
        the contingent remainder vested under this scenario after the lives
        in being plus 21 years, the contingent remainder is invalid.

        Strike the interest and restate the title:

        Lionel has a life estate, and
        Michael has a reversion in fee simple absolute.

15.   David has a life estate,
David's first child to reach age 21 has a contingent remainder in
        fee simple, and
Pamela has a reversion in fee simple.

Put the contingent remainder in David's first child to reach age 21
to the test. Using 'create, kill and count,' can you create a scenario
in which the interest will vest, but only after the lives in being plus
21 years has passed?

No. Even if you create a new child for David, child X, and kill all
the lives in being, when you start the 'count' stage of the analysis
child X will reach age 21 before the lives in being plus 21 years
has expired. There is no way to delay the vesting until *after* the
lives in being plus *21 years*. The interest will vest in child X the
day before the period runs at the latest. There fore, the contingent
remainder is valid.

16.   Mel has a life estate,
Mel's first grandchild has a contingent remainder in fee simple,
        and
Danny has a reversion in fee simple.

Put the contingent remainder in Mel's first grandchild to the test.
Using 'create, kill and count,' can you create a scenario in which
the interest will vest, but only after the lives in being plus 21 years
has passed?

Yes. The key is the person you created, X, should have been a new
child for Mel. After you kill off all the lives in being at the time of
the conveyance, it is conceivable that more than 21 years later X
can have a child – who would be Mel's first grandchild. This
scenario would vest the remainder but after the lives in being plus
21 years. Therefore, the contingent remainder is invalid.

Strike the interest and restate the title:

Mel has a life estate, and
Danny has a reversion in fee simple absolute.

17.   Tony has a life estate,
       Kirby's first grandchild has a contingent remainder in fee simple,
             and
       Kirby has a reversion in fee simple.

       Put the contingent remainder in Kirby's first grandchild to the test.
       Using 'create, kill and count,' can you create a scenario in which
       the interest will vest, but only after the lives in being plus 21 years
       has passed?
       No. The key is that the conveyance is a devise – which means it is
       in Kirby's will. Because the conveyance does not become
       effective until Kirby dies, you cannot create a new child for Kirby.
       The person you create would have to be a new grandchild for
       Kirby, thereby immediately vesting the interest. You cannot delay
       the vesting until after the lives in being plus 21 years. Therefore,
       the contingent remainder is valid.

18.   Brock has a life estate,
       John's first child to graduate from law school has a contingent
             remainder in fee simple, and
       Al has a reversion in fee simple.

       Put the contingent remainder in John's first child to graduate from
       law school to the test. Using 'create, kill and count,' can you
       create a scenario in which the interest will vest, but only after the
       lives in being plus 21 years has passed?

       Yes. Create a new child for John, child X. Kill all the lives in
       being at the time of the conveyance, count 21 years – is it possible
       that X could go to law school and graduate, thereby being John's
       first child to graduate from law school? Yes. This scenario would
       vest the remainder but after the lives in being plus 21 years.
       Therefore, the contingent remainder is invalid.

       Strike the interest and restate the title:

       Brock has a life estate, and
       Al has a reversion in fee simple absolute.

19.   George has a life estate,
        George's widow has a contingent remainder in life estate,
        George's children who survive George's widow have a contingent
              remainder in fee simple, and
        Rosemary has a reversion in fee simple.

   (A) Put the contingent remainder George's widow holds to the
        test:

   Can you create a scenario in which the interest will vest, but only
   after the lives in being plus 21 years has passed? No. The
   contingent remainder in George's widow will vest immediately
   upon George's death. There is no way to delay the vesting until
   after the lives in being plus 21 years. Therefore, the contingent
   remainder in George's widow is valid.

   (B) Put the contingent remainder in George's children who
        survive George's widow to the test.

   Can you create a scenario in which the interest will vest, but only
   after the lives in being plus 21 years has passed?

   Yes, create X, a new life in being who grow up and marries
   George, and then have them have a child Y (another new life in
   being). Kill all the lives in being at the time of the conveyance.
   Then count 21 years. Is it possible that X, George's widow, will
   die after the 21 years? Sure. When George's widow dies after the
   lives in being plus 21 years, the contingent remainder in George's
   children who survive George's widow (Y here) vests. Therefore,
   the contingent remainder in George's children who survive
   George's widow is invalid.

   Strike the interest and restate the title:

   George has a life estate,
   George's widow has a contingent remainder in life estate,
   Rosemary has a reversion in fee simple.

20.   George has a life estate,
        George's widow has a contingent remainder in life estate,
        George's children who survive George's widow have a contingent
                remainder in fee simple, and
        Rosemary has a reversion in fee simple.

        (A) Put the contingent remainder George's widow holds to the
             test:

        Can you create a scenario in which the interest will vest, but only
        after the lives in being plus 21 years has passed? No. The
        contingent remainder in George's widow will vest immediately
        upon George's death. There is no way to delay the vesting until
        after the lives in being plus 21 years. Therefore, the contingent
        remainder in George's widow is valid.

        (B) Put the contingent remainder in George's children to the test.

        Can you create a scenario in which the interest will vest, but only
        after the lives in being plus 21 years has passed?

        No. The contingent remainder in George's children will vest upon
        the creation of George's child Y and there is no scenario in which a
        child can vest in the interest but only after the lives in being plus 21
        years. Even if George has more children, their interest will vest the
        moment they are born, and when George dies there is no way to
        delay the vesting of any new children until after the lives in being
        plus 21 years (do not worry about new reproductive technology –
        such developments are beyond the scope of this introductory
        coverage). Therefore, the contingent remainder is valid.

CHAPTER 12 PROBLEM SET – EXECUTORY INTERESTS

1. A has a fee simple subject to a condition subsequent, and
    O has a right of entry/power of termination in fee simple.

    (O's future interest is *not* subject to the Rule.)

2. A has a fee simple subject to an executory limitation, and
    B has a shifting executory interest in fee simple.

    Put B's interest to the test. It is possible to create a scenario where
    the interest vests but not until after the lives in being plus 21 years?
    No, the express condition is tied to a life in being. Where the
    express condition is tied to a life in being (A), it is impossible to
    delay the vesting until after the Perpetuities' period. The executory
    interest is valid.

3. A has a fee simple subject to an executory limitation, and
    B has a shifting executory interest in fee simple.

    Put B's interest to the test. It is possible to create a scenario where
    the interest vests but not until after the lives in being plus 21 years?
    Yes, the express condition is *not* tied to a life in being. Where the
    express condition is *not* tied to a life in being, create an heir for A,
    heir X, and an heir for B, heir Y. Kill the lives in being, O, A and
    B; count 21 years, and ask, "is possible that the condition will
    occur?" Sure, it is possible that X could stop farming the land,
    thereby vesting the executory interest in Y but not until after the
    Perpetuities' period. The executory interest is invalid.

    Strike the interest and restate the title:

    A has a fee simple determinable, and
    O has a possibility of reverter in fee simple.

4. A has a fee simple subject to an executory limitation, and
    B has a shifting executory interest in fee simple.

    Put B's interest to the test. It is possible to create a scenario where
    the interest vests but not until after the lives in being plus 21 years?

Yes, the express condition is *not* tied to a life in being. Where the express condition is *not* tied to a life in being, create an heir for A, heir X, and an heir for B, heir Y. Kill the lives in being, O, A and B; count 21 years, and ask, "is possible that the condition will occur?" Sure, it is possible that X could stop farming the land, thereby vesting the executory interest in Y but not until after the Perpetuities' period. The executory interest is invalid.

Strike the interest and restate the title:

A has a fee simple absolute. (Notice where the fee simple is cut short by the condition subsequent words of limitation, typically the condition is struck as well.)

5.   O has a fee simple subject to an executory limitation, and
     A has a springing executory interest in fee simple.

Put A's interest to the test. It is possible to create a scenario where the interest vests but not until after the lives in being plus 21 years? Yes, the express condition is *not* tied to a life in being. Where the express condition is *not* tied to a life in being, create an heir for A, heir X (who is also a new child for A), and an heir for O, heir Y. Kill the lives in being, O, A, and A's two children; count 21 years, and ask, "Is possible that the condition will occur?" Sure, it is possible that thereafter X could have a child, thereby vesting the executory interest in A's first grandchild but not until after the Perpetuities' period. The executory interest is invalid.

Strike the interest and restate the title:

O has a fee simple absolute.

6.   A has a life estate,
     O has a reversion in fee simple subject to an executory limitation, and
     Whoever is then the President has a springing executory interest in fee simple.

Put the President's interest to the test. It is possible to create a scenario where the interest vests but not until after the lives in being plus 21 years? No, although the express condition is not tied to a life in being, it expressly provides that the interest will vest 5 years after a live in being dies. You cannot delay the vesting until after the lives in being plus 21 years. The executory interest is valid.

7.   O has a fee simple subject to an executory limitation, and
A has a springing executory interest in fee simple.

Put A's interest to the test. It is possible to create a scenario where the interest vests but not until after the lives in being plus 21 years? Yes. Regardless of how many daughters A has, create a new one for her (X). Kill all the lives in being (O, A, and any daughters who were alive at the time of the conveyance). Count 21 years. Is it possible that thereafter X will get a tattoo, thereby vesting the executory interest? Sure. The executory interest is invalid.

Strike the interest and restate the title:

O has a fee simple absolute.

8.   A has a fee simple subject to an executory limitation, and
B has a shifting executory interest in fee simple.

Put B's interest to the test. It is possible to create a scenario where the interest vests but not until after the lives in being plus 21 years? No, the express condition is tied to a life in being. Where the express condition is tied to a life in being (A), it is impossible to delay the vesting until after the Perpetuities' period. The executory interest is valid.

9.   A has a life estate,
O has a reversion in fee simple subject to an executory limitation,
        and
A's first child to graduate from law school after A's death has a
        springing executory interest in fee simple.

Put the executory interest in A's first child to graduate from law school after A's death to the test. It is possible to create a scenario where the interest vests but not until after the lives in being plus 21 years? Yes. Create a new child for A, child X. Kill all the lives in being, O, A, B, and C. Count 21 years. Is it possible that thereafter X will attend and graduate from law school? Yes. A scenario exists where the interest vests but not until after the Perpetuities' period. The executory interest is invalid.

Strike the interest and restate the title:

A has a life estate, and O has a reversion in fee simple absolute.

10.   A has a fee simple subject to a condition subsequent, and O has a right of entry/power of termination in fee simple.

(Although the conveyance has both words of determination and condition subsequent terminology, the courts favor the condition subsequent characterization to avoid the automatic forfeiture of the property interest – and the future interest is not subject to the Rule against Perpetuities.)

11.   Nelson holds a fee simple subject to an executory limitation, and Stedman holds a shifting executory interest in fee simple.

Can you create a scenario in which the interest will vest (as applied to executory interests, this means has the right to become possessory), but only after the lives in being plus 21 years has passed? Yes. Create X, and heir for Nelson, and Y, an heir for Stedman. Kill all the lives in being at the time of the conveyance, and count 21 years. Is it conceivable that X, Nelson's heir, will stop using the land for agricultural purposes so that Y, Stedman's heir, will be entitled to claim possession of the land under the executory interest? Yes. Because the executory interest could become possessory after the lives in being plus 21 years, the interest is invalid.

Strike the interest and restate the title:

Nelson holds a fee simple determinable, and
Oprah holds a possibility of reverter in fee simple.

12.   Donor has a fee simple subject to an executory limitation, and
        Whoever is the President of St. Louis University High at the time
            Donor's estate is distributed holds a springing executory
            interest in fee simple.

        Can you create a scenario in which the interest will vest (as applied to
        executory interests, this means has the right to become possessory),
        but only after the lives in being plus 21 years has passed? Yes.
        Create an heir for Donor, X, and also create at least two other parties,
        Y, and Z – all new lives in being who grow up. Y becomes President
        of the school. Kill all the lives in being at the time of the conveyance.
        Z becomes the personal representative for Donor's estate. Is it
        conceivable that Z will be so slow in distributing Donor's estate that
        it will not occur until after the lives in being plus 21 years? As
        implausible as it seems, yes. Therefore, the executory interest is
        invalid.

        Strike the interest and restate the title:

        Donor holds a fee simple absolute.

13.   Sara has a life estate,
        JoJo has a vested remainder in fee simple subject to an executory
            limitation, and
        Emma has a shifting executory interest in fee simple.

        Can you create a scenario in which the interest will vest (as applied to
        executory interests, this means has the right to become possessory),
        but only after the lives in being plus 21 years has passed? No.
        Emma's executory interest can only become possessory if *JoJo* sells
        liquor on the land. The condition is tied to a life in being. There is no
        way to create a new life in being who will affect the condition. Once
        we kill JoJo, there is no way the condition can occur 21 years later.
        Therefore, the executory interest is valid.

14.   Owner holds a fee simple subject to an executory limitation, and
        Donald holds a springing executory interest in fee simple.

        Can you create a scenario in which the interest will vest (as applied to
        executory interests, this means has the right to become possessory),

but only after the lives in being plus 21 years has passed? Yes. Create an heir for Donald, X. Kill all the lives in being at the time of the conveyance. Count 21 years. Is it possible that thereafter Donald's heir, X, will decide to exercise the option to purchase? Sure. The executory interest would become possessory but not until after the lives in being plus 21 years. The executory interest is invalid.

Strike the interest and restate the title:

O holds a fee simple absolute.

15.   George has a fee simple subject to an executory limitation, and Zuzu holds a springing executory interest in fee simple.

Put Zuzu's interest to the test. It is possible to create a scenario where the interest vests but not until after the lives in being plus 21 years? No, the express condition is tied to a life in being. Where the express condition is tied to a life in being (Zuzu), it is impossible to delay the vesting until after the Perpetuities' period. The executory interest is valid.

CHAPTER 12 PROBLEM SET – VESTED SUBJECT TO OPEN

1. A has life estate, and
    A's children have a vested remainder, subject to open, in fee simple
        absolute.

    Put the vested remainder, subject to open, in A's children to the
    test. Create a new child for A, X. As soon as you create the new
    child, the interest vests in the new child. It is impossible to delay
    the vesting until after the lives in being plus 21 years. The vested
    remainder, subject to open, in A's children is valid.

2. A has a life estate, and
    A's grandchildren have a vested remainder, subject to open, in fee
        simple.

    Put the vested remainder, subject to open, in A's grandchildren to
    the test. Create a new child for A, X. Kill all the lives in being, O,
    A, B, and C. Count 21 years. Is it possible that thereafter X will
    have a child, another grandchild for A, whose interest will vest but
    not until after the lives in being plus 21 years? Sure. Because a
    party can vest in the class gift but after the lives in being plus 21
    years, the vested remainder, subject to open, in A's grandchildren is
    invalid.

    Strike the interest and restate the title.

    A has a life estate, and O has a reversion in fee simple.

3. A has a life estate, and
    A's children who reach age 30 have a vested remainder, subject to
        open, in fee simple.

    Put the vested remainder, subject to open, in A's children who
    reach age 30 to the test. Create a new child for A, X. Kill all the
    lives in being, O, A, B, and C. Count 21 years. Is it possible that
    thereafter X will reach the age of 30, thereby vesting but not until
    after the lives in being plus 21 years? Sure. Because a party can
    vest in the class gift but after the lives in being plus 21 years, the

vested remainder, subject to open, in A's children who reach age 30 is invalid.

Strike the interest and restate the title.

A has a life estate, and O has a reversion in fee simple.

4.   A has a life estate, and
A's grandchildren who reach age 20 have a vested remainder,
        subject to open, in fee simple.

Put the vested remainder, subject to open, in A's grandchildren who reach age 20 to the test. Create a new child for A, X. Kill all the lives in being, O, A, B, and C. Count 21 years. Is it possible that thereafter X will have a child, another grandchild for A, who will grow up and reach the age of 20? Sure. X's interest will vest but not until after the lives in being plus 21 years. Because a party can vest in the class gift but after the lives in being plus 21 years, the vested remainder, subject to open, in A's grandchildren who reach age 20 is invalid.

Strike the interest and restate the title.

A has a life estate, and O has a reversion in fee simple.

5.   A has a life estate, and
A's children who reach age 20 have a vested remainder, subject to
        open, in fee simple.

Put the vested remainder, subject to open, in A's children who reach age 20 to the test. Create a new child for A, X. Kill all the lives in being, O, A, B, and C. Count 21 years. Is it possible that thereafter X will reach the age of 20, thereby vesting but not until after the lives in being plus 21 years? No. X will vest the moment he or she reaches age 20. The vesting cannot be delayed until after the lives in being plus 21 years. The vested remainder, subject to open, in A's children who reach age 20 is valid.

Subject Matter Index

Alternative contingent remainder, 70
alternative phrasing, 73
look-alike, 80
premature termination
  of finite estate, 73, 78
merger, 74

Analytical scheme, 3
possessory estates, 9
future interests, 25

Class gifts, 150
Rule of Convenience, 160
Rule against Perpetuities, 174

Condition precedent, 60, 100, 124

Condition subsequent, 60, 103, 124

Destructibility of contingent remainders, 65, 74, 79 152

Divestment, 103, 127

Doctrine of Worthier Title, 150

Equitable interests, 3

Executory interests, 23, 30, 98
Rule against Perpetuities, 190

Fee simple absolute,
defined, 6

Fee Simple Absolute, *continued*
Modern trend, 11
words of limitation, 8
transferability, 13

Fee simple defeasibles,
nature, 17
types, 18
analytical scheme, 18
future interests, 25
Transferability, 34
Flowchart, 35

Fee simple determinable, 19
nature, 20
words of limitation, 21
future interest following, 26
transferability, 34

Fee simple subject to a condition subsequent, 19
nature, 20
words of limitation, 21
future interest following, 23, 26
transferability, 34

Fee simple subject to an executory limitation, 23
nature, 24
future interest, 23
shifting vs. springing, 30
transferability, 34

Fee tail, 44
male/female, 45

Finite estates, 42
nature, 42
future interests, 47
modern trend, 49
transferability, 49
flowchart, 51
premature termination, 73

Forfeiture, 74

Future interests,
defined, 1-2
analytical scheme, 4, 25

Future interest only
   conveyance, 99

Gap scenario, 101

Legal interests, 2

Life estate, 43
life estate defeasibles, 137
life estate determinable, 139
life estate subject to executory
   limitation, 140

Merger, 74

Possessory estate, 1

Power of termination, 20, 23

Remainders, 47, 58
test for vested, 58
contingent, 58
destructibility, 65
alternative contingent, 70
transferability, 82
class gifts, 158
Rule against Perpetuities, 178

Renunciation, 74

Reversions, 47

Right of Entry, 20

Rule against Perpetuities, 174
contingent remainders, 178
executory Interests, 190
class gifts, 201

Rule in Purefoy's Case, 152

Rule in Shelley's Case, 146

Rule of Convenience, 160

Shifting executory interest, 30,
   99

Springing executory interest, 30,
   99

Term of years, 46

Vested remainder subject to
   divestment, 103, 126

Vested remainder test, 58
born, 59
ascertainable, 59
no condition precedent, 60
class gifts, 158

Words of limitation
defined, 4
common law approach, 8
modern trend approach, 11

Words of purchase, 7